MR. FIX-IT
INTRODUCES
YOU TO
YOUR
HOME

MR. FIX-IT INTRODUCES YOU TO YOUR HOME

Lou Manfredini
With Curtis Rist

BALLANTINE BOOKS • NEW YORK

A Ballantine Book
Publishing by The Ballantine Publishing Group

Copyright © 2002 by Lou Manfredini
Illustrations copyright © 2002 by Harry Trumbore

www. ballantinebooks.com

The Cataloging-in-Publication Data for this title is available from the Library of Congress.

ISBN 0-345-44987-8

Interior design by Michaelis/Carpelis Design Assoc. Inc.

Manufactured in the United States of America

First Edition: March 2002

10 9 8 7 6 5 4 3 2 1

Acknowledgments

Writing a book, I have discovered, is a lot like building a house—only it requires more time, and an even bigger work crew to assemble it all. Naming everyone I'm indebted to in this adventure would more than fill a page, but I'd like to single out a few people.

To Jon Harris and Brian DeFiore, thank you. To Curtis Rist, my co-author, and Harry Trumbore, our illustrator: I'm amazed at your ability to make a tough job seem easy. To my great friend Kathy Neumeyer, who researched the facts and details for this book, once again I'm astounded at your grace under pressure. And to the great people at Ballantine, thanks for helping turn a rough-hewn idea into the finished book you're now holding.

Above all, I owe everthing to Mary Beth, without whom our house just wouldn't be a home.

Introduction   x

It's not how a house looks that matters, says Mr. Fix-It, it's how a house feels. Spend your repair and renovation dollars with this in mind, and you'll end up with a solid home that appreciates in value—and is far more comfortable to live in.

1   ### HOW A HOUSE WORKS   1

A house is more like a living, breathing organism than a pile of lumber and concrete; here's an anatomy lesson

2   ### WATER, WATER EVERYWHERE   17

Can't make sense of that tangle of plumbing? Follow Mr. Fix-It as he traces every drop, from water main to sewer line

3   ### A WIRED WONDER   35

The average home contains some two miles of wiring— Mr. Fix-It can untangle every inch

4   ### HOT AND COLD   53

Here's how to keep your home cool when it's hot, and warm when it's not

5   ### AN OPEN-AND-SHUT CASE   75

Windows and doors bring in the light while keeping out the wind and rain; here's how to manage them

6   ### GETTING FLOORED   93

As the most heavily used surface in a house, floors deserve some special attention

7   ### WALL POWER   111

It's not what's on the walls, it's what's in them that will add the most to your home

contents

8 **A VIEW FROM BELOW** 129
Basements can be scary places—unless you know how to tame them

9 **A VIEW FROM ABOVE** 147
Like a shingled umbrella, a roof protects your home from the elements; here's how it works

10 **SPECIALTY OF THE HOUSE** 165
More than just a place to cook, the kitchen has become the focal point of the household

11 **BATHING BEAUTIES** 183
Want an inviting bathroom? First take care of mold, mildew, leaks, and foul air

12 **ROOMS TO LIVE IN** 201
What you need to know about setting up rooms—from décor and lighting to closets that work

13 **AN EYE FOR DETAIL** 219
It's the little things—from paint to woodwork—that bring out the best in a home

14 **THE GREAT OUTDOORS** 233
Your home should be connected to the land that surrounds it; here's how to devise a plan

15 **SIXTY-MINUTE INSPECTION** 249
Mr. Fix-It takes you on a tour of your home and helps you make a list of what to tackle first

MR. FIX-IT INTRODUCES YOU TO YOUR HOME

Searching for our dream home a few years ago, my wife, Mary Beth, and I knew only vaguely what we wanted—until we walked up to a slightly tired-looking brick Georgian. The place was far from trendy; in fact, it had been built back when FDR was president. There was no hot tub in the backyard, no "family recycling center," and no skylights. It had the original kitchen, the original furniture, and even the original owner—a kind lady who had lived there since 1941. Yet as we stepped inside on that wintry day, I closed the two-inch-thick front door behind us and heard a sturdy thunk, like an old Mercedes. "This is the house," I instantly whispered to my wife. "What are you talking about? We haven't even been *through* it," she responded. But I persisted: "I'm telling you, this is the house!"

And I was right. With Mary Beth's enthusiastic approval, we bought the place—metal kitchen cabinets and all—the next day.

Lots of people, especially real estate agents, think they can divine exactly what a house should be in order to appeal to people. They might come up with an ideal square footage, promote a certain bedroom-to-bathroom ratio, and go on and on about the value of a deck versus a patio. I think that's mostly nonsense. Because when it comes down to it, the only thing that's truly important in a house is the way it feels—a place that feels solid, not tinny; a home that keeps you cool in the summer and toasty warm in the winter; a house that will stand up for the ages, rather than fall apart before the decade's out. Whether you're renovating a home, building an addition, or simply maintaining what you've got, I believe it's a lot better to let yourself be guided by that principle rather than try to add a few haphazard things that might attract some future buyers.

More than anything, I want you to think of your house as a place to treasure and care for, not patch together. We all allow ourselves on occasion to do slipshod things to our cars, for instance, whether we skip the occasional oil change, hold off on the scheduled maintenance, or even pocket the insurance money instead of repairing that bashed-in fender. Unfortunately, too many people take the same approach to a house. Yet while a car will eventually end up on the scrap heap, a well-maintained house will only grow in value. This investment goes far deeper than simply owning a few shares of some dot-com or blue-chip stock. It's an investment in ourselves and our quality of life. As the very symbol of family life, a house demands respect from the people that live in it.

That sense of respect is what I hope you can develop by reading this book. As you'll discover, this is not a typical how-to volume, with tips on how to fix a broken bathroom tile, regrout a kitchen backsplash, or patch a leaky roof. There are probably plenty of those already on your bookshelf—and if you're like most homeowners who try to wade through them, you probably find yourself lost in a bewildering vocabulary of floor joists, wall studs,

R-values for insulation, and the secret coding of blueprints. It's as if these books were written in another language. Instead, this is a book that will help you begin to understand a house in its entirety, in a language you can follow. While you may not find the exact details you'll need for every project you want to undertake, you'll walk away with something far more important: an intuitive understanding of your home that will empower you to make the right decisions for its future as well as for your own.

I'll start by taking you on a tour of your house, from the ground up. We'll look at how a house works—it's more like a living, breathing organism than a pile of brick and lumber. We'll untangle the mess of wiring that lies coiled behind your walls, and the plumbing that snakes its way to sinks and bathroom fixtures. We'll focus on basements and attics, kitchens and bathrooms, rooms to live in and rooms to sleep in. And for those apartment dwellers among you, trust me—there's an awful lot going on behind your walls that you need to know about, too. The aim is to give you a greater appreciation of the things that are covered up by paint and paper on your walls, and the systems that flow just beneath the plush carpets and polished wood of your floors. Why do you need to know these things? Because it is this unseen portion of your house that does more to make you feel comfortable and secure than any cushy sofa or swath of fabric hanging in a window ever will. And if the hidden things aren't working properly, before long that lovely paint will be peeling off the walls and those plush carpets will be damp and moldy. Who needs that?

I began in the construction business eighteen years ago, and since then I've seen thousands of houses go up, and renovated countless more. I've worked on every aspect of the home, from sewers to shingles, from basement footings to chimney tops. What I'd like to do is share with you my sense of what a house is and how it works and help you avoid the many mistakes I've made over the years. Everyone wishes they had a friend in the home improvement business, whether that's a carpenter they could trust or a hardware store guy who could really answer their questions. My aim is for you to begin to feel that way about me.

I'll have plenty of advice for you as we move along, but first I want to tell you about what I think is the golden rule of home improvement: Whatever you do to your house, whether repairing it, maintaining it, or renovating it, you have an obligation to make sure the job gets done right. That means getting the training you need to tackle it yourself, or hiring someone qualified to do it for you. My goal when I work on a house is simply to do the best work possible. When the next person comes along to renovate in twenty or thirty years, I want him to look back and say, "Wow, the last person who worked on this really did a great job." As a builder, I know it's the only mark that's worth leaving. And as a homeowner, you should have the same standards. Because, ultimately, a good home is tactile. You can feel it in the weight of the knob when you close a door, the sturdiness of the handrail as you climb the stairs, and the way the kitchen drawers glide smoothly as you pull them open. And all that translates into value, by creating a home that is a pleasure to live in. Sloppiness is always offensive, but good craftsmanship—regardless of the style, taste, or décor—is always a pleasure.

Although I hate to think about it, I know that someday, when it's time, Mary Beth and I won't have any trouble selling our home. The new buyers will surely quibble over our color scheme and choice in carpeting. But when that front door closes, they'll know—as I did—that the best home really is a castle. My hope is that this book will help you turn yours into the fortress of your dreams.

MR. FIX-IT INTRODUCES YOU TO YOUR HOME

chapter ONE

How a House Works
A home is more like a living, breathing organism than a pile of lumber and concrete; here's an anatomy lesson

I'll admit it—to call myself an expert on matters of the home is a little presumptuous. When I think of experts, I imagine people like Stephen Hawking rather than some guy named Lou.

Yet for all of my professional life, I have indeed been involved with home maintenance and renovation. And for most of this time, what I have focused on are the mistakes that homeowners make. When I began working at a hardware store in high school, my job was to answer people's questions—and inevitably these concerned problems that they had themselves created: Why was the new faucet that they just installed dripping? Why was the paint that they just spread on the exterior of their house now peeling? And why were the walls in their newly renovated bathroom already beginning to turn gray with mold and mildew? Everyone seemed to have drafty windows, screen doors that wouldn't shut right, and cracks in their living room walls. I always swore that if ever got the chance to build a house, I would build it in such a way that it didn't have any of these problems.

houses

I got my wish some years later during college—not an entire house, perhaps, but at least a significant portion of it. Looking for a summer occupation, a friend and I started our own company—gloriously named Home Care Services—and promptly found work doing odd jobs for his mother, who worked as a real estate broker. We fixed mailbox posts, planed the occasional closet door, and one day were called to look at a peeling deck on the back of a house new to the market. "Do whatever you can to make it look better," my friend's mother told us, and we set to work. Using my hardware store skills, I noticed right away that the problems seemed to extend far beyond the crackled finish. For one thing, the wood beam connecting the deck to the house appeared to be thoroughly rotted. Crawling around some more, I noticed that this connecting board as well as the structure of the deck itself were made from ordinary pine (the kind that rots) as opposed to pressure-treated wood (the kind that does not). Obviously, the deck had been built by some hapless weekend carpenter who had taken a great set of plans from a do-it-yourself manual. While that was okay, he must have skipped a few pages regarding wood selection. He'd also missed the part about pitch: The whole deck angled not away from the house, as it should have to drain rainwater, but directly toward it. After a few years of having rainwater slosh against them, both the siding of the house and the structure beneath it were beginning to decay. In short, the entire deck was junk, and worse, it was literally ruining the house.

What was to have been about a $75 deck staining job suddenly turned into a $1,500 emergency repair project—and the beginning of a crusade on my part to help people understand how to care for and maintain their homes. What causes mistakes such as this? Mostly ignorance. If things are done incorrectly—whether it's because people are trying to save money or because they really just don't know any better—they can create so many additional problems. That deck was a good example. At a quick glance, it looked okay. But there were two key flaws that anyone should have easily understood—the deck had the wrong pitch, and it was made with the wrong wood. Because of that, all those hours of work and all the money that had gone into it were wasted. Ironically, the repairs ended up costing far more than it would have cost to build the deck correctly the first time.

It's not as if there are a million concepts to learn regarding a home. There are actually only a few key principles to keep in mind, which then have many easy-to-follow variations. In this sense, learning to maintain your home is a lot like learning to cook pasta. If you put the spaghetti into a pot of cold water and try to boil it from there, you end up with a big congealed mess in the pot. You do this exactly once in your life, then never again. Instead, you learn to put it in boiling water, and you come out with perfect pasta every time. With houses, as with pasta, there's a natural logic and order in the way things should be done. Taking the time to learn this, as we're about to do in this book, will empower you to care for your home wisely and with confidence. Before diving in, however, let's take a quick tour of a house and focus on some basic elements.

Meet the House

We tend to think of houses as we know them as something fairly recent—dating back to the Colonial era, perhaps, or maybe all the way back to the Renaissance. Yet the origins of four walls and a roof actually go back much further than that.

The first identifiable houses are some fifteen thousand years old and are indeed unique. They amounted to a cluster of homes, found in what is now Ukraine, created out of the tusks and bones of wooly mammoths (unfortu-

Living in Style

One of the worst things that can happen to a home is if it is renovated without any consideration given to its style. I've seen classic brick Georgian houses from the 1930s all but ruined by white clapboard additions, and the porches of Victorian houses made charmless when white filigree posts are replaced with square chunks of pressure-treated wood. You may think you're improving the value of your home by building an addition or making repairs. But in my opinion, you've just devalued the place by about 20 percent.

We can't all be historic preservationists, of course, but we owe it to our houses —as well as our neighbors—to renovate with care and cultivate a little respect for the style of the house, both on the outside and on the inside. To help, here's a quick tour of some major house styles that you'll find around the country, which are often echoed in the designs of new houses as well:

The Saltbox.

Hello, New England! This home looks like a standard two-story Colonial from the front, but it slopes down to only one story in the back.

The Georgian.

A refinement of the Colonial style— and made popular again a century ago—this is usually built of brick with a formal and ornate entry.

The Greek Revival.

This style first became popular in the United States in the early 1800s and can be found across the country. Look for examples both with and without pillars.

Spanish Style.

Stuccoed exteriors and orange or red tile roofs mark these homes common throughout the South, Southwest, and West.

The American Foursquare.

This common house found in older towns and small cities has a pyramid-shaped roof, a big front porch, and a square floor plan (hence its name).

The Bungalow.

Built in a variety of styles, from Craftsman to Chicago, these have low-pitched gable roofs, front porches, and long, narrow floor plans.

nately, this is no longer a materials option). Things evolved quickly after that, and you can find references to palatial houses with swinging doors and finely polished floors worthy of a spread in *Architectural Digest* going all the way back to *The Iliad* and *The Odyssey* some three thousand years ago. Indeed, the desire to live in a well-crafted and comfortable house is one of the things that marks us as civilized humans—as does the frustration over not always having things in our home work and feel just the way we want them to.

What exactly is a house? It's heavy, that's for sure, and in order to remain stable it needs to be connected solidly to the ground. If you build a house flat on the ground with nothing supporting it from underneath, all that weight will soon start shifting and sliding and the whole structure will eventually fall down. Instead, houses sit on top of foundations, which can range from fully excavated ones or shallower crawl spaces to concrete slabs. What type of foundation you have mostly depends on what part of the country you live in. If you live in the North, where the ground freezes in the wintertime, you need a full foundation or crawl space that extends down several feet to what is called the frost level or the no-freeze zone. Built this way, the foundation will be immune from all the bucking and heaving as the ground alternately freezes and thaws—an action that could otherwise buck and heave your home right off its foundation, like the losing cowboy in some real estate rodeo. If you live in the freeze-free South, your foundation is more than likely a concrete slab laid right on top of the earth, with no major excavation required. Either way, the foundation has to be set in what is called undisturbed soil, which has settled to the point where it is completely compacted. If you build it on top of a recently filled area, the soil will inevitably settle—as will your house, and in ways not likely to enhance its value.

Now comes the structure of the house, which is usually called the framing. Like the skeleton in our bodies, framing gives a house support and keeps it standing upright. When you think about it, a house has to withstand a great deal of pressure. Not only is its sheer weight bogging it down, but it has to hold up against the onslaught of shifting winds and—depending on where it's located—the weight of winter snows, the occasional hurricane, and even an earthquake tremor or two. The framing has evolved into an intricate design of vertical, horizontal, and diagonal supports that can hold up pressures applied from any direction.

Let's consider a wood-frame house. The framing begins on top of the foundation, with pieces of wood called the sill. On top of the sill, horizontal boards called joists carry the weight of the floor above them and also help to lock the rising walls in place. The walls themselves are built of vertical pieces of wood called studs, which are connected on both ends to rows of wood running around the perimeter of the house, called the plates. Then come more floor joists, which form the structural base of both the floors and the ceilings of a home. If you've got a second story,

We've Been Framed!

What's under the roof and beneath the walls of a house? Its structure, of course. Here's a quick look at the framing and the elements of the foundation that give your home the support it needs.

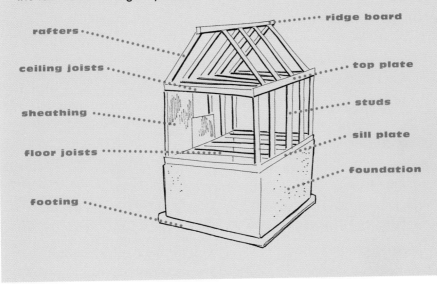

rafters · · · · · ·
ceiling joists · · · · · ·
sheathing · · · · · · ·
floor joists · · · · · · · ·
footing · · · ·

ridge board
top plate
studs
sill plate
foundation

this process repeats until it's capped off with angled boards called rafters, which rise to form the roof. If you have a solid brick or stone home, you won't have studs, but you'll still have joists and rafters.

The joists and the rafters work in complementary ways to keep the walls standing upright. The joists are actually compressed from the weight they carry, which causes the fibers within them to tense—thus pulling the walls in tightly. The weight of the roof also presses down and out on the roof rafters, but with the opposite effect on the walls: It tends to push them outward. Since the walls are being pushed outward by the rafters and pulled inward by the floor joists at the same time, the forces cancel each other out. Happily, the net force is zero—and so the walls remain standing. Sturdy as it is, however, this arrangement would quickly fall over if the house were buffeted with a sideways force. To further buttress it, the sides are covered with plywood sheathing or with pieces of lumber nailed diagonally across the studs. Built this way, a house is far stronger than the sum of its individual components. It can withstand any pressure—downward, sideways, and any combination thereof.

What comes next are the various systems that make our home life easier and healthier. The gaps in the walls between the studs become filled with one network of pipes that supplies water and a separate network for draining waste. Wires bring electricity to every outlet and light switch, and heating and cooling ducts or radiator pipes snake their way to every room. Doors and windows provide light and access, and insulation in the walls helps buffer changes in temperature. The roof and the exterior siding provide a block against wind, rain, and even sun. The goal of all these systems is to create an indoor space that's distinct from the outdoors—one in which we, and not nature, can control our comfort, moderate changes in the seasons, and regulate for ourselves the arrival of night and day.

The Number-One Enemy

So with a structure as beautiful and strong as a house, what could possibly cause it to deteriorate? The answer lies in a simple molecule containing one

oxygen and two hydrogen atoms—in short, water. You can live in a home built of the most massive beams, and water will lay it to waste within a matter of years. It can seep into the tiniest cracks beneath shingles on the roof, drip through uncaulked gaps around windows, and pool in basements, where it forms rot-causing swirls of humidity. Short of a cataclysmic fire, there's nothing that is more destructive to the long-term health of a home than water.

The most obvious trouble comes from water that pours into the house from outside. Water isn't evil; it's just adhering to the laws of simple gravity and heading downward. If you have a house where water drains from the roof and drips away from the house down a gentle slope after it lands on the ground, your home will be dry. If you have a home situated at the base of a hill or surrounded by a driveway or walkway that pitches toward the foundation, then your home will be wet. Once water comes in contact with wood, it turns something hard and dry and inhospitable to life into something soft and damp and inviting to everything with roots, rhizomes, pincers, and teeth.

In addition to old-fashioned inundation, there's a more subtle yet no less destructive form of water infiltration at work in many houses. As a problem, this is sometimes harder to pinpoint because the water originates inside the home and begins to rot it from the inside out. To see how this could happen, let's take a step back to look at what goes on within a home. Today's homes are sealed with insulation, weatherstripping, and caulk to reduce heating and cooling losses. Unfortunately, this also reduces the ability of moisture to escape from a house. Take a shower in the morning, boil a pot of water, open up the dishwasher and release a

Before You Say "I Do" . . .

For most of us, our homes rank as our largest single investment—as well as our largest single source of frustration, since they tend to be filled with things that break and need to be repaired. Balancing our desire to own a home with the patience needed to maintain it can be a challenge, especially since people often have their vision clouded by greed. In the late 1980s, real estate became practically synonymous with junk bonds—a risky, high-yield investment that often came crashing to the ground. The result was that houses themselves suffered. Homeowners made cosmetic changes in the hopes of making a quick profit, without giving houses the structural attention they truly needed.

Fortunately, the days of trading one house for another and being guaranteed a profit are over, which I think is a good thing as far as the houses are concerned. Real estate still makes a great investment, but instead of feeling like we're playing the lottery we can now begin to value houses for what they are: a work in progress, a place for a family to live, and the fundamental element of a neighborhood. If you want to make a quick dollar, look elsewhere for guaranteed returns. You'll never be able to muster the patience, the determination, and the will to manage a place of your own with any finesse. The real estate landscape is littered with relics where people tried this but failed. Talk about ugly! But if you want to place your money in something that will steadily improve in value as you care for it and renovate it in smart ways, then you're ready for a home. Whatever you buy, be prepared to think in terms of years and decades rather than months. In home ownership—as with all relationships—nothing beats a long-term commitment.

cloud of steam—all of these activities release moisture into the home. That may not sound so serious, but combine this with a basic fact of physics—that warm air holds far more moisture than cold air—and you'll begin to recognize what sort of problem can emerge.

In a heated house, warm, excessively moist air gradually penetrates into the walls and ceilings, where it comes in contact with colder surfaces that are chilled by outside air. Where these two surfaces meet, the air suddenly dumps its load of moisture in a process that we all know is called condensation. But what not all of us know is that the moisture ends up lingering right inside the walls. I've ripped apart the walls in some relatively new houses during the course of renovations and found that the structure has been completely rotted as a result of this process. Again, there was no obvious leak that needed to be patched; it was simply damage resulting from chronic condensation. I'll go into greater detail about the causes and remedies for this—which include installing ventilation fans and constructing walls in ways that block the water vapor from penetrating in the first place—in coming chapters.

The Air We Breathe

We take many things for granted in our homes—right down to the air that we breathe. Where does it come from? And how can we be sure that it is pure?

An Approach to Maintenance

People eagerly set money aside for fancy remodeling projects—that bubbling bathtub, for instance, or those new kitchen countertops. But they never seem to set anything aside for maintenance, such as the $100 to have the furnace or boiler cleaned each year or the $400 needed to seal the driveway or fix the roof. Neglecting repairs such as these can cost you dearly in the long haul, however. Imagine driving your car without ever budgeting any money for its maintenance in the vague hope that you'll somehow be the first driver in history to reach 150,000 miles before you have to buy a new one. You'll be lucky if you make it to 15,000 miles, and the same is true with a house. Maintenance problems don't heal themselves; instead, they only get worse and more expensive to repair. Our homes thrive on prevention and early detection of problems. Make sure you save and plan for this, and spend money first on projects that allow

Instructions for Instructions

Recently, I needed to switch the clock in my kitchen stove to Daylight Savings Time—and discovered I didn't know how. It contained a series of buttons that needed to be alternately pressed and twisted in just the right order. Without the instruction manual, my family would have stayed in Central Standard Time while the rest of Illinois sprang forward. Look around at your home, and you'll find literally dozens of things that require manuals in order to run them—and not just the VCR. Try adjusting the temperature on the water heater without one, or even getting through the front door if you have an alarm system.

As Americans, we're notoriously bad about reading instruction manuals, but you can't let that prevent you from taking a different approach with your home. Save all the instructions in one place—whether a folder in your file cabinet, a cardboard box stowed in a closet, or a drawer in the kitchen cabinets. You don't need a fancy organizing system, but as long as you have all your manuals together you'll be able to find the one you're looking for when you need it.

Nothing is as healthy as a drafty house. The air inside it is exchanged every few minutes, and it is always fresh. Any impurities—from things such as formaldehyde emanating from glues in carpeting and in kitchen cabinets to excess moisture that can lead to mold and mildew—simply vent away with the breeze. Most of us, however, have long ago opted against drafty houses. Beginning with the oil crisis in the 1970s and continuing with the rise in home heating prices, it has become a necessity to add insulation and weatherstripping to contain that expensive heated or cooled air. The more expensive fuel becomes, the more people seal their homes up.

Working properly, a house should naturally exchange all the air in it at a rate of at least about once an hour. This means that air is drawn in through tiny cracks, rises through to the top of the house as it is warmed, and vents through the roof. You'll always have enough oxygen to breathe, but your home may be too "tight"—the word refers to too much insulation and not enough airflow. In some cases, homes can become sealed so tightly during peak heating and cooling seasons that the occupants are practically living in a giant Tupperware container. They may be keeping that heated and cooled air inside, but they've also managed to trap everything else—including fumes from fireplaces and toxic cleaners, and even illness-causing viruses and bacteria. So bad has indoor air quality become that the federal Environmental Protection Agency has labeled being indoors one of the most severe exposures to tainted air in the course of a person's day. In some cases, even the air along expressways has fewer particulates than the air inside a house.

We've all heard of "sick building" syndrome, which usually applies to office buildings in which the air becomes stagnant and polluted and literally makes people sick. But this can happen in houses as well—especially those that are tightly insulated. Commercial buildings solve the problem by having an outside air intake, in which they're constantly mix-

An Alarming Situation

We all want our homes to be safe and secure—and to this end, many of us turn to a built-in security system. While this may bring us some extra peace of mind and actually lower insurance premiums, security systems do have some drawbacks—chief among which are false alarms. It's estimated that between 95 and 99 percent of all alarms sound for no reason, and all that crying wolf takes a toll. Police respond to real emergencies in about three minutes, according to the International Association of Chiefs of Police, but that falls to about fifteen minutes when responding to a house alarm. That's more than enough time for the crooks to pack up your jewelry, your computer, and your stereo and flee— even with that siren blaring.

What's a good way to protect yourself further? To begin, consider installing perimeter lighting outside your home that's tripped by a motion detector. That way, if someone approaches the house at night the lights suddenly go on, which should give him a jolt. Make a habit of locking the doors and closing the windows, since nothing could be a more obvious invitation to a break-in. Talk to a contractor about ways to make your house more resistant to break-ins; for example, 3-inch screws hold door hinges much more securely than 1-inch ones and can make a door harder to kick in. And keep in mind that the best alarm system of all is a barking dog—just remember it's the size of the bark, not the size of the dog, that matters.

ing fresh air with the building air so that it doesn't become stagnant, smell stale, and make people sick. Office building windows don't usually open, but the air can be made fresh by bringing outside air in through an exchanger such as this. This is also a simple remedy that many houses could benefit from, and should be the first thing you consider.

What else can you do about all this? The next thing to consider is a filter. Filters on furnaces and air-conditioning systems remain one of the most neglected aspects of a home. People think they're permanent, for one thing. Or they think they can get away with having the cheapest, nastiest filter money can buy—something costing all of 79 cents that couldn't even trap a piece of sand, let alone a piece of dust. Fortunately, you can do much better. There are pleated filters that trap much smaller particles, and even electrostatic filters, which give the particles an electric charge that makes them easier to catch.

While no one solution will work for everyone, the key is to understand that you can no longer assume you will have a good supply of breathable air just because you're living on the planet. Instead, you have to guarantee that this is the case, in ways that I will show you in coming chapters. By taking steps to make sure you're getting an adequate supply of high-quality air in your home, you'll ward off a great deal of trouble.

House Smart

Houses can often seem like complicated, overwhelming affairs—especially to those who don't take the time to study them. There are certainly some technical aspects of the home that require special attention, such as the wiring, the plumbing, and the heating and cooling systems. But the basic premise is hardly confusing: It has four walls and a roof to shed water, which is not all that different from what Laura Ingalls Wilder had in her little house on the prairie. If you live in an apartment, you have essentially the same thing—it's just that the individual apartments are stacked up like boxes. The sooner you realize this, the sooner you will begin to grasp the concepts that will help you create a home that's both free of trouble and more comfortable.

As we move through the coming chapters, I'm going to work to take the mystery out of your home's individual components. You don't necessarily need to know the intricacies of construction or the details of, say, how a furnace works to become an exceptional homeowner. Yet whether you're planning to renovate your home or simply maintain it, do the work yourself or hire someone to do it for you, understanding the basics will give you the ability to make sure things are being taken care of the right way.

Think of this as the instruction manual you always wish your home had come with. Once you read it, you'll truly become the master of the house.

chapter TWO

Water, Water Everywhere

Can't make sense of that tangle of plumbing? Follow Mr. Fix-It as he traces every drop, from water main to sewer line

As homeowners, we often like to pretend that we can get along just fine without understanding the more complicated aspects of our homes. Take plumbing, for instance. We turn on the faucet and the water comes out. We flush the toilet and everything goes away. Who knows—and who really cares—why?

Which brings me to the strange misadventure of my friend Jim, for whom I built a home a few years ago in Chicago. This was a great piece of real estate, if I do say so myself, and the house was beautifully built. About six months after they moved in, however, a city work crew moved into the neighborhood and tore up the streets to tie in new sewer connections to every home. Everything seemed to work fine, but shortly after that there was a horrendous rainstorm, the kind that leaves the streets flooded in a matter of seconds. During the storm, my friend was home and practicing piano in the living room. Midway through a song—the theme from

plumbing

Handel's *Water Music,* no doubt—he heard an ominous gurgling coming from the lavatory off the entrance hall. This was followed suddenly by what sounded like a fire hydrant coming unplugged. In moments, a rush of water spilled from under the lavatory door and flowed down the hallway and into the living room. My friend jumped up to see what was going on, and opened the lavatory door to find an enormous geyser of water gushing up from the toilet bowl. "It's like Old Faithful in here!" he boomed at me from his cell phone in the middle of the deluge. "What did you do to my house?"

Fortunately, it wasn't my fault. Those city workers had accidentally misconnected the new sewer line. As a result, every drop of rainwater that collected in my friend's gutters and downspouts roared back through his sewer lines and shot out the toilet, which was the lowest drain in the system. Bizarre as this story is, it underscores a point: I have a love-hate relationship with plumbing. I love it, of course, because it makes life so easy and healthy. On average in the United States, we use an astounding 350 gallons of water at home every day—which includes water used for everything from washing clothes to cooking, flushing the toilet, and showering and taking baths. And oh yes, that includes the 2 or 3 pints per person we actually drink. Modern plumbing and sewerage systems have made diseases such as cholera and dysentery a thing of the past.

Yet despite all these benefits, plumbing is by far the most troublesome system you'll ever own. The typical home contains some 1,000 feet of supply pipes, waste drains, and vents, some portion of which will inevitably fail. When it does, you could find yourself confronted with leaks, pipes that make wild knocking sounds, and drains that back up with foul-smelling water—not to mention the occasional home-wrecking geyser. To sort out how to manage it all, let's take a look at plumbing systems drip by drip.

What's It All About?

The modern plumbing system is a marvel of engineering that has been arrived at by many centuries of trial and error—with an emphasis on

The Anatomy of a Plumbing System

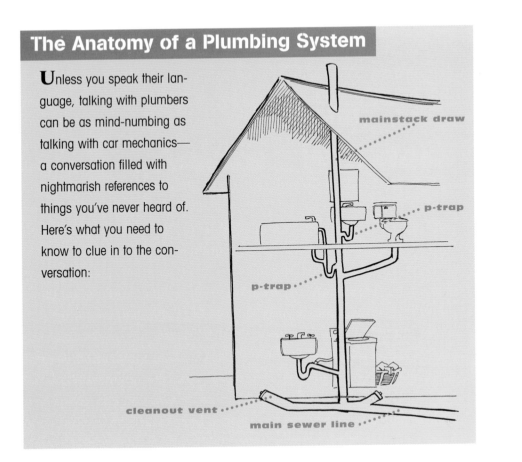

Unless you speak their language, talking with plumbers can be as mind-numbing as talking with car mechanics— a conversation filled with nightmarish references to things you've never heard of. Here's what you need to know to clue in to the conversation:

mainstack draw

p-trap

p-trap

cleanout vent

main sewer line

error, to be sure. What has emerged is just about perfect. The plumbing system is, in fact, two entirely separate systems that work together. The first is the water supply; the second is known as the drain-waste-vent system, or DWV in plumber lingo. This sounds more complicated than it is, and I guarantee it will not be hard to understand. Let's begin at the point where water enters your home.

Whether you have a well or a public water supply, water enters your home from a main line somewhere down below the first floor. Water has to flow under pressure, otherwise it will just sit in the basement instead of, say, rising to the faucet in your second-floor master bathroom. If you have a public water supply, that pressure is often created by water being pumped into a water tower—these are those giant things looming on the highest hill of just about every town in the nation and are usually painted pale green. If you have a well, you have a pump that not only draws water from the well but pressurizes it, too. In either case, the normal pressure for water running through a pipe is between 30 and 60 pounds per square inch, or psi. When you turn on the faucet at the kitchen sink, or flush the toilet, or run the bath, a valve opens and this pressure forces the water to spill out. Turn on several faucets at once and you'll likely see the water pressure drop because it gets divided among all of them—which explains why in certain houses if someone flushes the toilet while you're in the shower, the flow becomes a trickle.

Getting the water into your home is the easy part. Getting it out requires a greater effort. For starters, we're not draining water, we're draining what is politely referred to as "wastewater"—which runs the range from the benign to the vile. Wastewater is under no pressure whatsoever other than our own urgency to have it flow out of the house as unobtrusively as possible. It simply follows the laws of gravity to flow downhill, which in this case is down through drainpipes to the lowest part of your home. There it flows into the main sewer line (if you're connected to a city sewer) or to a septic system (if you live in a small town or rural area).

If draining this wastewater were as easy as just having it run down a pipe, indoor plumbing would have emerged centuries ago. But there is a complicating factor. Specifically, drain systems smell terrible, even if they're functioning perfectly well. Without some clever engineering, those smelly gases would back up from the sewer right into your house. Believe me, an outhouse, inconvenient as it may have seemed, was the far better alternative for our ancestors than smelly indoor plumbing. Fortunately, some ingenious engineering has evolved to prevent this backup.

The most important device in the entire drain system, I would argue, is known as a P-trap, which is that squiggly pipe you can find beneath every sink. This takes its name from the fact that it sort of looks like the letter P, lying on its side. Most people think the P-trap is shaped this way to catch stray wedding rings and the like that accidentally tumble down the sink, but it actually has a much more significant purpose. When wastewater drains through this pipe, some of it stays behind and fills the downward-facing P part of the trap, which forms a little trough. Water trapped here forms a bottleneck that prevents foul-smelling gases from belching back into your house. Simple

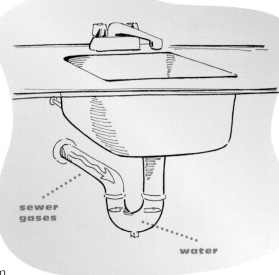

as this sounds, it is hugely effective at blocking odors. If there were a contest for the single greatest invention in the history of plumbing, the P-trap would get my vote.

Even the water in this P-trap, however, wouldn't be enough to stop all sewer gases such as methane from bubbling through the bottleneck. To protect against this, a plumbing system needs to be vented. If you take a look at the roof of your home, you will see one or more pipes rising through the roof. These look like little smokestacks, and most people think they are somehow connected to the bathroom ventilation fans. They are not. Instead, these connect to the main drainage pipes and allow noxious fumes to pass without notice to the outdoors rather than gurgling through the P-traps. In addition, these vents allow wastewater running down drains within a house to flow faster, since the vents help draw air into the waste pipes. This can be a tricky concept to understand, but there's a very clear way to illustrate it. Imagine a big can of juice. If you punch one hole in it, the juice pours out very slowly. Yet if you punch a second hole, the juice rushes out much faster because air can be drawn in to displace the water. In the drain system, that second hole is provided by the vent.

Emergency, Emergency!

Let's say a pipe suddenly bursts somewhere in your home and begins shooting water everywhere. This is a rare occurrence, to be sure, but a devastating one that can indeed happen. You could call a plumber to bail you out, but in the hour or two it will take him to get there, water will have destroyed your carpeting, furniture, walls, and floors. Instead of standing by and watching helplessly, this is one crisis you can resolve yourself—by shutting off the main water valve.

This valve—which astonishingly few people know about—is located just inside the house where water enters by a pipe either from a well or from a municipal water supply. If you live in an apartment, you'll find a similar valve either beneath the kitchen sink or in the bathroom. No matter where it is located, by turning it off, you cut off the entire water supply to every pipe in your home. No water, no leak. The valve comes in handy only if you know where it is located, however. Go find it before an emergency strikes.

Heating Water

Here's one of those everyday phenomena that's easy to ignore: You turn on the faucet on the left, and out jets hot water. The water certainly doesn't enter your house this way. Flowing from a city main or from a well drilled into your yard, it's probably around 55 degrees. Raising that to proper bathwater temperature requires a water heater—which is a cylindrical tank that usually sits off alone in a corner of your basement. Cold water flows in, is heated using natural gas, propane, fuel oil, or electricity, then is stored in the tank until needed.

Simple as this sounds, a water heater is probably the most troublesome—and short-lived—of all the major appliances in your home. It requires continual maintenance to keep it operating efficiently and safely. Water heaters often corrode because of a buildup of minerals contained in the water. When they do, they slowly lose their heating efficiency, and inevitably leak. This process is all but unavoidable, and as a result water heaters have become more or less disposable, lasting an average of just 7 years. To slow this quick and inevitable process of decay, manufacturers install magnesium or aluminum anode rods into the tanks; these chemically attract corrosive minerals and elements in the water that would otherwise settle to the bottom of the tank.

Depending on how mineral-laden your water is, these anode rods may exhaust themselves in as little as five years. Amazingly, the cost of replacing these simple little rods is usually more than the cost of actually replacing the entire tank because the rods are so inaccessible. Many plumbers, in fact, won't even attempt to do it. One way to preserve these rods

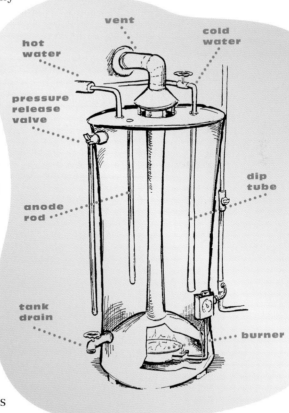

Clean the Screens

What's the number one cause of low water flow from a faucet? A buildup of grit trapped by screen filters that screw onto the tips of most faucets. Amazingly, even a tiny amount of sediment trapped against the screen can plug the flow a lot, and before you know it you will have only a trickle of water.

To fix the problem, you simply unscrew the filters from the faucets and wash them off. Your faucets will be reborn, and you should have a steady flow of water. Some screens can't be removed so easily, however, especially those in washing machines. Here, the water supply hoses have to be unscrewed from the back of the machine with a wrench and the filter screens vacuumed free of grit. An annual cleaning should take care of most troubles.

and extend the life of the tank is to drain a few gallons from the bottom of the tank once each year, using the drain valve designed for this purpose. It looks like an ordinary garden hose spigot. Doing this flushes away some of the corrosion-causing sediments.

Still, don't get too attached to that old heater. Even if it doesn't start to leak, the fuel efficiency of heaters drops from between 75 and 80 percent for brand-new models down to about 60 percent after five years, and an appallingly bad 50 percent after ten years. While you may think you're being penny-wise by scraping by with an old heater, you won't think you're so smart when you do the math. An efficiency of 50 percent means that 50 cents of each hot-water heating dollar is going to waste. Since an average family spends about $300 a year for hot water, that means a $150 annual loss due to inefficiency. New heaters cost only between $300 and $400 installed, so the correct course of action should be very clear.

One big improvement in water heaters is known as a tankless water heater—which avoids many of the problems with corrosion and efficiency that plague ordinary heaters. In a tankless water heater, hot water is not heated and stored, but rather produced steadily only as you need it. These suitcase-sized units, which are popular in Europe, produce about 2.2 gallons of hot water per minute—which is slightly more than is needed to give a good flow out of a showerhead. They use about 30 percent less energy than a conventional water heater, but there is a drawback: You can't use hot water in two places at once. So if you're trying to wash dishes at the sink while someone else is filling the bathtub, forget it.

I have a tankless water heater myself and have found that this is a small inconvenience compared to the benefits and savings. While these

Get the Lead Out

Copper piping is the standard of excellence in water supply systems dating back to the 1940s, but before that the material of choice was lead—going all the way back to the days of the Romans. The word *plumbing*, in fact, is actually derived from plumbum, the Latin word for lead. Lead piping had its advantages, since it could easily be twisted into the walls of a house. Unfortunately, we now concentrate more on its disadvantages, particularly as a toxin that can seriously affect the developing brains and bodies of young children.

If you live in a place built before the 1940s, the chances are very good that you have lead piping as your main supply line. When homeowners hear this, they often flip and think they have to rip everything out and start over even if the system is working perfectly well. Don't. The amount of lead that dissolves into water running through a pipe is very small, far below anything that would cause alarm. The longer water sits in the pipe, however—such as overnight—the more lead that dissolves. One good precaution in a house with lead piping is to let the cold-water tap run for about thirty seconds in the morning before drinking from it. This will reduce the amount of lead you and your family are exposed to.

If you're concerned, have your water tested by an independent laboratory to find out just what your exposure to lead is.

units typically cost about $700 to install, which is a little bit more expensive than a regular water heater, they make a better long-term investment. They remain far more efficient than conventional heaters over the years, and don't have the problem of corrosion and leaks. Trust me, when it's time to replace your heater, look into one of these.

An Approach to Plumbing Problems

The number one problem with a plumbing system involves the drains—they clog. Here, Mr. Fix-It's rule is straightforward. Never, ever pour chemical drain openers or cleaners down a drain to try to free up a clog. These are extremely corrosive and dangerous to use, which shouldn't be much of a surprise since their active ingredients are either lye or sulfuric acid. If they worked, we could probably live with the risks of messing around with something this caustic. But the irony, I have found, is that these products seldom actually eat away whatever it is that's plugging up a drain. They are exceptionally good, however, at eating away your skin, which you will discover firsthand when you inevitably splash yourself with them while pouring them in. Plus, the vapors are harmful and terribly caustic to your lungs.

What you end up with then, when you pour these into a drain, is an additional problem to work around. Not only do you have the clogged drain, it is now a clogged drain filled with a caustic liquid that cannot be touched by humans. If you try to use a plunger to further unplug a clog, you will end up with a cascade of caustic water splashing back at you. This is extremely risky, especially if it hits your eyes. If you call a hapless plumber after contaminating your plumbing system in this way, he will invariably take apart the drain—and this same water will splash out all over them and the floor. Please, at all costs, avoid this stuff.

Instead, as a responsible homeowner, you'll do much better by preventing blockages in the first place and by arming yourself with the right tools if they happen to occur. First, let's talk about prevention. The

Caring for a Forgotten Basement Pump

In a drain-waste-vent system, wastewater is fed by gravity to the main sewer line. That works fine for drains on the first and second floors—but what happens if you have a laundry room or bathroom in the basement, where the drain often lies below the main sewer line? Wastewater can't jump, so it needs a pump to lift it up and out of the house. These are called ejector pumps, and are contained inside small plastic boxes, about 5 gallons in size, that lie on the basement floor. When they fill up with waste water, a flotation ball inside triggers the pump to start up, and out the waste goes.

For many people, this black box is a mystery, and one that they would prefer to leave entirely alone. That ejector pit, however, needs to be serviced every year—especially to remove lint buildup from a washing machine. This involves lifting the lid off and scooping out any foreign matter, which is definitely a job calling for heavy-duty rubber gloves. Keep in mind also that no pump lasts forever, especially one that sees a lot of use. Typically, the switches that turn them on and off fail. Since they're inexpensive to replace, it's better to have a plumber put new switches in every three years rather than wait for them to fail and risk having the ejector pit back up. By the way, all small pumps have a distinct life span. If yours is ten years old, I'd say it's time to shop for a new one.

number one rule is that you need to limit the amount of solid material that goes down the drain. The toilet, for instance, should be used for toilet paper only, never as the equivalent of a bathroom garbage disposal for dental floss, scraps of paper, or anything else that you happen to have in hand that doesn't belong there. Bathtubs are also prone to clogs. Here, install a hair trap right in the drain. It may gross you out to have to remove the matted ball of hair that accumulates there every few days, but it's a lot better than having it accumulate farther down the drain. And never pour hot grease down the kitchen sink. Not surprisingly, this will congeal when it hits the cold water in the P-trap,

where it will constrict the flow of fluid—like an artery gone bad. Instead, pour grease into a can and throw it out.

Now, let's talk about the tools you'll need. A plunger is essential, and I'll go into the specifics of how to use it when we get to the bath-room in Chapter 11. Suffice it to say that this will unplug most clogs you encounter, especially in the toilet. If it doesn't, you will be doing yourself a favor—and saving plumber's fees—if you buy and figure out how to operate a snake, which might cost all of $25. Made from bendable steel, a snake is maneuvered into a drain with a crank handle that can sometimes be attached to a power drill. Unlike a plunger, it can reach clogs up to 25 feet away and break them apart with gentle twists and tugs from you. While this may sound like advanced plumbing, it is in fact extremely easy to use. With these two tools, you sure won't be squandering your money on chemical drain cleaners, and you may never need an emergency visit from the plumber.

One very large exception to this do-it-yourself approach to drains concerns the case when every single drain in the house backs up. This is a sign of something serious, which will indeed involve calling a plumber. Several things could be wrong here. For one, the main sewer line could be clogged—and it shouldn't come as a surprise that freeing this is as messy an affair as it gets. You sure don't want to be experimenting with your little plunger and snake. Sometimes, the main sewer

Sewer Cameras: The Ultimate Home Video

If you have a connection to a city sewer system, one of the worst things that can happen is that the line clogs up with tree roots. They grow into it and block the flow, which causes water to drain sluggishly or actually back up in your sinks, toilets, and bathtubs. Yuck!

In the past when this occurred, you would call a sewer contractor, who would try to snake out the line. He would feed a long, flexible rod into the pipe and grind away the roots and pull the pieces out. But if you had a broken pipe, the tree root would simply grow in again. Enter the sewer camera. This is similar to a snake, only the end is fitted with a little infrared videocamera. A sewer camera can inspect the sewer line as you go through, so you can see exactly what your trouble is—and know right where to dig if that becomes necessary.

Sewer cameras can work miracles and save you money, but there is one caveat. Some unscrupulous contractors have been known to try to pass off as yours a videotape from another homeowner's broken sewer line, just so they could claim there was a need to dig up the line. Imagine—fraudulent sewer videos! Is nothing sacred? So Mr. Fix-It's tip is this: If you're going to spring for the sewer cam, make sure you request a live broadcast of the action. You can always ask for a videotaped version as well. It'll be one home movie your family will never forget.

A Pipe Dream

Let's say you're just sitting down to a dinner party at your home, and—flush!—you hear a gush of water flowing through a drainpipe from the upstairs bathroom. This is not exactly a conversation starter, to say the least. One of the downsides of modern-day plumbing is that waste pipes are usually made of plastic. While this is easy and cheap for plumbers to work with, it offers no protection against noise. Older homes—say, those built before 1960—had

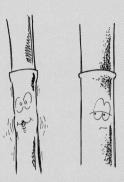

plastic   cast iron

waste lines made of cast iron. While more expensive than plastic piping, these heavy-duty pipes are very quiet. You can barely hear the water flowing within.

Unlike lead piping, cast-iron waste lines can still be found in every plumbing supply store. If you're renovating or building an addition, by all means ask your plumber to install them in areas where silence matters—such as through the dining room walls, or in the family room, media room, or home office. It will take twice as long to cut the pipes and solder them together than plastic and therefore cost you more, but you'll appreciate every drop you don't hear.

line becomes bent and doesn't drain—which would cause lines to be slow. If you are tied into a municipal sewer system, the problem could be that the main line has become clogged with tree roots or even collapsed altogether—which would involve major excavation to repair it. If you have a septic system, backed-up drains are inevitably a sign that it is time to have the septic tank pumped out. It has become too full of what I will politely call "solids" for wastewater to drain properly into it. No matter what, call a plumber to help in these instances. And above all, leave the liquid drain cleaner on the supermarket shelves, where it belongs.

A Septic System Primer

With a municipal sewer system, anything you wash or flush down the drain is neutralized at a sewage treatment plant. But what happens if you own a septic system instead?

In this case, wastewater enters an underground tank, which is about the size of an upright piano. As the waste flows in here, bacteria actively decompose it; this is a critical part of the process. Solid materials—such as coffee grounds and celery strings—settle, and fats and other floatable things rise. The liquid part in the middle layer of this effluent is then siphoned off by gravity to a leaching field, where it drips through pipes buried beneath the ground.

Obviously, a system such as this requires some delicate treatment. Every three to five years those solid materials that accumulate in the septic tank need to be pumped out at a cost of about $200 or more. If you use a garbage disposal regularly, you may even have to have the tank cleaned out every year. If you don't have this done, your drains will be sluggish and then stop altogether, since wastewater can't flow freely. Worse, solids could start to be siphoned off into the leaching field, where they plug up those buried pipes. If this happens, you'll be looking at a repair bill in the thousands.

Keep your septic system running smoothly by reducing the amount of solids you dump down the drains—such as dental floss in the toilet or coffee grounds in the sink. And avoid using liquid drain openers and chlorine bleach. These will kill the all-important bacteria that decompose solids, and hasten the need for the tank to be pumped.

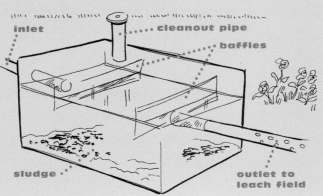

Making Water Soft

Depending on where you live, you may discover that your water is hard. This does not mean hard as in ice, but rather hard because it contains a lot of dissolved minerals. Things such as calcium, magnesium, and iron precipitate out of the water and build up in pipes, greatly restricting the flow of water. These same minerals also reduce the lathering ability of soap and instead combine with it to form a sticky scum that coats bathtubs, sinks, showers, and washing machines. A common fix for this sort of problem is a water softener. What this does is substitute sodium (from sodium chloride, which is salt) for these minerals. Since sodium does not precipitate out in pipes or react badly with soap, the hard water troubles are eliminated.

If you're like me, you're thinking, "Wait a minute, isn't this the same sodium that is supposed to cause high blood pressure?" Exactly, which is why you should take a few precautions when connecting a water softener. You don't want to drink this water—partly because of the health risk, and partly because water coming from a softener tastes weird and ever so slightly briny. A good compromise is to have a plumber connect the water softener only to the hot-water pipes. You'll still end up with good drinking water running through the cold-water taps, and soft water for bathing and washing clothes in hot.

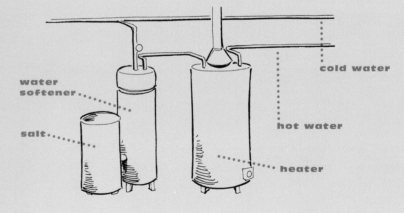

A Knock-Knock That's No Joke

One of the most irritating problems that can occur in plumbing systems is a knocking pipe. Unsuspecting houseguests become supremely embarrassed whenever they slip quietly into the lavatory, and an early riser in the house (such as myself) will jar everyone awake. In fact, this ranks as one of the most vexing issues that people ask me about. Fortunately, there's a surefire cure—it doesn't require a plumber and costs you nothing to tackle it.

To begin, you have to shut off the main water valve in your home, which will cut off the flow to every faucet and fixture. With the water supply off, you then have to run around the house and open up every faucet and flush every toilet until there is no more water coming out of the pipes anywhere. When everything has been drained dry, you go around the house again and close all the faucets. Then go down in the basement and slowly open the main valve to fill the system back up. Your knocking pipe problem will have disappeared.

Sounds like Houdini, right? Here's why it works. The water supply pipes in your home are under pressure—you turn on a faucet and water flows out. What you don't see are air chambers within your pipes that act like shock absorbers to cushion the pressure when you turn the water off. Over time, however, the air needed in your pipes naturally dissipates, and the water—when you turn off the faucet—slams

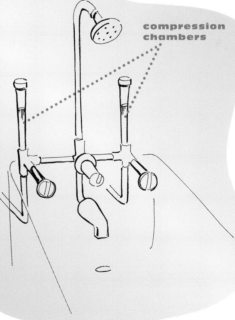

compression chambers

against it at full force. Imagine a Three Stooges routine where everyone runs around and around through a doorway until somebody closes the door and Curly slams into it. Exactly the same thing happens to the water, which is why you hear a knock.

By draining the system, you're replacing the air in the compression chamber and eliminating the knock. This may not make you the next Houdini, but you will certainly be able to impress your friends.

chapter THREE

A Wired Wonder

The average home contains some two miles of wiring—Mr. Fix-It can untangle every inch

As much as we care about our homes, we often don't give proper respect to the things that we cannot see.

Take wiring, for instance. I have some friends who dreamed of buying an old house and fixing it up once they got married. Looking around, they found a gem—an American foursquare, a classic house built in the 1920s, with a great front porch. The place was loaded with charm, which is something you can't easily build into a new house. But like all places loaded with charm, it also needed a ton of work. Since they didn't have a huge budget, they asked me what I thought they should tackle first. That was easy. "Upgrade the electrical system and rewire the house," I said. The place had been built with an old knob-and-tube system, which is to electrical systems what the *Hindenburg* was to air travel—namely, a disaster waiting to happen. In this, wires are stretched through the walls and held in place by porcelain knobs, then covered in cloth sheathing. If the two wires touch, as they invariably do during the earthquake known as renovation, they heat up. This is the same principle that turns the element in

electricity

Anatomy of an Electrical System

An electrical system amounts to a collection of separate circuits through which electrons flow. Electricity arrives by a power line, goes through the electric meter into the service panel, and then is distributed to receptacles, switches, and meters throughout the house. Here's a quick tour:

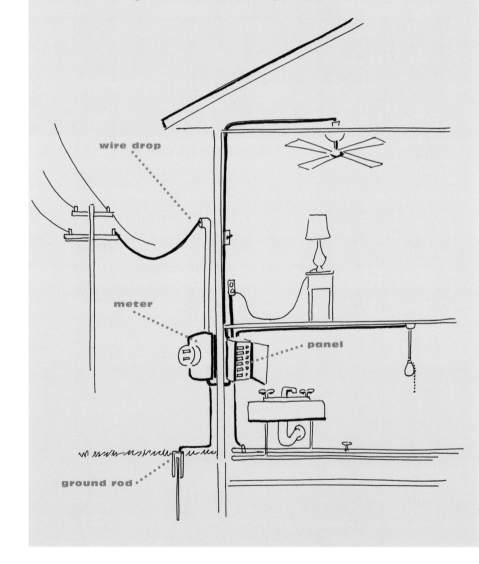

wire drop

meter

panel

ground rod

a toaster red-hot. Your only hope to avoid a fire is to replace the wiring.

Not everyone listens to me, however, especially when it involves spending about $10,000 to upgrade something that's more or less invisible. Instead, my friends opted to spend their money on the things that made the place look more appealing, such as having the floors refinished, adding new windows, and spending every night working until midnight stripping paint from walls and woodwork. After two years, the place looked great. But when they were all finished, as if on cue, a pair of wires in the wall of a second-floor bedroom came loose from their sheathing, touched, and started a fire. Fortunately, no one was hurt when this happened. Unfortunately, after the fire department left with their hoses, the place looked worse than ever.

Electricity, like plumbing, is one of those aspects of a house that most of us would rather avoid having to understand. Yet by ignoring it, we open ourselves up to lots of potential dangers, from house fires to electrocution. We'll blithely rig up extension cords like so many snakes touching head to tail, clip off the third prongs of plugs if they don't happen to fit into an old two-pronged outlet, and install light fixtures and ceiling fans without bothering to turn the power off at the circuit breaker box. There's a terrible downside to this. One in eight house fires, it has been shown, result from faulty wiring and overloaded circuits. In an average year, home electrical problems account for ninety thousand fires, more than seven hundred deaths, and $700 million in property damage. Clearly, we need to pay more attention to the wiring systems in our houses—and the only way to do this is to plug in and begin to figure it out.

Circuits, Circuits

To understand electricity, we have to start with the atom. As every third-grader knows, these contain protons, neutrons, and electrons, but the electrons don't always confine their orbits neatly to the atom, the way they do in drawings. Instead, some of them, called free electrons, have

How It Works: Switches

Touch a switch and it turns on a light—but how? Behind those wall plates, all switches are mechanical devices that simply make a connection between two wires. Specifically, they connect the hot wire coming from the electrical panel to a neutral wire coming from a light or other electrical device. A piece of metal within the switch joins these two wires together. When it's in the on position, the connection is made and the circuit is complete. When it's off, the circuit is broken. Popular types of switches include:

Single-pole switches. The most common switches of all, these simply click on when pushed up, and off when pushed down.

Three-pole switches. These are always installed in pairs and make it possible to turn a light on or off from two different locations, which makes them useful for opposite ends of a hallway or at the top and bottom of a set of stairs.

Dimmers. These connect to a light fixture just like a single-pole switch. Inside, however, they contain circuitry that uses resistance to reduce the voltage flowing to a light. In the process, these create a harmless amount of heat—which you can feel when you touch the dimmer.

what amounts to an unlimited travel pass. They're free to zip around wherever they want, as long as they have a conductive loop to travel in. So if you make a continuous connection of metal wiring, these electrons will circle around endlessly. The loop formed by these wires is known as a circuit. It's like a Hula-Hoop, with the electrons doing a never-ending shuttle inside. One such loop is formed by the wiring in your house, which connects to the power lines strung along your street and, ulti-mately, to the power company itself. While it sounds as if it must take electrons a long time to head from the power utility to the filament in your light bulb and back again, think again: They move at the speed of light, which is 186,000 miles per *second*.

Besides racking up an impressive collection of frequent-flier miles, these electrons are willing to pay their way by doing some work. If you connect something to a circuit for them to run through, whether it's a light bulb or a motor for a fan, they'll flow through in the form of elec-trical current and turn it on. When the deed is done, they retreat to the other half for the trek back to the power plant—spent, exhausted, and in need of a recharge. Now, let's work on a little vocabulary that will help you communicate all this to an electrician.

Electrons, like some assistants I've had, need plenty of prodding to do their chores—and they get it in the form of voltage. Voltage is like the water pressure in a garden hose, which forces the water, or in this case the electrons, to rush along. The higher the voltage, the greater the pres-sure of the electron flow, and the more work they can do. A thunderbolt contains a tremendous amount of voltage—some 100 million volts—which is why it is so destructive. By contrast, a small AA battery contains just 1.5 volts, which makes it all but harmless. The voltage to your home lies somewhere in between. Overhead power lines usually carry 7,200 volts, but if you were to direct that into the delicate wiring of your house, it would fry every circuit instantly. Instead, a transformer, which you can see as a small drum attached to the top of a utility pole or as a metal box where the cables are buried underground, lowers the voltage for use in your household. Small items, such as lights and kitchen appliances, run on 120 volts. Bigger ones, such as refrigerators and dishwashers, take 240 volts.

Two other terms also come into play. When electricity is put to work at an outlet or light fixture, the electrons flow through the circuit and the voltage is discharged as heat or light or motion. This electrical current is measured by a unit called the ampere, which is better known by its nickname, the amp. Circuits in a house tend to come in two varieties. There are 15-amp circuits, which run to lightswitches and ordinary outlets. And there are larger 20-amp and 30-amp circuits, which power the electrical workhorses such as electric clothes dryers and dishwashers.

Finally, the energy actually consumed by the electrical gadgets in your home is measured in watts. It takes maybe 100 watts to run a light bulb, and 1,000 watts to run a refrigerator. Your monthly electric bill is calculated by the total number of watts you use per hour, in blocks of 1,000. This is known as the kilowatt-hour, and it's what all those dials spinning wildly on the electric meter outside your house are measuring.

Taming the Electrical Beast

To complete an electrical circuit you need two wires. A hot wire—which is the dangerous one—brings the electrons to the outlet or fixture with full voltage. A neutral wire draws the spent electrons and transports them back where they came from. Every outlet or fixture has both a hot wire and a neutral wire, but these should never touch. If they do, the electrons discharge their voltage right at that spot, which causes the wires to heat up and spark. If a wire becomes overheated, the circuit breaker (or fuse, in older houses) acts as a safety mechanism. As the temperature builds, the connection within the circuit breaker is temporarily severed, which causes a break in the electron loop. Since electrons can't flow without a completed circuit, the wire will immediately cool down. Circuit breakers are the first line of defense in preventing an electrical fire.

Another problem occurs, however, in that electricity doesn't run only through the copper wiring that is insulated with rubber or plastic. If it encounters an easier way to discharge its load—which is known as a short circuit—it will take it. This is dangerous not just because it can set the house on fire but because it can kill people. Human bodies are about 90 percent water, which is an excellent conductor of electricity—far better, in fact, than copper wiring. If you come into contact with a short cir-

How It Works: Receptacles

Modern electrical receptacles each have three holes. The two parallel slots are different sizes: The shorter one is the hot slot, from which electricity flows. The longer one is the neutral slot, which is required to complete the connection. The third hole, shaped like an inverted U, is for the grounding prong of a three-prong plug. By inserting a plug into the receptacle, you complete the electrical circuit— and electricity flows. If nothing is plugged in and nothing is turned on, then there is no flow at all.

People sometimes worry that electricity might "run out" of receptacles when they're not being used. But when nothing is plugged in, the circuit is broken, and electricity is stalled. Still, empty outlets provide a dangerous invitation to

young children. If they stick a piece of metal—even something as innocuous as a paper clip—into the hot slot, they can easily suffer a life-threatening shock. Each year some three thousand children end up in hospital emergency rooms as a result of this sort of tragedy, and you sure don't want yours to be among them. In households with kids, childproof receptacle covers are an excellent idea. These plastic devices press safely into the outlet and block the flow of electricity.

cuit and happen to be standing on a damp surface, the electricity will pass through you, which can be disastrous. While the circuit breaker will stop overheated wires from setting fire to the house, it won't protect you from getting electrocuted because it doesn't shut off the current quickly enough. Something that will save you, however, is grounding.

In terms of electrical safety, the three most important things are grounding, grounding, and grounding. Given a choice, electricity would like to head to the ground rather than to the power company. That's what happens with lightning, after all—it discharges its voltage and dissipates harmlessly once it strikes the ground. Electrical systems in houses are also grounded. In a well-designed system, a wire is connected to each and every outlet and receptacle, and is then literally attached to a metal rod that runs it into the ground. This is what that "third hole" at the bottom of an outlet is for. This means that any leaks in the electrical system will be siphoned off to the ground instead of discharging their voltage through you when you touch, say, a blender with a frayed cord. Ungrounded outlets, which exist in many houses built before the 1950s, will still work, but won't protect you from shocks such as these. This is also why it's so reckless to cut the third prong off the plug of an appliance wire or extension cord if you only have a two-hole socket to fit it into. You'll be operating it with no grounding and, therefore, no protection.

Probably the greatest invention in recent years is the ground-fault circuit interrupter (or GFCI) outlet. Required by electrical codes in all new construction since 1993, these are circuit breakers that are positioned directly in the outlet in places where you could come in contact with both a short circuit and wetness. They're put in bathrooms, near kitchen sinks, and outdoors. The beauty of these is their quick response time. If they sense a drop in the current flow to the neutral wire—which means, in effect, that you yourself have become the neutral wire—they shut off the circuit in one-fortieth of a second, which is fast enough to prevent serious injury. Don't experiment with this, however; just trust me on it. These outlets can be easily added to an older house and make one of the most cost-effective safety upgrades on the planet. Anyone who doesn't have them should make an appointment with an electrician to have them installed before reading another paragraph.

How It Works: A Circuit Breaker

Inside a circuit breaker, there is a piece of metal, half copper and half steel, making the electrical connection. When cool, the metal lies flat and the circuit is open. When it heats up, however, the metals expand at two different rates, causing the piece to distort and "throw" the circuit. You don't have to replace the circuit breaker when this happens, since the metals quickly cool and return to their normal position. Instead, after finding and fixing the cause of the problem, you simply click the circuit back into the on postion.

Upgrading Service

Mercifully, electrical systems have evolved over the years—and depending on the age of your house, yours should, too. Beginning around the 1900s, houses were first fitted with knob-and-tube wiring, and the power companies connected them to 60-amp and later 100-amp circuits. While this may have sufficed in the 1930s, when each house had just a few light bulbs and maybe a radio in the living room, it sure wasn't adequate for much else. The result, as electrical demands grow, is that people add extension cords and adapters to make up for a shortage of outlets in these antiquated systems, which can dangerously overload circuits. Then they rely on fuses—rather than the more efficient circuit breakers—as a safety mechanism.

If you've got fuses in your electrical service box, which have to be screwed in like tiny light bulbs, I have a few words of advice: Change them to circuit breakers! Some people argue that you can have a perfectly safe system with fuses, so there's no point in doing this. But I disagree. There's no way an old system can be safer than a properly installed new one. And when it comes time to sell your house—as it one day will be—prospective buyers are going to blanch when they or their home inspector takes a look at what you've got hidden in the service box. Do yourself a favor and upgrade the box. It's going to give your family

What It Means When the Lights Flicker

Electrical systems will tell you when they're overloaded, as long as you know how to listen to them. The biggest sign of trouble is flickering lights. If they flicker when a power-hungry appliance such as a refrigerator or a dishwasher switches on, you've got problems. This is a clear sign that the circuits are dangerously overloaded. Call an electrician. The solution may involve nothing more than stringing independent circuits to the big appliances, without having to rewire the entire house.

extra peace of mind, and it will add value to your house in a way that new wallpaper and a fresh coat of paint simply will not. And if you have an old service box, with no room to add additional breakers, you'll want to consider adding a larger panel to create more flexibility. That way, when you want to overhaul the kitchen or put in a workshop out in the garage, you'll have the electrical capacity you'll need to make it hum.

People get tricked into thinking that their electrical upgrades stop at the service box. And, true, for a couple of thousand dollars they end up with a great new hookup, a shiny new electrical box, and a bunch of circuit breakers rather than old fuses. In some cases, however, this acts more like a face lift that alters the appearance of a system without changing the underlying decrepitude of the system itself. You may still very well have a tangle of old wires running through the walls, with decaying insulation and overloaded circuits ready to burst.

The only way to discover this is to hire a licensed electrician who can make a detailed inspection. Done right, this involves taking apart all the electrical boxes in the walls and ceilings, figure out the wiring, and telling you what needs changing. If it's knob-and-tube wiring, you have only one choice: replace it. In other systems, you may be able to run separate lines for big power-draining items, such as the refrigerator, the dishwasher, and portable air conditioners. That will ease up the load on the existing circuits, and you won't have to rewire everything. This is the least expensive way to fix a lot of electrical problems in an old house—and it can be done without smashing through every wall.

The Need for Safety

When I first started in the home construction business, I ended up working as an electrician's assistant one afternoon. My job was simple. It involved holding a piece of 2-by-4 in my hand and standing by him while he worked on a ladder to install a high-voltage motor in an overhead garage door opener. "If I get hung up," the electrician told me, referring to the grabbing power of electricity that would literally keep him clinging to the wire if he got zapped, "hit me in the head with the board so I fall off the ladder."

Professionals know how serious the risks involved with electrical work can be. Keep in mind that electrons move at the speed of light. It's not likely you'll be able to duck them—especially since you can't see them. And the smallest amount of electricity can kill you. This is something that average homeowners don't think about when all they want to do is, say, put the dining room chandelier on a dimmer switch. There are many things that I eagerly recommend homeowners do for themselves, since they can be rewarding and money-saving. Mucking with the electrical system is not among them. Unless you're willing to get some training, perhaps by taking a course at a community college, stay away from it. Even a simple task can turn into a life-threatening event. In just about every case, it's more than worth it to call in a licensed expert.

By necessity, you have to keep the electrical systems in your house to the highest standards. This is the one area in which you absolutely do not want to cut corners, no matter how tight your budget. Stuffing obvious problems, like age-decayed wires, back into the walls and keeping your fingers crossed is asking for trouble. The one thing that can guide you to make the right decisions is the National Electrical Code, which is pro-

Working Smart

If you know nothing about electrical systems, hire an electrician rather than trying to get on-the-job-training yourself. It's the only way to guarantee the work is done safely and properly. If you're going to tackle smaller tasks—such as replacing a worn-out outlet or installing a new ceiling light—follow one rule: Always turn off the circuit breaker controlling the circuit. Then double-check that it's off by plugging a light into the outlet or turning on the light switch. If you're still not sure you've hit the right breaker, turn off the main breaker, which is the big switch at the top of the service box. You'll be putting the entire house in the dark, but at least you'll be able to work with confidence.

duced by the National Fire Protection Association. It's in effect in all fifty states—with the occasional local provision thrown in as well.

Like all regulations, the code can sometimes be maddening and seem like overkill. It requires certain elements in the home to have their own dedicated circuits—things like a refrigerator, dishwasher, washer, and dryer. That way, they're not draining electricity from other equipment in the house, which reduces the risk of fire. The circuit breakers required by code also make it possible to isolate the circuit that has a problem without shutting down the power to the rest of the house. The requirements for the spacing of outlets—every six feet, and applied on every bit of wall two feet or more in width—also add to safety. Having many separate circuits and many outlets prevents the system from becoming overloaded no matter how many gadgets you plug in.

Surge Relief

Even if your electrical system is up to code, there can still be a problem that you have to take additional measures to defend against—and that's something called power surges. In an ideal world, the voltage running through circuits in your home would remain constant, at either 120 or 240 volts. We're not in an ideal

world, however, and this voltage can fluctuate dramatically. There are slight surges that can occur every time an electric motor in a refrigerator or air conditioner switches on, and then there are the 10,000-volt behemoths that result from lightning striking a nearby utility pole.

In the past, these smaller surges posed little threat. While they might have blown out the occasional light bulb, they caused little damage—certainly not to outlets and switches. Then came the age of the microprocessor. We now have chips in our computers, stereo equipment, TVs, and VCRs, all of which are extremely sensitive to voltage fluctuations. Even small surges, over time, can shorten the life of and eventually destroy computers and other electronics. These things can be protected by a surge protector strip, which comes between your equipment and the outlet. If the voltage from the outlet surges above the accepted level, the surge protector diverts the extra electricity into the outlet's grounding wire rather than having it course through your microprocessors. A surge protector is rated by a unit called a joule, which is a measure of how much energy it can absorb and divert before it fails. A higher number indicates greater protection; look for at least 600 joules.

Far more destructive than surges that originate within your house, however, are larger power surges resulting from lightning or from erratic power delivery from utilities. These can result in large blips of upward of 400 volts, which is something those small surge protectors attached to outlets are powerless to stop. Power surges are alarmingly common. In the United States,

it's estimated that we try to draw about 5 percent more electricity than utilities can produce. This results in brownouts, in which power producers temporarily cut back the voltage to some customers to make up the deficit. While that alone can damage sensitive equipment such as computers and high-tech stereos, these undervoltages are inevitably followed by overvoltages or spikes that cause even more damage. We may not always be aware of it, but we live in a near continual state of such fluctuations—and they seem to be increasing rather than decreasing.

In a world such as this, the only way to protect equipment properly is to install a surge protector that covers the entire house. These fit right next to the service panel, and work by siphoning off excess voltage and sending it directly to the ground, rather than through wiring in your house. It might cost you $200 to have a surge protector installed, but it will cover every outlet and fixture in your house to far better effect. Good ones can handle surges up to 20,000 volts. But even with the whole-house surge protector, you'll still need the smaller units indoors to protect against little surges originating from within your household.

Backup Power

When I was growing up, a power failure was dealt with by having a flashlight and a few candles lying around. It was actually kind of fun. But

A Fifteen-Second Inspection

What's the worst thing you can find in an electrical system? A rusted circuit breaker box, which is common among those positioned in chronically damp crawl spaces or basements. This is more than just a cosmetic flaw. The corrosion can penetrate the circuit breakers themselves, forcing them to stay in the open position even if a circuit overloads. When that happens, you're operating without any safety backup—which is an invitation to a fire. Take a look at the box every year and flick the breaker switches off and then on to make sure they still work. If they don't budge, or if you see signs of rust, call an electrician.

now, considering the amount of work people do at home, the complexity of their lives, and the shortage of free time, a power failure is more often greeted with dread. Add to this the specter of brownouts and rolling blackouts as power companies struggle with shortages, and it becomes hugely desirable to find a way to provide an emergency power supply when you need it.

Enter the backup generators. Instead of relying on the utility to provide you with voltage to pressure those electrons in your wiring, you can accomplish the same with a portable generator. The least safe method of doing this is to have a gasoline-powered generator set up out in the garage, with an extension cord rigged up to the circuit breaker box. Some foolish people continue to do this, but it is terribly risky and you should never, never attempt this. Not only do you risk filling up the garage with deadly carbon monoxide fumes, but you will blow out the generator or worse when the power comes back on. A big improvement in the past fifteen years has been the emergency transfer switch, which isolates certain circuits—say, to the refrigerator, a few lights, the sump pump, and the TV—and allows you to power them separately during a blackout. While you do have to throw the switch manually to make the shift to the generator and then turn it off again when the power comes

Don't Try This at Home

If you use a lightweight extension cord for a heavy-duty appliance, you're asking for trouble. Thin cords are usually rated for 6 amps—even though the outlet and the circuit breaker that they connect to may be rated for 15 or even 20 amps. That means that the cord itself can overload and become dangerously hot without the circuit breaker tripping. If you use a thin extension cord to connect to a heavy-duty appliance such as an air conditioner or a refrigerator, the insulation in the cord will start breaking down, creating a real fire hazard.

back, the safety this adds is enormous. The generator itself might cost you around $1,000 to produce 4,000 watts of electricity, with another $250 for the installed transfer switch. And remember, to avoid an accumulation of deadly fumes the generators have to be positioned outside, rather than in the garage or basement. Obvious as this may seem, it is truly startling how often people ignore this.

Mr. Fix-It's Law, however, dictates that when the power goes off you won't be home to connect the generator and throw the transfer switch—meaning your basement will flood without the sump pump and the food in your freezer will spoil. As a remedy, some companies have developed automatic transfer switches, which run with generators powered by either gasoline or natural gas and positioned permanently outside. These are so sophisticated that they will sense a drop of electricity within five seconds and fire up the system automatically. The cost is considerably more—perhaps $7,000 for those same 4,000 watts—but the foolproof aspect may be priceless to some.

An alternative to this is to have a battery-powered backup positioned in the basement. While just as expensive—at about $7,000 for 4,000 watts—it has the advantage of being maintenance-free, as well as being silent.

Conventional generators make a good deal of noise—on par, perhaps, with a lawn mower. While that may sound like a racket, it will be music to your ears as your neighbors' milk turns to cottage cheese in their refrigerator. Many municipalities, however, have laws restricting noise-producing machinery. This has led to the popularity of battery-powered energy sources. They also run without producing any emissions, which makes them feasible for city or apartment living.

Not everyone needs a backup generator, to be sure. Some neighborhoods rarely have blackouts, and when they occur they last only briefly. You sure wouldn't want to spend a few thousand dollars just to be sure that you don't lose, say, a half hour of TV to the darkness. For others, blackouts happen far more frequently, and the stakes can be much higher. A twelve-hour blackout in the Northeast in wintertime, for instance, could burst pipes as the water within freezes. And a friend of mine lives in a rural area that gets at least a blackout a month, which can drag on sometimes for a day or two. Also, if anyone in your household requires any round-the-clock medical equipment, a backup system is truly essential. In these cases, the money for a backup generator seems like money well spent—and the system will become a plus to buyers whenever the house goes up for sale.

A Plan of Attack

No matter what age your house is, remember that electrical systems aren't built to last forever. Eventually, they will all need maintaining and upgrading. You could have obvious problems, like knob-and-tube wiring, or more subtle ones, like a lack of GFCI outlets in wet areas. Either way, in the rush to care for and improve your house, this is one area you don't want to neglect—as my friends with the hapless foursquare found out.

For them, the fire could have been prevented had they spent their money first on having their wiring replaced. It might have cost them $10,000, which is money that could have easily been recouped if ever they wanted to sell their house. As it was, their house suffered terrible smoke damage, the roof had to be redone, all the plaster and the drywall had to come down, and the whole place ended up doused in water by the firefighters. The damages amounted to about $75,000.

Fortunately, they weren't hurt, and the insurance covered just about everything. This was truly an avoidable catastrophe, however. And when they went to repair the damage, a new electrical system went right where it should have been in the first place—at the top of their to-do list.

chapter FOUR

Hot and Cold
Here's how to keep your home cool when it's hot, and warm when it's not

Sometimes ignorance about our homes can lead us to make the silliest mistakes, especially when it comes to our comfort.

When I first started building new homes, for instance, I worked for a builder on a great place—a job I was proud of because I knew the work had been done well. In the middle of the winter, however, the owner called my boss with a complaint. "This place is freezing!" he griped. "It just never gets warm." We sent the furnace guy out to have a look. The furnace was producing hot air, just as it should, and a forced-air blower was sending it through the house, just as it should. Still, the complaints continued. I went with the builder to have a look one day, and he made an unusual diagnosis. "Too much furniture," he said, which startled the homeowner as much as it did me. "What do you mean, too much furniture?" the homeowner fumed. "What *else* did you think I was going to put in my house?"

As it turned out, the problem wasn't really the amount of furniture, but the position in which it had been placed. Forced-air heating systems send hot air through vents in the floor and draw it back in through intake vents also positioned near the floor. These need to be free of obstructions to flow smoothly. But in this house, every single one of these was blocked by furniture. There were sofas and draperies blocking the vents in the living room, bookcases blocking vents in the family room, and beds and bureaus blocking everything in the bedrooms. While the furnace worked fine, the forced-air blower could barely wheeze, let alone fill an entire house with warm air. After a few minutes of rearranging things and freeing up those vents, the house suddenly felt as balmy as a day in Florida.

Of all the aspects of a house, comfort can be the most important. You can have the grandest house in the world, as these people did, yet have it be a misery to live in. Or you can own the most humble work in progress, but if it keeps you warm as toast in the middle of a blizzard or creates a cool oasis for you in the middle of a July swelter, you'll find it the homiest haven of all. Discomfort is easy to pinpoint. All you have to do is feel for drafts in the winter and stifling heat in the summer. Comfort, however, is harder to define, because in a comfortable house the specific details just disappear. Instead, things seem exactly as they should be, not too hot, not too cold. Fortunately, this condition doesn't have to be arrived at by accident. Insulation of walls and ceilings and weatherstripping of doors and windows, which I discuss in Chapter 5, can go a long way toward eliminating drafts. But let's take a closer look at some frequently overlooked components of comfort, which can turn even the lowliest bungalow into a dream house.

Feeling Warm, Feeling Cool

What makes you feel comfortable? The right temperature, of course— somewhere between 68 and 72 degrees in the winter, and slightly warmer in the summer, maybe between 73 and 75 degrees. The actual temperature of the human body is 98.6 degrees, as we all know, so why, then, do we feel most comfortable at these lower temperatures? The reason has to do with our skin temperature, which is actually only about 74 degrees. Here's where a little bit of physics enters in to the

A Fan of Fans

While central air conditioners keep things cool, nothing matches the beautiful simplicity of ceiling fans. These work not by lowering the temperature but by swirling currents through the air so that moisture evaporates from your skin faster. This cools you down, and with a lot less 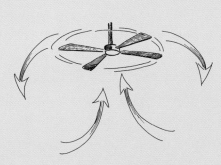 electricity than an air conditioner requires. Yet ceiling fans can also make air conditioners work more effectively. Cool air tends to flow from vents and settle near the floor, where it stays. But if you run a ceiling fan on slow and in reverse, it will pull colder air up from the floor and mix it better in the room. This keeps you more comfortable, and, since the condensing unit on the air conditioner will run less, it also saves you money. The same is true during the heating season. Remember earth science class in school? Heat rises. By running the fans slowly, you can keep that warm air circulating. Not only will you be more comfortable, but your furnace will run less which will save you money.

comfort equation. Heat travels from warm things to cooler ones, never the other direction. That means that if you can get the temperature in the room as close to 74 degrees as possible, you'll feel comfortable. You won't heat up, the way you would if the temperature far exceeds 74 degrees. And you won't cool down, the way you would if the temperature drops much below that. Like Goldilocks, you'll have found something that feels just right.

Temperature, however, isn't the only factor in the comfort equation. The other thing to consider is humidity. Take a trip to Arizona when it's 105 degrees in August, and you won't instantly expire. Why? Because, as the joke goes, it's a dry heat. There's literally very little humidity in the air. That means that moisture can evaporate readily from your skin, and when it does it draws heat from your body and cools you down. Now, make a visit to Chicago, where I live, on a 95-degree day, and you'll probably find yourself gasping not because of the heat but because of the humidity. A lot of moisture in the air means that nothing evaporates from your skin very quickly, and so no heat can be drawn out of your body to cool you down. With a lot of humidity, you're more or less simmering in your own juices.

Now, let's apply this to the home. In winter, the goal is not only to raise the temperature but to raise the humidity as well—which can easily be accomplished with an assortment of humidifiers, including whole-house models. A range of 30 to 40 percent relative humidity is ideal, although this often drops to 10 percent in a home, especially those with forced hot-air systems. With humidity that low in the winter, you'll feel cold no matter how high you jack up the heat. The high end also poses a problem, however. We're naturally creating humidity just by living in a house. The average family of four creates 4 gallons of moisture a day just by taking showers, boiling spaghetti, and even through the simple act of exhaling. In new homes built with thick and supertight insulation, this moisture can accumulate to an unhealthy degree. If you actually see it beading up on the windows, you know you've got a problem that could lead to mold and mildew. In a house like this, you can't just crank up the humidifier to 40 percent, or you'll very quickly feel like

A Whole-House Approach

One clever way to cool down a house is with a whole-house fan. Positioned in the ceiling of the top floor so that it vents into the attic, this moves air at an astonishing rate—just two minutes is all that's needed to exchange the entire volume in a house. To operate it, you open the downstairs windows at night, once the outside temperature begins to drop. Cooler air is instantly sucked into the house, and continues to be drawn in all night. Then, in the morning, you turn off the fan and close the windows. Cool air is then trapped in the house, in the most cost-effective way possible. Whether you use a central air conditioner during the day or not, a whole-house fan can make a sensible addition to a house.

you're living in the bayou. Instead, you have to work to strike a balance between comfort and health.

In summer, you're after the opposite goal. You want low humidity so that moisture evaporates from your skin and your body naturally cools down. While air conditioners do indeed reduce the temperature of the air they circulate, they also reduce the relative humidity—and that means it feels cooler. This is why dehumidifiers are so effective in making a room feel comfortable, even though the air they churn out is the same temperature as the air around them. Ignoring humidity limits the effectiveness of your heating and cooling systems and means that you'll be wasting a lot of money trying to raise and lower the temperature in a futile effort to feel comfortable.

A Home in Balance

We have some notion that when we turn on the heat or the air-conditioning from a single thermostat, we're taking care of the entire house. But the fact is, you're dealing with three different atmospheric conditions in any home—not just one. Regardless of the season, you've got the basement, where cold air settles; you've got the second floor, where warm air rises; and you've got the first floor, sandwiched between these two temperature extremes. This is basic physics, and you don't need to be Einstein to grasp the principles: Hot air rises; cold air falls. In the summertime, any air-conditioning you have on rushes down the staircase—which is more or less a giant duct in the middle of your home—and settles into the basement, turning it into a refrigerator. In the wintertime, all of that heating you're spending your money on rushes up to the second floor, leaving the first floor—and especially the basement—cold. Simply cranking up the heat or blasting the AC isn't going to change this balance. In fact, the larger temperature differential it creates is just going to aggravate things. The air will rush faster—and make things seem even hotter and colder than they were.

Instead, what you need to learn to do is balance the heating and cooling systems you have, so that they deliver more heating or cooling to the rooms where it's needed. When you're talking about heat, you want more distributed on the first floor of your home and even in the basement than you do upstairs. If you have cooling, you want more spread out upstairs than downstairs. Fortunately, this is a lot easier to accom-

Maintaining Ducts

One of the biggest sources of indoor pollution can some-times lie unnoticed—the air ducts that move hot or cold air through your home. Filters remove some of the dust, pollen, and mold spores that fly through these ducts, but much more clings to the side as it settles out of the relatively slow-moving air. To safeguard the system, the first line of defense is to filter the air to keep the stuff out of the ductwork in the first place. But older ducts—twenty years and up—may need a bigger fix. Professional duct-cleaning services can reach in with superlong vacuum tubes and clean everything out. How do you know if you need this? Check your nose. If you or someone in your household has chronic or mysterious allergies, the cause may lie within the ducts.

plish than it sounds. In the summertime, cool air is forced through vents. You'll want to close off the vents in the basement and partially close them on the first floor. That will force more cool air up to the second floor. (Of course, if you only have a one-story house, you'd leave the vents on this floor wide open.) In the wintertime, you'd do the reverse—specifically, limit the flow of hot air to the upstairs ducts so that more will go to the lower parts of the house and counteract all that heat rushing up the stair-case. This works for hot-water systems as well, since you can easily adjust the water flow through most radiators, which a lot of people don't even realize. Do this by gently turning the valves, which are connected right to the radiators.

In new houses, contractors can install dampers right in the ductwork that can give you more effective control over your system. This is definitely something you'd want to discuss with them if you're building a new home or addition. Some systems are so sophisticated, in fact, that you can control the temperature in every room, courtesy of a separate thermostat and damper in each. These are nice, but you'd need to be Michael Jordan—or at least a Rockefeller—to afford it.

Even without this sort of technology, balancing the system is something you can easily do yourself, especially since it's more of a trial-and-error process than an exact science. Just allow several hours—say, five or six—for things to adjust before you can be sure you're technique is working. It may take some time to sort out, but when you do it will make a huge difference. And best of all, it won't cost you a thing.

Heating Things Up

No matter what type of fuel you use, most houses are heated in one of two ways—with a furnace, which accounts for about two-thirds of all heating systems, or with a boiler. The difference between the two is simple: Furnaces heat air, while boilers heat water.

Let's start with furnaces, which are connected to a forced-air heating system, as we saw above. In this system, air from the home is filtered, then drawn through a duct into the furnace, where it is heated to some 800 degrees by a blast of flame. This superheated air is then blown through ducts and emerges through vents, usually positioned in the floors. Furnaces used to be simple contraptions. The thermostat told them to turn on or off, and they did. Now they're sophisticated pieces of equipment filled with computer technology, which includes sensors to check that the air is not too hot or too cool as it leaves. In fact, the technology in the typical new furnace is so sophisticated that it is about two to three times more complex than the computer systems used to run Apollo 11!

At the heart of the furnace lies the heat exchanger, in which heat from the flame is transferred to air in the ducts. This keeps the fumes from the fire separate from the air you breathe —a vital safety feature, since your home would other- wise fill with deadly carbon monoxide and other toxic fumes. Instead, these fumes rise and go out the flue or chimney harmlessly. Of all the things that can go wrong with a furnace, the worst would be to have a crack in a heat exchanger—which hap-

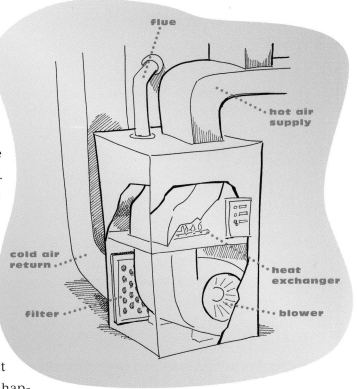

pens occasionally in systems twenty years of age and older. When the heat exchanger cracks, the fumes that should be headed upward instead begin to seep into the ducts and circulate through your house. If you sud- denly smell fumes in your home, which could be a sign of a heat exchang- er failure, shut the furnace off and head outside at once.

Fortunately, this is a rare event—especially if you have your furnace serviced each year by someone, such as your local fuel supplier or heat- ing contractor. Not only do they check the heat exchanger for signs of trouble, they adjust the furnace so that it runs at peak efficiency and make sure it's soot-free so that it won't suddenly konk out at 3 A.M. in the middle of a January freeze. It may cost you $100 to have the furnace serviced each year, but it's about the best money you'll ever spend. Because technology increases so rapidly, and because furnaces are more efficient than ever, it will probably make sense to replace your

Adding a Little Humidity

Because of their modest cost, forced-air heating systems are among the most popular of all—accounting for about two-thirds of all heating systems installed. But when air passes through the furnace heat exchanger, it does more than heat up. That heat also bakes all the moisture out of the air, resulting in dry air that can not only make you feel dried out but leave you feeling cold as well. Rather than installing individual humidifiers in every room, a better solution is to have a humidification system installed in the forced-air blower just as the heated air is sent through the house. Some systems send the air across a spongelike plate dripping with water; others inject an atomized spray into it. The best ones let you perfectly adjust the relative humidity of the air—so if you want it between 30 and 40 percent, which is ideal in winter, you can simply dial it in.

furnace if it's fifteen years old, and it will certainly make sense if it's more than twenty-five years old. You may have to spend $8,000 or so for a new furnace. But the money you spend will be quickly recouped by dramatically lower fuel bills, as well as increasing comfort. It will also add value to your home—particularly if you plan on selling in the near future and can tell prospective buyers your furnace is less than five years old.

A boiler forms the heart of the other major type of system, which is called radiant hydronic heating. Rather than heating air, a boiler heats water, which is then pumped throughout the house either through radiators or circuits of tubing that lie just beneath the floor. As with the furnace, the boiler also has a heat exchanger—but the flame is heating pipes containing water rather than air. Among central heating systems, hydronic ones are the oldest and certainly the most comfortable as far as I'm concerned. In fact, they were just about the only choice until the 1930s, when forced-air systems first became popular.

Forced-air systems have their advantages. Or, rather, they have two specific advantages. The first is that they cost less to install than hydronic systems, by about a third. The second is that the ductwork used to pump hot air can also be used to pump cool air. All you need to do is fit the system with a $1,500 to $2,000 outdoor condenser, as I'll show, and you've got central air-conditioning. But hot-water heat is by far my favorite way to go—regardless of the extra cost. For one thing, it's as quiet as heat can get, since there's no blower shutting on and off. There are also fewer drafts, so you won't feel air blowing on you while you're sitting on the living room sofa. Forced-air systems also tend to kick up a lot of dust and allergens as they vent air through the house; hydronic systems do not. Mostly, I believe, the advantages of a hydronic system come down to a matter of comfort. Forced-air systems pulse on and off, which means that you're usually either too hot or too cold. But the water that runs through hydronic systems—whether it's through baseboards, tubes set beneath the floor, or even cast-iron radiators—stays hot, so you get a far more even and efficient heat.

Boilers have a slight safety advantage over furnaces as well. Even though heat exchangers in boilers can fail, the risk to your health is less because the heat exchanger is filled with water, not air. If there's a leak, you'll notice a steady stream of water dripping out, rather than smelling fumes around the house. As with furnaces, boilers need regular professional maintenance, which should be done

Sweep That Chimney

While it may sound like a romantic notion, chimney sweeps—as in Dick Van Dyke in *Mary Poppins*—are very much needed if you have a working fireplace. Burning wood produces creosote, which clings to the lining of the chimney. When enough accumulates, it can catch fire— and produce superheated flames that can burn down the entire house. Many houses don't exist anymore because of chimney fires. Don't let yours be one of them. Call a chimney sweep at least once a year in the fall. It's probably the best low-cost fire insurance there is.

once a year. That will ensure that all the burners are clean and running as efficiently as possible and that the pumps are working adequately to move hot water through radiators.

Furnaces and boilers have one major drawback, which is that they require oxygen to burn. And where do they get this? From the air inside your home. In an old, drafty house, this poses little problem. There's plenty of oxygen floating around to fuel both you and the fire to heat your home. A drafty house, it turns out, is in many respects a healthy house. But in a tightly insulated house, a major problem occurs. Just where will the oxygen come from to fuel the heating system? It comes from within the house, but it can draw with so much force that it actually depressurizes the house. When this happens, air is sucked inside from places it shouldn't be—such as down the fireplace flue, backward through the bathroom exhaust vents, and even down the chimney connected to the boiler or furnace. This can contain not only foul smells but also dangerous toxins such as carbon monoxide. In short, this is not air you want to breathe, trust me! If you have a well-insulated house, you'll want to consider having an outside air source connected to the furnace or boiler. This can be installed by your

radiators

expansion tank

water loop

exhaust pipe

gas

pressure release

circulating pump

Return of the Swamp Thing

In the age before air conditioners, people in some parts of the country switched on evaporator coolers—better known by their nicknames, "eevaps" and "swamp coolers." These old-fashioned chillers still have some advantages over air conditioners. They cost half as much to install as central air-conditioning, for one thing, and they consume a third as much energy. Evaporative coolers work on the same principle as a sweaty person standing in front of a fan on a hot day. As sweat vaporizes, it takes heat from the skin and cools you down. In these systems, hot air from the outdoors is passed over a filter soaked with water (rather than sweat). The hot air evaporates the water, which cools the air inside the house. A good evaporative cooling system can chill the air 30 degrees or more and force warm, humid air out through windows or ducts in the attic. The key to these systems is to install them only if you live in an area filled with hot, dry air—like the arid Southwest. An estimated 15 percent of all homes in the United States could use them, the EPA estimates, but right now they account for only about 1 percent of all cooling systems.

heating fuel supplier for $200 or $300, and will help protect the air you breathe.

Keeping Your Cool

It's amazing sometimes how quickly a new technology can move from a gimmick to a necessity—think of cell phones, the Internet, and central air-conditioning. Originally designed as a refrigeration tool for food, air-conditioning has steadily become more popular in houses built since World War II. While these systems do indeed cool the air, their biggest contribution to your comfort is that they also lower the humidity. That means that water from your skin evaporates faster than it would in a more humid environment, which means that you actually feel cooler.

Central air conditioners don't use boilers and furnaces, but instead

The Cheapest Form of Electric Heat

Electric radiant heat is the easiest of all to use—it clicks on, with no maintenance and no refueling needed. But it's expensive, as you discover each time you get your monthly electric bill. A compromise, which works well in milder climates, is to heat and cool your home using a device called a heat pump. Instead of creating a heat source the way boilers and furnaces do, heat pumps use electricity to move heat to the inside or outside of a home. During the summer, a heat pump captures heat from inside a house and transfers it to the outdoor air through a condensing unit. During the winter, the process is reversed. Heat is captured from the outdoor air, compressed, and then released inside.

Obviously, there are some limitations. Where it is freezing outdoors, there won't be much heat to transfer, and so conventional electric baseboard heating is needed to supplement the heat pump. Depending on the climate, heat pumps can be as much as three times cheaper to use than electric radiant heat alone.

rely on electricity to run a unit called a condenser. This is usually a large, sometimes noisy unit that is usually positioned outside by the foundation of a house. Air conditioners work in exactly the same way that a refrigerator does—except that they chill your entire house rather than just a little box. The key ingredient is something called a refrigerant, which goes through a phase change from a liquid to a gas and back again to a liquid.

Just how does this end up cooling anything? Let's take a tour and find

A Cool-Looking Solution

In my view, nothing makes a house look tackier than having a portable air conditioner sticking out of a window. This is the ugliest thing you ever want to see, especially in an old house! One great alternative is a ductless central air conditioning system, which does not involve snaking ducts through the walls—and makes an ideal choice for homes with hot-water, steam, or electric heat. The cooling portion of these units fits beneath a window inside the house—similar to the kind of unit you find in hotel rooms. The noisy condensing part of the system lies outside, similar to those used in conventional air conditioning systems. The outdoor condensers are connected to the indoor coolers by a small tube, which enters the house through an inconspicuous hole about half an inch wide. You can hook several of these units up to a single condenser, which allows you to cool specific rooms in your home—and preserve the look of the exterior.

out. The condenser takes the cool refrigerant in its gas phase and compresses it. This hot, compressed gas then runs through a condensing coil, where it is cooled by air blown over it from a fan positioned in the outdoor unit. This is the sound you hear when it switches on. As the refrigerant in the coil cools, it condenses and turns into a liquid. Now comes the fun part. This liquid then moves from the condensing coil into an expansion valve. Imagine, if you will, what used to happen in your high school gym class: You and your classmates would file down a tight corridor, then when you got into the big gymnasium you'd run like wild. The same thing happens here, only on a molecular level. The liquid runs through the tight coil, and when it gets to the expansion valve the molecules evaporate suddenly to form a gas. And a very cold gas, at that.

From here, the cold gas runs through a set of cooling coils that allow the gas to absorb heat and cool down the air inside the home. At this point, the technology for cooling is very similar to what happens in a heat exchanger in a furnace—only that air sucked from ducts throughout the house becomes cooled, rather than heated, and is then circulated back through the house. The air conditioner does more than just cool the air, however. As the air cools, the humidity contained in it is reduced, and water literally drips out of it. The cooler air circulating through your house now has a lower humidity—and that's what makes you feel more comfortable. Once the refrigerant has become a gas and done its job cooling the air in your home, the gas is then compressed into a hot liquid again, and the cycle repeats endlessly.

While this works marvelously well, one problem can occur. The cooling coil can occasionally freeze, which means that a coating of ice forms on the outside. This greatly limits the effectiveness of the system, since ice can't absorb heat the way the gas inside the cooling coil can. While this might suggest that there is too much refrigerant in the system, the opposite is in fact true. If you've got freeze-ups, there's not enough

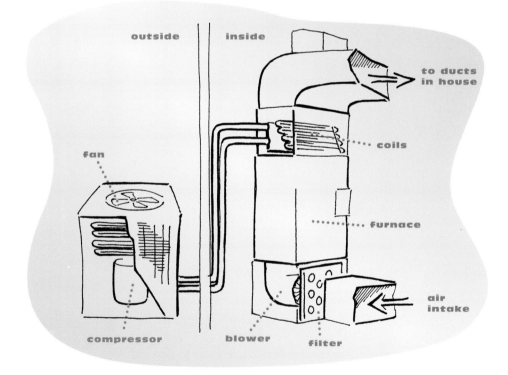

refrigerant in the system. Fortunately, an air-conditioning service company can easily add more to the system.

If you have a forced-air heating system, it is very easy to have a central air conditioner hooked up because it uses the same ductwork. It's no problem, and this is one of the great benefits of these systems. But if you have a hydronic system, there is a problem—you need ducts, not pipes, to run air through to cool off the house. Fortunately, there is a clever alternative to standard forced-air ducts called a cold air handler, or space pack. This involves snaking flexible ducts about two inches in diameter through the walls into every room in the house. Radical as this may seem, it's actually one of the most noninvasive procedures there is, and you won't have to patch a lot of walls once it's been added even if you have a very old or historic home. One caveat: The space pack is a high-pressure system compared to ordinary ducts; if you're walking by a vent and are wearing a toupee, the breeze will definitely flip it over.

All central air conditioners should be inspected by a professional every year. It is not uncommon to have the refrigerant leak out of your system, which means it loses its efficiency—and costs you extra money to cool your home, and could also burn up your compressor. Beyond this, the gas acts as a way to lubricate the motor. So without enough, it would be a lot like running your car's engine without motor oil. You wouldn't go very far. These systems need to be recharged by adding more refrigerant and patching any leaks. On your own, make sure you check the condenser outside periodically and remove any leaves, grass clippings, or other debris that have a habit of blocking the air intake vents. This puts extra strain on the blower—just like furniture blocking the vents inside—and cuts down on its cooling abilities.

If you're installing a new system, make sure the condensing system is free to breathe on all four sides and on the top. It requires a huge volume of air to work efficiently. You never want to install a condensing unit under a deck, for instance. Remember that the whole point of the condensing unit is to cool the refrigerant and turn it into a liquid before sending it back into the system. If the airflow going to the condenser is limited, the fan won't be able to cool the refrigerant enough. If that happens, your system will run longer to try to keep your home cool, which will both shorten the life of your condensing unit and cost you more money in electricity.

Building a Better Thermostat

Thermostats used to be simple things. More often than not, they amount to a single round dial that you set somewhere between 68 and 72 degrees and hope for the best. The problem is, as every homeowner has probably long suspected, these types of themostats are terribly inaccurate. Their ability to sense the temperature is flawed, and many of them can have a swing of up to 8 degrees before the furnace or boiler turns itself on and off. Set it for 70, for instance, and you could find your house swinging between a nippy 66, and a *warm* 74. Far better are electronic programmable thermostats, which can be easily swapped with an existing one. These tend to have an accuracy within 1 degree, so if you're setting it for 70, it will range between 69 and 71. That's far better than the old system, and if you can feel the difference of 1 degree, then—like the princess and the pea, or, closer to home, Mrs. Fix-It—we're never going to make you feel truly comfortable.

Electronic thermostats offer an additional benefit: They also allow you to vary the temperature automatically throughout the day, without having to remember to switch it yourself. Let me show you why this matters. If you're heating a house, you can program an electronic thermostat to automatically lower the temperature when you're at work and your kids are at

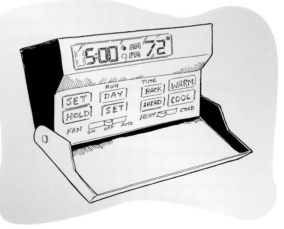

school, or when you're asleep at night. This can save you a great deal of money. Daily temperature manipulations of 5 or 10 degrees can save you up to 30 percent on your heating and cooling over the year.

Interested in swapping thermostats? I thought so. This is an easy task, and one you can do yourself (or have an electrician do it for you). The only tricky part is making sure you're buying the correct thermostat. Specifically, if you have both central heating and central air-conditioning, you have to buy a programmable thermostat that can accommodate both. Remove a thermostat and you'll find four wires—a red one, a white one, a green one, and a black one. On the back of the new thermostat, you'll find four letters that correspond to those colors, namely, R, W, G, and B. Attach the wires, screw the thermostat to the wall, and you're in business. This is a low-voltage gadget—on the order of a flashlight—so there's no danger at all in making the connection. The instructions that come with programmable thermostats are fairly easy to understand, and anybody can make the swap. You might, however, need a master's degree to be able to figure out how to program the unit!

The Fireplace Fiasco

There's nothing more romantic than a fireplace. Who doesn't yearn for the glow of the fire at the hearth, snuggling close on a cold evening, and the way a fireplace becomes the centerpiece of a room? Plus, we've all deluded ourselves into thinking that they actually add to our home's overall warmth. Sadly, fireplaces have a very big downside. In fact, they're just about the most inefficient thing you can have in your house, and one that will surely disrupt your comfort unless you take care of some very important details.

Fireplaces may look great, but they do two undesirable things. First, they suck out all the oxygen from your home, and I'm not exaggerating by much. Fires need air to burn, lots of it—some 20,000 cubic feet per hour, or the equivalent of the entire volume of air in your home once every forty-five minutes. Now, you don't need to worry about running

out of oxygen, since as air (which you've already spent money to heat with a boiler or furnace) is sucked up and out the chimney, more air is being drawn in from outside. No matter how well insulated or weatherstripped your house is, cold air will be pulled in behind switchplates and outlets, behind baseboards at the bottoms of walls, and even through things such as dryer vents in order to feed the fire. The hotter the fire gets, the more oxygen it burns and the more it sucks cold air into your house. If you react to the growing chill by tossing yet another log on top, you're only worsening an already bad situation.

Second, fireplaces also create problems by creating a heat source—and a massive one—concentrated in one spot in your home. Most of the time the fireplace is in the living room, which is right next to your dining room, which 90 percent of the time is where your thermostat is. So the fireplace makes the living room nice and toasty warm, and the heat spills over to the dining room. But when it raises the temperature there, the thermostat says to itself, "Well, gee, it's pretty hot, so I'm going to turn the furnace off." When it does, the rest of the house cools down. So while you and your mate are snuggling on the living room floor, the bedrooms on the second floor where your kids are sleeping are freezing because the furnace isn't clicking on.

What's the way out of this? For starters, just know that a fireplace is

Five Ways to Save Money on Energy

I can't do anything about the rising cost of heating oil, natural gas, or propane, and electricity prices are going up—but I can help you use less energy. Follow these tips to keep your bills as low as possible:

- Service your heating system every year. It might cost $100 to have someone clean the unit and change the filters, but it's the best money you can spend to keep your system running smoothly with no surprises.

- Install a programmable thermostat. This is a must-have with energy costs rising. Outdated thermostats are the weakest link in conserving energy. New thermostats range from about $40 to $100 but can save you up to 30 percent in energy costs. This news is catching on way too slowly. According to the U.S. Energy Information Administration, only about 11 percent of all homes are equipped with modern programmable thermostats.

- Check the arrangement of your furniture. Really. Couches and chairs placed over the vents and in front of baseboard radiators can reduce the efficiency of both your heating and cooling systems. Your furnace or boiler, as well as the central air conditoner, will have to run longer, thus using more energy to heat your home.

- Be smart about the temperature you choose. Turning down the thermostat just 1 degree in cold weather can save you up to 3 percent on your fuel bill, according to the Environmental Protection Agency. A setting of 68 degrees should feel perfectly comfortable if you follow all these tips.

- Let the sun help heat your home. This costs nothing. During the day open up drapes and blinds to let the sun heat your home. At night draw the curtains to keep the heat inside.

all romance. You can never use one to actually add heat to your home, because you'll always end up losing more heat when you light it than you gain. As for what to do about all that oxygen being drawn out of the house, you need to have an external air supply—a vent that draws air from outside your house and connects right inside the firebox, where the logs burn. This is something you'd probably need to hire a contractor to do. In addition, you need to have glass doors installed. These close off the fire from the room, which guarantees that the air used for burning the logs comes through the external air supply. The doors also keep too much heat from radiating into the room, which will stop the flames from playing havoc with your thermostat. These two things—the doors and the external air supply—can be retrofitted into just about any fireplace, which will vastly improve its efficiency.

And for those romantic moments when you crave the nearness of a fire, you can do what I do: Open the glass doors. Just remember to close them again before heading to bed for the night.

A Comforting Thought

As you can see, there's a lot more to comfort than throwing up a few batts of fiberglass insulation or jacking up the thermostat a degree or two. There's mechanical upkeep, balancing systems, working with new thermostats, bringing your fireplace up to date—and even making sure you have your furniture positioned properly. These are things no one a generation ago had to worry about. But with fuel prices what they are nowadays, and only climbing higher, they're what all smart homeowners need to consider.

chapter FIVE

An Open-and-Shut Case
Windows and doors bring in the light while keeping out the wind and rain; here's how to manage them

So often, the things we love about our homes have less to do with the way they make things look than with the way they make things feel.

About four years ago, for example, I was renovating a house in Chicago when a friend who happened to be looking for a new home wanted my advice. That's one of the things I love about being Mr. Fix-It: Just as doctors get queried about bad backs at cocktail parties, I get grilled about septic systems. In any event, my friend and his wife were looking, looking, and looking but just couldn't find a place they thought was well built. I invited them over to take a look at what I was working on—not to try to sell it to them but to show them some of the details I think help make a place a solid investment.

The house had plenty of natural light from a profusion of wonderful windows, and the doors between the rooms were solid. "What do you mean, solid?" my friend asked as he and his wife

Cleaning Windows

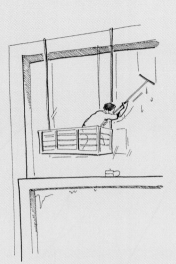

There's a lot of controversy over what's the best way to clean a window, and people tout everything from Glass Wax to newspaper. I've never found that newspaper worked very well for me; it gets soggy and leaves a trace of black ink around the window edge, which is hardly attractive. Instead, I go for the squeegee. You can attach a pole to it for second-story windows, dip it in a bucket of water with some dish detergent in it, and have a field day both inside and out. It's exactly like what those guys do to your windshield at a full-service gas station—just make sure you roll a towel at the bottom of the window indoors to catch the drips. I hate to admit this, but it's even kind of fun.

took a tour, careful to dodge the squadron of carpenters nailing up trim. "Well, feel this with your hands—go ahead and knock on it," I said, opening a bedroom door. He did, and a resounding thud filled the room. Many builders use hollow doors, I explained, which are wafer-thin pieces of wood separated by cardboard or paper mesh. Not exactly heirloom quality. I mentioned some other things to look for, including hardwood floors, nice cabinets, crown molding, and a good paint job, then sent them on their way for a weekend of house hunting. Monday morning, to my surprise, I received a phone call from my friend, telling me that he and his wife wanted to make a full-price offer on the place I was renovating. "What? This isn't even in the neighborhood you wanted!" I said. "Lou," he countered, "we looked at a dozen places, and none of them could pass the solid-door test. Once we knew what to look for, we just couldn't settle for anything less."

A house can be memorable because of its style or location or great landscaping. But for the most part, it's the quality of the things you touch every single day that makes you feel at home—and doors and windows rank at the top of the list of what's most important in this respect. You just can't cut corners here. After all, doors and windows are in constant motion. Other than the floors, no aspect of the house gets quite as much wear and tear as these do—especially if you've got children. If windows are drafty and hard to open, and if doors do nothing to block sounds being transmitted from room to room, you'll find yourself vexed no matter how great things look. Luckily, this is one area you can easily upgrade—by replacing doors and windows, or by working to upgrade the ones you've got—to produce a home that's noticeably more appealing. Let's start with doors and go over the basics of what you need to know.

Doors to Adore

Close a solid door, whether it's the entry to your house or to a bedroom, and you'll feel a satisfying sense of security. Close a hollow door, filled with cardboard, and you proba-bly won't feel so confident, to say the least. Solid doors were once made out of solid planks of wood—and still are, if you have a few unused digits in your budget. But solid doesn't necessarily have to mean expensive anymore. You can have a door that produces that same feeling even if it's made with nothing more than a hardwood veneer applied over a solid core of

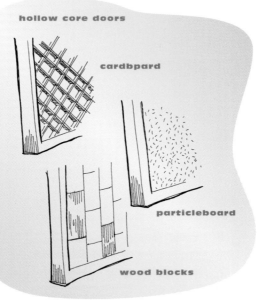

hollow core doors

cardbpard

particleboard

wood blocks

Types of Windows

Everybody knows what a window is—or do they? I'm amazed how many people think a window has to be a standard double-hung when in fact there's a huge range of styles that you can add to a room to turn it into something wonderful. Here are a few examples that I hope will give you some ideas for your remodeling projects:

Double-hung. These are the classic windows, in which the upper and lower sash glide past one another. The beauty of these is that they provide natural ventilation. Warm air inside the room rises and goes out the top of the window; cool air from outside is drawn in through the bottom. Most new double-hungs now come with full screens for better ventilation; older ones contain only partial screens that fit into the bottom or top of the window.

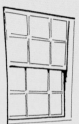

Casement. With a few cranks of a handle, these windows swing open. Like sails on a boat, they catch breezes that flow by a house, and draw them inside. Plus, they're easy to clean since both sides are accessible from inside the house.

wood fiberboard. Since this is the case, then why do hollow doors even exist? That's something I've often wondered. When houses are built by large developers, they look to cut costs wherever they can. So instead of spending $100 for a great solid door, they spend $30 for a hollow one. There might be twenty doors in a house, for a $1,400 savings, multiplied by a hundred or two hundred or a thousand homes they're building. That may work out well for the developer, but there's a problem—they don't have to live in these homes, and you do. Every day, you bear the burden of this savings by having to touch and look at shoestring doors that make your home feel like an echo chamber. This is not

Awning. Like casement windows, these swing open—but from the bottom rather than the side. Because of this, they are the only window that can safely be left open during a rainstorm, since the water cascades off them.

Fixed windows. While these can't be opened for ventilation, they are useful—and inexpensive—for positioning in groups.

Bays and bows. These extend from the house through a slight cantilever and provide wonderful space inside for a window seat if they're large enough, or for smaller areas—such as a sunny shelf for plants above the kitchen sink. Most contain a combination of fixed windows that can't be opened, along with casement, awning, or double-hung windows that can.

an uplifting experience, and if it's privacy you're looking for, you couldn't possibly do any worse.

I know I am not alone in my feelings, since my friends discovered this same thing. As a result, I think one of the best things you can do for your home if you have hollow interior doors is to upgrade them. This is not a frivolous improvement, since your house will be a lot more pleasant to live in—and solid doors are something that will add to a home's appeal whenever you decide to sell it. People often ask me what they can do to increase the value of their homes—whether they should redo the bathroom or build a new master bedroom. I think doors are overlooked as an

Screen Gems

Screens, like window glass, come in a great variety of styles, but there are two materials I particularly like. Screening made of aluminum mesh is the most durable of all—and a good choice if you have cats or if you want extra protection for a sliding door that sees a lot of wear. They're not the most see-through material, however. That title belongs to black fiberglass mesh, which is the type of screening most commonly available on new windows. It's not particularly strong; you can easily poke through it if you're not careful. But fiberglass mesh all but disappears once it's in place—meaning you'll be able to see clear through to the outdoors.

improvement project. If your house was built sometime after World War II, when building sizes became standardized, this can be a very easy thing to do. Doors come in standard sizes—whether 24, 26, or 28 inches wide—so it's not like you would have to rebuild the door frames in order to hang them. You simply attach them to the existing hinges, or add new hinges and make some simple adjustments to make sure they close. For a carpenter, this is about as simple as a task gets.

Even more than the interior doors, you want the front door of your house to shine. The front door amounts to a welcome mat to the world, a sign that says "This is who I am, and this is my family's home." A lot of builders try to make this statement by putting a flat panel door on the entryway, which couldn't be any more boring. You might as well put up a sheet of plywood on hinges, because that's about how appealing it looks. Again, you can get an attractive door to fit whatever budget you want. There are doors that come with windows, called lights, cut right into them, as well as sidelights. Some have six panels arranged in a Colonial style, or more elaborate clusters for a Mediterranean look. Doors come in everything from fiberglass, which mimics the look of wood, to steel or wood, which is my favorite. And most of them—even the wooden ones—come wrapped around an insulated core. This way,

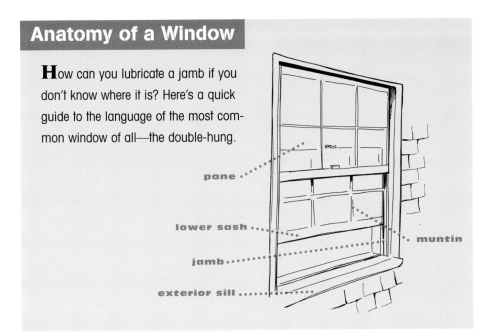

Anatomy of a Window

How can you lubricate a jamb if you don't know where it is? Here's a quick guide to the language of the most common window of all—the double-hung.

pane

lower sash

jamb

muntin

exterior sill

not only do you get an attractive door, but you can also improve the insulation efficiency of your home at the same time.

A good door elevates the character of your house not just in the way it looks but also in the way it feels—and the same can be said for doorknobs. Who wants to grab hold of a cheap, rattling piece of metal with a corroded brass finish, something that looks as if it fell out of the hardware store bargain bin? I sure don't. Yet this is what many people force themselves to live with every day. Do yourself, and your guests, a favor and get good doorknobs to match the solid doors. These cost more, it's true. But, again, they'll add a feeling of solidity to your house that's far more valuable. How do you tell good knobs from cheap ones when you're shopping for them? Price is one indicator. If you're spending $9 on a doorknob, let's just say that you're probably not getting a very good doorknob. But beyond price, just pick them up and compare them. Good doorknobs feel heavy because they're built with heavy steel and brass components that keep them from falling to pieces. Most of the good hardware is solid brass that comes in an infinite array of finishes, from shiny chrome to black antique. Cheap doorknobs have all the weightiness and appeal of a piece of plastic—hardly something that calls out to be touched.

Fortunately, it's very easy to swap doorknobs, either by doing it yourself or by having a carpenter spend a few hours and do them for you. New doors and knobs can really change the look of a house, even if you're not up to making other renovations throughout the place. The noises will be muffled and you'll feel like you live in a new home, even if you don't make other substantial renovations.

Coming Unhinged?

How a door looks is one thing; how it operates, however, is equally important. Let's face it, doors get a great deal of abuse. We slam them shut, they get banged around by furniture as we move it, and children—or, at any rate, my four little darlings—sometimes view them as extensions of their toy box, to be swung from at will and all but battered down on occasion. This stress is transferred to the hinges, and it shows itself in a number of ways. You can end up with doors that don't latch closed, doors that don't stay open, and doors that squeak. Sometimes the problem is a structural one. As the house ages, it begins to sag. This isn't necessarily a sign that it's falling down, just a sign that things settle, which everyone, myself included, recognizes as an inevitability of age. When this happens, the door no longer fits properly because the frame has become slightly twisted out of its rectangular shape.

A typical problem is that a door simply won't latch shut—but the problem usually lies with the hinges rather than the latch. And it almost always involves the top hinge, which holds the bulk of a door's weight and is under tremendous pressure from all that leverage. If the hinges are worn or broken, you'll have to replace them. But if the screws have simply worked loose, you can try tightening them again. Often, the wood that you're trying to tighten these into has become splintered and weakened,

An Expensive Break

In the old days, if someone launched, say, a baseball through your window, you could fix it by tapping out the broken bits of glass and installing a new pane with glazing putty. Not so with modern windows. When one of these breaks, the thermopane seal breaks along with it, which means that the entire sash has to be replaced—which can make for a pricey repair. While the increased energy efficiency of new windows far outweighs this breakage risk, it would probably be a good idea to move the backyard baseball diamond a little farther afield.

and so you'll need Mr. Fix-It's high-tech remedy: Take a few wooden toothpicks, break them into bits, coat them with a little carpenter's glue, and stuff them into the empty screw holes. Let the glue dry for twenty-four hours then rescrew the hinge to the frame.

With heavy doors, the screws will eventually wear loose again. A more durable method than the toothpick trick is to install 3-inch-long screws that go through the jamb of the door and hit the framing. The long screws really grab into the wood and hold the door solidly. It's the difference between grabbing your kids by the hands as you swing them and grabbing hold of their wrists and locking hands for the same maneuver. You get a far greater holding power.

If the hinges still seem out of kilter, you may have other problems that would involve chiseling into the wood to hold the hinges in a different position. This is not advanced carpentry by any means, but unless you've got some finesse with tools, I'd recommend staying away from this. Like a beaver, you could whittle that door down in no time and end up with bigger problems than you started with.

Beyond hinges, the single most common thing that can happen to a door is that it needs to be trimmed. You may have bare floors, then pick up a great bargain rug at a yard sale, and suddenly the door no longer closes without scuffing. You can shave the door with an electric planer or a circular saw if you know what you're doing. If not, stick to an elec-

A Cool Solution for a Hot Storm Door

Storm doors give extra insulation to exterior doors and make it possible to open the door on a sunny winter's day to let in light. Still, like a greenhouse, they can trap a lot of heat when a south-facing door is closed—enough to melt vinyl or plastic grilles or cause paint to blister. We're talking hot, even if it's below freezing out! You can moderate this heat buildup by drilling a pair of quarter-inch holes into the bottom of the storm frame, and two more up high. This will help vent away enough of the heat by drawing in cooler air from below, and prevent the storm door from becoming a smelting factory.

tric belt sander—which you can rent for about $20 a day from any hardware store. Imagine the track on a bulldozer or tank, and this is exactly how the sandpaper spins around one of these tools. They give you great control, and you'll get the job done quickly as well as neatly. Remove the door by tapping out the metal pegs that hold it into the hinges, carefully clamp it to a pair of sawhorses without gouging the wood, and get to work. You may have to keep at it for a while, but you won't risk splitting the wood or cutting off too much even if you're a novice.

Also, keep in mind that doors swell and contract with the seasons. They're made of wood, after all. If they stick in the summer, you can sand them or plane them down to fit. Whether you're trimming a door to allow it to pass over a carpet or just sanding a portion of an edge to make it fit the frame, be sure to seal the newly exposed raw wood edges with paint or polyurethane immediately. Otherwise, the wood will continue to "breathe," which means that the cellulose fibers absorb or evaporate moisture depending on the surrounding humidity. In wintertime with its dry air, you could very well find you have the opposite problem: doors that have shrunk and are now too small for their frames.

Windows of Opportunity

To me, a well-designed house is one that brings in as much natural light as possible. Light makes even the smallest home feel large and airy by bringing the outside world indoors. This, of course, is accomplished by windows—but specifically by their size and positioning. As a builder, the first thing I do when I renovate a home is to take a look at the house and figure out how to bring in more light. There's a simple reason for this: A house with great light will sell in an instant. It's what homeowners love. These are changes you can make fairly easily to any home.

In many houses, especially older ones, windows seem to have been designed almost as an afterthought. It's as if the builder said, "Well, here's a bedroom, we must have a window." The result is often a hodge-podge of ill-planned openings that can make a home feel grim. Fortunately, it's never too late to make window corrections that can drastically change the mood of your home's interior. The biggest change is the disappearance of the old "you can't do that" philosophy. This is the rule that said you couldn't put furniture in front of a window, so you ended up with small windows raised high off the floor just so someone could put a couch or a bureau beneath it. The reality is, who cares if you put anything in front of the windows? If you want to open up your kitchen by adding a bow window over the sink, or turn the living room into a quasi-solarium with big floor-to-ceiling windows, go ahead and do it. My feeling is you'll be making a wise investment—as long as the work is done well and it's part of an overall plan for your home.

How do you avoid installing windows that are either too large or too small in your home? That's not as hard a task as it might seem. What you need to do is get a big 3-foot-wide roll of brown paper, the kind that is used in a butcher's shop. You take that paper and tape it up on the walls to the size of the windows you like. This will help you get a feel for just how the windows might look, and will give you a chance to try various configurations—something you sure can't do once the windows are installed. When you think you've determined the size and position, leave

What to Look for in a Garage Door

Most of us don't spend a lot of time inspecting garage doors, but there's something you should know: Not all are created equal. You can buy wood doors, fiberglass, and metal—and even have them custom-made. One company I know of, for instance, specializes in creating doors that mimic the side of the house, so that when they're closed you don't notice them. For a brick house, for instance, they apply brick veneer to the doors.

Most of us, because of the cost, stick with metal doors—but here, too, there is an important choice to make between uninsulated and insulated ones. Too many people choose uninsulated doors by default, because they're trying to save a couple of hundred dollars. That's too bad, because not only are these doors more prone to dents, they're much noisier. Slam one of these shut, and it sounds like Fred Sanford's red jalopy rolling down the street, with all that clanging and banging. Insulated doors, by contrast, contain a foam core that not only strengthens the door but makes it quieter to live with. My advice: Spend the extra dollars, and the door will work a lot better for you—as well as your neighbors.

them there for a while to be certain. Invite your friends and relatives over to comment, which should certainly make for some lively conversation. This will really give you a feel for what will look good in a room. It's possible to get carried away, of course. If you're living with neighbors just a half dozen feet away, you certainly wouldn't want to have an entire wall of windows; this would turn your home into the proverbial goldfish bowl. You'll have to work to balance the need for a lot of light with your need for privacy, but making the effort to do so will help you create a home that you love.

Sealing Cracks

Much as we love windows, they make up the biggest heat-loss agents in a house. Little gaps and cracks around doors and windows may seem insignificant when you spot them, but they can add up to a major air leak. Just imagine the wind that would pour in from a giant hole, about 2 feet across, knocked into the side of your home. This is essentially what you'd be dealing with if you were to add all those tiny cracks together. Not only do they limit the effectiveness of your heating and cooling systems, but they also cost you money because you'll be heating and cooling that much more air. The remedy is to add caulking and weatherstripping to cut down on air leaks.

One good way to determine where you need weatherstripping and caulking is to see how drafty the old ones are by using the candle test. On a cold day, when the air currents are most extreme, light a candle, then carefully run it around the inside perimeter of the windows. If the candle flickers, you've got leaking air. Once you've done this, you'll have a clear idea what areas need attention. Your next step is to caulk and weatherstrip.

Caulk comes in dozens of varieties and is usually squirted from tubes around window frames to keep air from passing through. Once something is caulked, however, you can't open it again without destroying the seal. This limits its usefulness, except for temporary puttylike caulking that can be pressed around windows in the winter, and removed each spring. A better approach for the moving portions of windows as well as doors is weatherstripping. This ranges from a soft rubber material, similar to what you find around a refrigerator door, to flat metal strips that spring together to form an air lock when a window is closed. Older windows have plenty of areas that need to be weatherstripped—and the

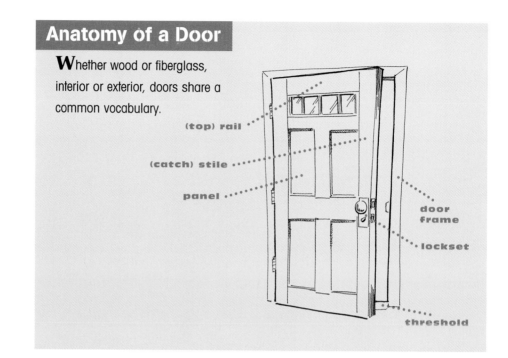

Anatomy of a Door

Whether wood or fiberglass, interior or exterior, doors share a common vocabulary.

(top) rail

(catch) stile

panel

door frame

lockset

threshold

hidden channels that hold the weights, pulleys, and chains that operate them often need to be insulated as well. New windows, however, usually defy the need for additional weatherstripping. If installed correctly, they're designed to work for decades.

Sometimes you can have really drafty windows that seem to defy weatherproofing. If you're squeezing in four tubes of caulk and still coming up with a breeze, you're definitely heading for new windows. But if you want to get through a tough winter, you can remedy this using a product known as window film. This is essentially a giant roll of clear plastic wrap. It attaches to the frame using double-sided tape, and then you heat it with a hair-dryer to make the surface completely taut and see-through. Done right, you won't know it's there, and it is very effective at eliminating drafts. You won't be able to open the windows without removing the window film, but the chances are you wouldn't want to open them until spring anyway.

Pane Relief

Among old windows, the biggest problem often lies in the glass. There's only a single pane separating you from the great outdoors. While this might keep the bugs out, it does hardly anything to keep out hot air in the summer and cold air in the winter. You might as well just put a bedsheet over the opening, because that's about the amount of energy efficiency you're going to get out of it.

Fortunately, a little more glass can go a long way. A second layer, called a storm window, vastly increases the insulation value of a window by creating a buffer of air in between. New windows take this a step futher with double-glazing. In double-glazed windows, also called thermopane windows, two pieces of glass trap air or a clear inert gas such as argon between them. Argon increases the insulating value of the window, and you pay more for it. My question, of course, has always been how the heck can I be sure the gas is actually in there if it's clear? I suppose you just have to trust the manufacturer. In any event, it is this stationary air, rather than the extra piece of glass, that creates an insulating buffer between the indoors and the out. With double-glazed windows, you don't need storm windows at all, the way you do with old-fashioned single-pane windows. That would be like putting a sweater on top of a down jacket; sure, maybe it would keep you a little warmer, but you certainly don't need it to be comfortable.

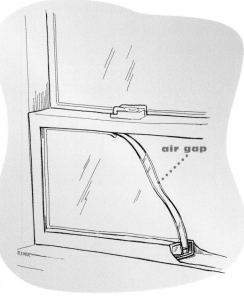

air gap

We live in an age when technology seems to change everything—even the glass within a window. Manufacturers have created different types of glass that can further increase a window's efficiency. An invisible filter that blocks ultraviolet light, called low-emissivity or "low-e" glass, is standard in most new quality windows, and can reduce UV rays—those nasty wavelengths that cause the colors in your carpets and furniture to wash out—by about three-quarters. With this glass, you don't have to draw the drapes ever again, and you certainly don't have to worry about your couch covers and carpeting fading if they're placed in front of a window.

One of my favorite gee-whiz technologies involves placing a thin layer of silver—a coating one molecule thick—on a film between the two layers of glass. Called heat mirror glass, this lets light through but reflects heat. It can raise the insulating value of windows, known as the R-value, to as much as 9—which is similar to the insulation value of many walls. It also reduces UV rays by 99.5 percent. What more could you ask from a window?

When It's Time To Say Good-bye

I constantly hear from people, "Oh, my windows are so old, I need to replace them." As I've shown, that's not always the case. Storm windows, weather-stripping, and caulking can go a long way toward making windows energy-efficient, and they are a lot more cost-effective. Yet in many instances it *is* time to replace the windows, whether because the frames are rotted, the mechanism is outdated, or they're simply not functioning anymore. Indeed, Americans spent about $8.5 billion in the year 2000 on replacing windows, a figure that is climbing between 15 and 20 percent every year.

If windows are drafty, that can be fixed. But if they're rotting, are difficult to operate, or slam down when you want them to stay up, that may be a sign it's time to go for a replacement. This is especially true if you want to go ahead and change the size, location, and number of windows you have anyway. Another sign of trouble is a white haze that builds up between the layers of thermopane windows. This is moisture, and a sure sign that the seal has failed—which greatly reduces their efficiency and means they should be replaced. New windows might cost anywhere from $300 to $1,500 per opening, installed. Renovating them can be as high as $300 or more. There comes a point when you have to wonder why you should bother spending money on old windows—especially when new ones will automatically have three, four, or even five times the energy efficiency of the old ones.

How do you know when that moment arrives? Start by taking a quick run through this checklist:

- Are your windows more than twenty years old?
- If we're talking double-hung windows, do you have to prop them open with a block of wood?
- Are there signs of rot around the exterior, near the sill, or around the molding on the interior?
- When you do the candle test around the perimeter of the window, is the flame extinguished?
- If you have thermopane windows, does a white cloud form between the two panes of glass—which would be a sure sign that the seal is broken and moisture is seeping in?

If you answer yes to three out of these five problems, I'd vote to replace, rather than spruce up, those windows. As always, do your homework to find a good contractor for the job, and buy the best-quality windows you can afford. That way, you can guarantee that you won't be ripping out faulty windows a few years from now and starting the process all over again.

Remember, however, that the real key in replacing windows in your home is not the window but the quality of the installation. A replacement window is only as good as its installation—have it done wrong, and your old, leaky, drafty windows will be transformed into new, leaky, drafty windows. Where's the savings in that? Compounding this problem is the difficulty in finding reputable window-replacement contractors. Anyone who has watched late-night TV commercials—in which windows are hawked with all the honesty of used cars—knows what I'm talking about.

You can avoid cheap windows and shoddy installation jobs by buying major national brands or good regional brands—and checking the refer-

Threshold of Pain

Imagine getting tromped on every single day, alternately doused with rain and exposed to relentless sun—and still being expected to look good. These are the demands we place on the threshold, which lies at the base of all exterior doors. More than just a symbolic entry into a house, over which bridegrooms carry their brides, this is actually a critical barrier against drafts and wetness seeping indoors. While metal thresholds require no maintenance, wooden ones can easily show signs of rot and wear. Check them yearly. Deep cracks can be patched with wood filler, followed by two coats of deck-quality paint. More serious decay may require replacement of the threshold itself—as well as an examination of the structural beams beneath it to make sure they, too, haven't deteriorated.

ences of whatever contractors you use. To avoid trouble, insist on the following:

- Look for a seal of approval from the National Fenestration Research Council or Energy Star. This will guarantee windows built to state-of-the-art standards.
- Is the manufacturer a member of a professional organization, such as the National Association of the Remodeling Industry (NARI)?
- Can the window manufacturer provide any third-party endorsements—especially from past and current customers whom you can contact yourself?
- Will the installer give you a solid completion date?
- Can the manufacturer provide start-to-finish installation with an ample warranty, such as five years on workmanship and ten years on product performance?

These insights should help you in your search for those new windows for your home. Now all you need to decide is what color to paint the walls and the trim and what kind of window treatments to hang.

chapter SIX

Getting Floored

As the most heavily used surface in a house, floors deserve some special attention

Floors sometimes strike me as being the Rodney Dangerfield of a home. Like him, they never get any respect.

An acquaintance proved this true when building a new home some years ago. He and his wife had to pare the cost of the house by a few thousand dollars to get a mortgage. But instead of targeting the luxuries, such as the granite countertops in the kitchen and the pegged cherry floors, they decided to chip away at the actual structure of the house. "Since we can't see it, we won't miss it," my friend thought. Obviously, he hadn't met me yet.

In any event, they scrimped on the size of the joists, which hold the floor up, and also on the thickness of the plywood subfloor beneath it. That, along with a few other cuts, saved them the money they needed, but at an unbelievable cost. The house came in on budget and looks great—until you walk across the floor. The living room has an unmistakable bounce to it, slightly reminiscent of a trampoline. And if you move across the kitchen at any gait other than a tiptoe, coffee cups on the kitchen table literally start to shake—the way that glass of water did in *Jurassic Park* just as the

floors

Tyrannosaurus rex made its approach. When the kids play upstairs, the ceiling fixtures rattle downstairs. Any movement at all, in fact, sends tremors throughout the house that would surely register on the Richter scale. "It's like living in a funhouse, only it isn't any fun," my friend moans. "I wish we had known!"

When people speak of flooring in their homes, invariably they're thinking about the floor finishes—the carpeting, wood, ceramic tile or stone that create the beautiful surfaces we walk on. Yet like so many other aspects of your home, it is what's underneath this delicate veneer that gives a floor its long-lasting solidity and helps maximize the life of the surfaces clinging to the top of it. The average floor faces a life of battle. It can be swollen by moisture wicking up from damp basements, abraded by dirt that's ground into its surface as we walk on it, and stained by everything from dripping pipes to seeping flowerpots. Then we tromp on it, day in and day out. Let's take a closer look at what creates a good floor—so you'll know what you need to think about, whether you're renovating, refinishing, or simply trying to clean and maintain this all-important element of your home.

Good Structure Makes Good Flooring

For the most part, our homes are framed using one of three materials. The most common, especially in homes a decade or more old, is what is known as conventional lumber. These are the 2-by-10s or 2-by-12s that are harvested from a forest, cut and shaped into the appropriate sizes, and then hammered together to create the structure of your home. Another method that is gaining popularity is to use what are called engineered products that are created not by cutting them from individual trees but by gluing many layers of wood together. These laminated boards are ultrastrong and ultralong as well, and can span much larger distances than conventional lumber. A third type of framing that is now gaining popularity, espeically in larger homes, involves using wood floor trusses, which are made from lumber held in place by a metal framework. Although the most expensive of all, these are extremely stable and can be fitted with electrical and plumbing systems very easily. We'll begin with the conventional framing.

Conventional framing has been around for hundreds of years, and the members that hold up the floor were originally rough-sawn timbers. In the old days, there was not much logic in the way they were spaced for the floor to go on top. Whatever the head carpenter decided looked right dictated how widely they were spaced. Since then, fortunately, building codes have developed in order to create some safety and stability in the home. This involves mathematical calculations to determine just how much load the floors can carry, so that it's no longer a matter of guess-work on the part of the builder.

The loads that engineers consider in designing floor framing can be divided into two categories—live loads and dead loads. Dead loads aren't as macabre as they might sound. These are defined as the weight of the structure of the floors, the joists, the sheathing, and anything else that is part of the actual house itself. Live loads are defined as the things that are added to a home. These include furniture, appliances, floor coverings,

Some Level-Headed Advice

Here's something I've seen so often it aches: A homeowner gets the idea to add a new tile floor to the kitchen and puts it on top of the old one. While the floor looks okay, the two-inch drop to the adjacent floor does not. If you want to have floors at varying heights and end up with a place that looks like some hillbilly house, go right ahead. But if you want to do it the right way, your floors should flow at an even level throughout your house. The solution here is to rip the old floor out completely, then adjust the height of the subfloor. This way, the surface of the new floor will exactly match up to the adjacent one. While this takes more time and money, it will spare you that slapdash look. I'm not saying you can't have a threshold to draw a line between two different types of material, but you sure don't want to have to step up or down a couple of inches to get from room to room.

people, and pets. Typically, residential homes are designed for a live load of 40 pounds per square foot, which means you could put a 40-pound bag of gravel on every single square foot of floor space and the floor would hold it. For a typical 2,500-square-foot house, we're talking enough strength to hold up 50 tons, or about six or seven adult African elephants. This is a tremendous weight, to be sure.

Jumping for Joists

The muscle behind all of this strength can be seen if you go down to the basement or crawl space and look up. You'll see a few large beams, perhaps with posts holding them up. Then across the tops of these you'll find a neatly spaced series of wooden boards positioned on their edges. These are the floor joists. Many people mistakenly call these rafters (but those are the structural members that rise at an angle into the roof). You find joists beneath every floor—including the attic floor—and they create not only the floors but the ceilings as well. If there's one structural element you pay attention to and learn about, let it be the joists. Understanding what goes on here will guide you through all of the floor-related projects you'll ever have.

In the modern-day home—say, one built within the last century—joists are made out of 2-by-6s at the small end of the scale all the way up to the much more solid 2-by-12s. They're usually spaced every 16 inches, although sometimes you find them spaced as wide as 24 inches. This wider spacing saves money when a home is built, but it results in a far shakier construction. Joists work by transferring the weight of the house and its occupants above to the beams, which then further transfer the weight to the posts and the foundation walls.

It's not just the thickness of the joists that gives a floor its strength, although bigger is so often better. Joists also need to be stabilized so that they don't become distorted. The area between the joists is called the joist bays, and in these, you'll see something called bridging crisscrossing through the bays. In older homes, these are 2-by-2s nailed in to form an X-shaped structure. In newer homes, the bridging is more typically made from cut-off ends of the joists themselves, which are cut to the width of the bay and nailed perpendicular to the joists every 8 feet. This bridging actually serves a very important purpose. Since the top part of the joist carries most of the burden, the bottom part bows and sways slightly. Stabilizing the joists with bridging ensures that the entire board can absorb the load more evenly. That will cut down on rattling in the floors above—which is something you'll appreciate, whether it's ordinary foot traffic or the shock of a living room full of guests on New Year's Eve doing the conga line.

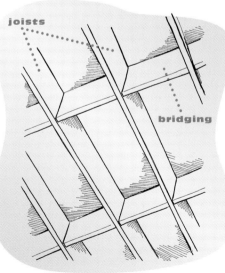

If you have bouncy floors that annoy

Keep It Clean

The best way to preserve floors is to clean and maintain them so that they don't get ruined in the first place. You don't have to go wild with cleaners and oils; simply get rid of the grit. No matter what floor surface you've got, grit will ruin it. It's the equivalent of having little pads of sandpaper on your shoes and socks as you roam around the house. It scuffs the color off vinyl, deteriorates the fibers in carpeting, and abrades the finish on wood floors. In fact, once a wood floor becomes embedded with grit, no amount of scrubbing will remove it; you have to refinish the floor. The only prevention is to sweep, vacuum, and damp-mop often. Be especially careful not to douse wood floors with water, however, since that can damage them even more than the dirt alone. Instead, damp-mop and dry with a terry-cloth towel. You'll get years more life out of your floors by keeping them clean, which will save you money and keep your house looking great.

you, take a close look at the bridging. Many times during renovations contractors will inadvertently knock them out. The heating and cooling guys, for instance, sometimes cut through them to create space for new ducts, and electricians love to drill through them to run conduit for their wires. By doing this, they may not be threatening the structure of the house, but they are weakening the stability of your floor. One remedy, of course, is simply to add more bridging to tie all the joists tightly together and control the sway.

In new homes, the difficulty of creating a stable floor is compounded by the frequent use of engineered lumber. These result in joists and beams that are far longer than those used in conventional framing. These engineered products are wood in the technical sense, but they are fashioned from smaller pieces of wood that are glued together. The result is very strong, and very long, pieces of lumber. What's nice about engineered lumber, from an environmental standpoint, is that they can be made from slightly inferior cuts of wood—which means that fewer trees have to be cut down, since those that are harvested can be used more efficiently. The problem, however, is that the longer the span these engineered wood products must cover, the bouncier the floors above them become. This is logical if you think about it. A baseball bat, for instance, is a lot more rigid than an 8-foot-long 2-by-4.

In new homes, you'll see more bouncing in the first floor than in the second. This is because the partition walls that form the upstairs bedrooms and closets actually help to keep things stable. Downstairs, there don't tend to be as many partitions, so the floor has less support. If your floors are bouncy, take a look at the bridging between the joist bays—and consult a carpenter to see if there's enough of it. If things continue to bounce, one way to further control the tremors is to add a partition wall in the basement beneath the offending floor, or by adding a supporting beam with a few posts. Just as it does upstairs, a wall such as this can help contain movement of the joists. You would probably want to consult a structural engineer in addition to a contractor before installing this, but it will be worth it. This sort of thing can be installed easily and would go a long way toward making a house feel more solid.

Installing New Floors

In our rush to get on with a new floor, we often forget the most critical element: the subfloor underneath.

The subfloor lies on top of the joists and forms the base on which the finished floor lies. While this may not sound critical, the subfloor is nothing short of the structural element that holds everything up, including you and all your possessions. The foundation, beams, joists, and subfloor work together to make your house stand up, like a pair of sturdy legs. Because of this, you need to take care, time, and effort in thinking about the subfloor, whether you're building a new house or renovating an old one.

In houses built before World War II, the subfloor consisted of 1-by-6 boards nailed together to form a smooth, stable surface. Then came ply-

Screen Savers

Wood floors often start to look dull before they need a full-fledged sanding. Instead of refinishing a floor, you can use a process called screening to renew the finish on the floor. This involves running a giant buffer over the surface that removes small scratches from the finish with a polyester screen instead of sandpaper—hence its name. When the screening is finished, you apply two layers of water-based polyurethane, and your floor will look like new again, at a fraction of the cost of refinishing it completely. Keep in mind that you can't do this on a laminate floor. The risk of penetrating the finish—and thus ruining the surface—is far too great.

wood, which was originally intended as a substitute for steel and was used to build small navy boats—including President Kennedy's ill-fated *PT-109*. After the war, plywood revolutionized the building industry, and sheets of it between 5/8 and 3/4 inch thick remain the ideal choice for a subfloor. An alternative to this is oriented-strand board (or OSB), which is essentially a wood mulch mixed together with glue. While OSB manufacturers swear it holds up, my experience with using it as a subfloor is that the nails from the hardwood floor don't hold in it as well as ordinary plywood. As a result, you will not find OSB used as a subfloor in my house.

Unfortunately, too many homeowners begin their renovations by choosing finish materials without giving much regard to the condition of the subfloor. They'll debate the merits of installing, say, Mexican saltillo tile or maple hardwood in the kitchen and ignore those squishy patches in the existing floor that are a sure sign of trouble. Believe me, the subfloor matters a great deal. Many times, it can suffer a great deal of damage from a variety of sources—which may or may not be visible in the finished floor above. When I'm renovating bathrooms, for instance, I routinely come across toilets that have been leaking water for years. While some of that water drips onto the floor, most of it has seeped into the subfloor. Not only does the wood rot, but I frequently find evidence of insect damage due to the constant moisture. This creates an environment in which pests, mold, and mildew can thrive. Sometimes things are so

bad that the joists and other framing members need to be replaced in addition to the subfloor.

Few people eagerly opt to take a look at the subfloor and replace it if there's damage, especially when they're working on a budget. They say things like, "Aw, I don't want to deal with the mess and aggravation to do it." They delude themselves into thinking that if the old floor seemed sturdy enough, the new surface will hold up just fine without any additional structural work. This is a mistake, of course—because ultimately the life span of the new floor is going to be shortened, and that ends up wasting more money than is saved. It's not that much work to do the necessary structural repairs once you already have the floor ripped up, and you'll have the confidence of knowing that you're getting things off to a solid start. If you don't, then you're playing the lottery with your floor's future—will it give way or won't it?

When rebuilding a floor, keep in mind that if your builder or renovator ever gives you a choice between two different sizes of material that you could frame with, always go with the larger one, even though it will cost you a little more money. Overbuilding where a structural member of the house is concerned is far better than underbuilding. And on the subject of the subfloor, make sure you don't scrimp on how it's attached to the joists.

Warm Floors

One of the most comfortable and increasingly popular heating types is radiant floor heat, or in-floor heating—which makes a great addition to a kitchen or bathroom renovation. This requires a boiler to heat water, rather than a forced-air furnace (see Chapter 4). But instead of circulating through a baseboard radiator, the hot water circulates through a long length of plastic tubing placed in a serpentine pattern just beneath the finished floor. It effectively turns the entire floor into a radiator, which is a great comfort if you've ever stepped barefoot onto, say, a ceramic tile floor in the middle of January in Chicago.

Heating floors is hardly a new technology. In fact, the ancient Romans pioneered it. What is new, however, is the plastic tubing that carries the hot water. Unlike copper pipes that can corrode and leak, the new tubing is guaranteed against leaks in some cases for a hundred years, and appears to be extremely durable. Under stone, tile, or vinyl floors the temperature of the water can rise to 120 degrees. Under wood floors, however, it has to be tamed so that the surface never exceeds 85 degrees—otherwise there's a danger that the wood might cup or crack. Watch out for carpeting, however. Thick-pile carpet and the pads beneath it actually insulate the floor and prevent the heat from rising. Also, the joist bays below the floor have to be insulated, which helps drive the heat in the tubes upward to heat the floor. Without insulation, the heat radiates in all directions—including downward—and reduces the warming efficiency.

For those who don't have a boiler, there's still the possibility of installing radiant floor heat by turning to electricity. For small areas, such as a bathroom, you can install an electric coil system beneath the tiles. The coils heat up safely, and the temperature can be controlled by a thermostat on the wall. While not economical for use in heating an entire house, these electric coils add a great deal of comfort to specific spots. Just remember: The coils have to go under the tiles on the floor, so this is only practical to add during new construction or a renovation.

Anatomy of a Floor

How do you know if your joists are wobbly unless you know where they are? Let Mr. Fix-It take you on a tour-de-floor:

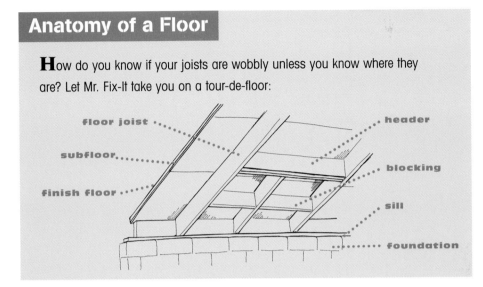

floor joist · · · · ·
subfloor · · · · · · · ·
finish floor · · · · ·
header
blocking
sill
foundation

If you nail a subfloor to the joists, it will eventually creak—no matter how skilled the carpenter who installs it. The best method to attach it is to first apply a layer of contractor's adhesive, followed up by decking screws. The combination will form a squeak-free bond for the life of the floor.

If there's one overriding rule for managing a floor renovation—or any other renovation in your home—it's this: Avoid shortcuts. As Mr. Fix-It, one of the most common questions I get from people is whether or not they can put a new floor such as vinyl tiles right over the top of an old one. This ranks as one of the shoddiest things you could do as a homeowner, and I would never recommend it. *Never!* And the reason is simple. If the old floor fails or deteriorates, it will take the new floor with it, so the $1,000 or $2,000 you've just spent on materials and installation is lost. To avoid this, you always want to rip out the old flooring and take the opportunity to inspect the subflooring underneath. If you don't, you're leaving a lot up to chance—as well as having a blind faith that the previous contractor laid the first floor correctly to begin with. That's an all but guaranteed way to lose time and money.

When I put down a new floor, I'm not going to trust anyone else's work from twenty or thirty or forty years ago. I check it for myself. That way, a homeowner doesn't turn around and complain to me when a floor fails, even if it was someone else's fault. The only time I want to go back into someone's house is to do additional work, not to fix a problem that I could have prevented with a little money and effort. It's an approach that will work for you, too.

Choosing Floor Coverings

Flooring comes in so many styles, I sometimes get dizzy thinking about them all. But rather than choosing something based on looks alone, you'll be doing yourself a favor by first considering how you live your life. If you have a houseful of kids, as I do, you'll want the most durable type of flooring you can get. Poured concrete comes to mind, but as you'll see, you can probably do better. Above all, think of practicality—especially in terms of how difficult it will be to maintain and how much it will cost to replace when it wears out. For instance, cork floors are somewhat popular just now; they look nice and have a springy comfort unlike anything else. But if you happen to have a giant dog running around, as I do, cork flooring is going to drive you crazy because it simply won't stand up to the abuse. My recommendation: Stay away from anything trendy. Instead, go with classic choices, which look good not just from a décor perspective but from an investment perspective as well.

Without a doubt, my single favorite floor material is wood. Nothing matches the beauty of its grain or that special glow it gets as it ages. Softwood floors such as pine show scratches and dings easily, so I prefer hardwood floors—which include familiar species such as oak and ash, and more exotic ones ranging from mahogany to teak. One especially great flooring these days is bamboo, which is odd because it's not a hardwood at all but actually a member of the grass family! Still, it looks gorgeous when finished, and holds up as sturdily as anything. What I like about wood floors is that they are a renewable surface. You can sand and refinish them, usually up to a total of four times before so much wood is

Squeak No More

As a wood home ages, the constant expansion and contraction of the wood causes nails to loosen. One common sign of this is a hardwood floor that squeaks. I like to call that squeak "character," because it adds a certain charm to a house. My wife, however, would like all squeaks to go away, because she says I wake everybody up when I roam through the house in the middle of the night. Since I can't argue with this logic, here are a couple of remedies that usually take care of the problem.

A squeak is caused by two pieces of wood rubbing against one another. One way to stop the sound is by reducing the friction of the moving pieces using a lubricant. We're not talking oil here, but rather a dusting with ultra-fine graphite powder. This is available at hardware stores, and for the most part it's used to free lock mechanisms. But if you pour a tiny bit of it on the floor so that it can work its way into the squeaking boards, it could very well reduce or eliminate the sound.

If that fails, you can always try a pair of well-placed nails. You first need to predrill some slender holes into the wood, angled slightly toward one another as in the diagram below. Then drive the nails in, being careful not to bang up the wood with the hammer. I'd use a type of nail called an 8d or 8-penny finish nail, which has a very small head. Then I'd sink it below the surface of the wood using a device called a nailset. True, you'll see the holes when you're finished, but you'll have tightened the Floorboard—and you can say good-bye to that squeak.

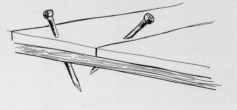

ground away that the nails holding it in place begin to appear. Because of this, wood floors add real value to a house. They're just the sort of feature in a house that will end up highlighted on a real estate agent's listing sheet when you go to sell it.

A common substitute for hardwood floors is known as laminate floor-

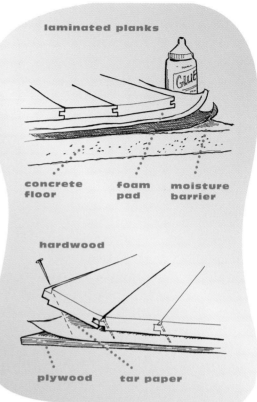

laminated planks

concrete floor   foam pad   moisture barrier

hardwood

plywood   tar paper

ing. This has a thin veneer of prefinished wood or even a photographic image of wood glued to a wood-fiber base. When it's installed, it looks identical to a well-done wood floor. I'm a pretty good fan of laminates, because they tend to be more durable than vinyl tiles or sheet vinyl flooring, and because the selection and quality are very good. But there's a numbers game at work here between wood and laminate floors that you should consider. It tips the balance in favor of wood every time. One surface I would avoid altogether, by the way, is a parquet floor. These generally contain pieces of hardwood about 3/8 inch thick glued to a square backing, and are glued down onto a floor like tile. They look good and are easy to install, and for this reason they have become a favorite with do-it-yourself home renovators—which is too bad, because in my experience parquet floors just don't hold up well. Inevitably, the strips of wood become unglued from their backing, and the floor sounds crunchy when you walk on it from all the pieces of wood popping in and out of place. You might as well be stepping onto a plate filled with Fritos.

In general, the range in cost to have hardwood flooring installed is between $5 and $9 a square foot, which includes sanding and finishing. Now, a laminate floor will cost you a little more, probably on the order of $7 to $9 a square foot to have it installed. The costs seem equivalent at first glance, it's true. But in five to ten years, when the laminate starts to wear out, you're going to have to replace it because it cannot be refinished. And by that time, it's probably going to cost you between $12 and $15 a square foot for a reinstallation. Let's contrast this with the cost of a hardwood floor. To refinish one of these floors, you'll probably spend no more than $2 a square foot. So in a decade, when your floor is really starting to show its age, you'll be able to renew its surface for about a quarter of what it would cost to install a new floor. There's no way around it: The wood floor makes a far better investment than laminate.

Tile and stone such as slate are also popular for flooring—largely because of their supreme durability. Here, however, you have to consider the weight of the flooring being laid down, and make sure that your subfloor is up to the task of holding it. If you have a kitchen with slightly sagging floors, for instance, this will surely not hold up two tons of slate satisfactorily. Instead, it will shift and wiggle, and before long it will cause the material to crack. You can install these sorts of material anywhere you like, as long as you pay attention to the preparation needed beforehand. Specifically, you need a solid subfloor. In addition, you have to lay something on top of the wood subfloor to limit the effects of the wood's seasonal expansions and contractions. This is often done by installing some

tile

adhesive
pad

concrete

slate

grout

stone

glue

cement

plywood

tar
paper

A New Look at an Old-fashioned Flooring

If you hear the word linoleum, you probably think of something that went the way of the milkman and the wringer washing machine. But great things have a way of making a comeback.

Linoleum makes a terrific choice for a kitchen, pantry, or mud room—any-where you might use vinyl flooring. Vinyl is a synthetic product made of chlorinated petrochemicals. Essentially, it's a plastic. The finish color is usually applied to the surface only, so when it wears, the color is scraped off. If you get ten years out of it, you're doing great, although five is more like it. Linoleum, however, is made with a special recipe dating back to 1863 that includes everything from linseed oil to ground-up cork. It's 100 percent natural, and there are no environmental toxins produced during manufacturing. Beyond this, the color in linoleum is marbled all the way through the material, so it wears far better. Instead of grinding off the top surface, foot traffic exposes different levels of color and gives it a burnished rather than worn-out look. Like the Energizer Bunny, a linoleum floor keeps on going—and will still look good after thirty or even forty years.

Why did people forget about linoleum in the first place? For one thing, the color choices used to be limited to just three: drab, drabber, and drabbest. Modern producers, however, have endowed linoleum with all the color vibrancy of a giant box of crayons. In addition, the material can be inlaid with borders of complementary colors to create a unique look. Of course, it does have its draw-backs. Because it is porous, its appearance and continued resilience depend on regular maintenance. New floors should be given one or two coats of acrylic sealer and a recoating once a year after that to keep them looking fresh.

type of concrete board over the subfloor, which is slathered with wet mortar. The tiles or stone pieces are then set into the mortar and should remain crack-free on this stable base.

Carpeting, too, remains a popular choice, particularly in bedrooms. There's been a huge consolidation among carpet manufacturers, so now there are about three main ones that produce just about every brand. Rather than focusing on a specific brand, you'll do better to let price be your guide. You pay more for carpets with tightly bound fibers that provide a denser, longer-lasting surface. While there are wool carpets available, most carpets—including even the best ones these days—are made from nylon which accounts for about 90 percent of the carpeting I see installed in houses. This may seem odd to anyone with a "natural is better" frame of mind, I know. But technology has changed so much in recent years that nylon fibers can now be produced with a plushness that wool just can't touch. Check it out with your own feet, and you'll see what I mean.

Not surprisingly, the key to long-lasting carpeting has as much to do with the quality of the pad as the quality of the carpet itself. If you're ever given an option when buying carpeting, upgrade the pad. Typically, a denser pad tends to spring back and keep its shape in the long term. That helps the carpet to lie flat, which reduces the friction on the fibers and carpet backing. You may spend a few dollars more per square yard for top-grade padding, but you'll ultimately save money because your carpet will hold up years longer. And don't overlook the importance of regular cleaning. Vacuum at least once a week to remove fiber-damaging grit, and hire someone on occasion to clean the carpets using steam extraction. In my experience, this works far better than dry-cleaning methods and can be used on either synthetic or natural fibers. How often you should have the carpets cleaned this way depends on how much traffic they get. With four kids in my household, the carpet cleaner shows up every year; if it were just my wife and myself, we'd probably cut it back to every other year. Tending to your carpets this way will add a fair

Mr. Fix-It's Favorite Floor Finish

I love wood floors, but you absolutely have to finish them with something or they'll soon be reduced to nothing but splinters. Every contractor seems to have some method for finishing floors he thinks works best—in this way, it's kind of like the old family meat loaf recipe. Here's how I like to do it.

After sanding a floor, I always use water-borne finishes, rather than oil-based ones. These provide a harder finish that dries faster. You'll need a total of three coats of finish. The first, called the sealer coat, will raise the grain of the wood as it dries. After it's applied, have the floors screened—a gently abrasive buffing that will even the surface. Follow this up with two more coats of finish, buffing between them. I like using a matte finish for two coats, then a semigloss for the third coat. It will give the floor a beautiful yet nonglossy sheen.

If you have an old floor that's being refinished, consider staining the wood before the finish goes on. Stains have a way of evening the finish look of old floors and can go a long way toward freshening them up. Here, you would use an oil-based stain because they work better than the water-borne stains. Keep in mind, that the darker the stain, the longer it will take to cure before the finish can go on—anywhere from one to three days.

One caution: I don't consider this a do-it-yourself job at all. Refinishing a floor involves using a giant drum sander, which looks easy to use but is not— especially around the edges and the corners. This is where amateurs tend to slip up, which results in uneven troughs that nothing ever covers up. You'll end up with a finish that looks sort of like the ripple effect of water on a lake. Don't even think of using a drum sander unless you have experience. And you sure don't want to gain this by using your own floors as the guinea pig.

amount of life to them—probably an additional three to five years.

No matter what flooring surface you choose, buy the best-quality materials you can afford, and make sure that you invest in a good sub-floor. These are things you'll appreciate with every step you take.

chapter SEVEN

Wall Power

It's not what's on the walls, it's what's in them that will add the most to your home

Here's a scene I have been a witness to so many times it's no longer funny.

An earnest young couple buys an old, peeling house and decides to give the outside a facelift. They spend an entire summer climbing up ladders, scraping old layers of paint, and neglecting their jobs and their families to get the task done. When they're finished, the house looks great—for about a month, until the paint starts peeling again.

Most often, the problem lies not in their painting and scraping techniques but in the walls themselves. Because of botched insulation, which we will learn about shortly, the walls themselves can become saturated with moisture. As the sun heats the walls from the outside, these water molecules want out and blast through the siding to get free—taking the paint with them in huge, heartbreaking chunks. Homeowners can scrape and paint all they want to, but nothing short of solving this moisture problem is ever going to keep the outside of their house looking good and remaining free of rot.

Walls are a funny thing, since we imagine them to be only a two-dimensional surface—one that needs painting on the outside or

walls

wallpapering on the inside and then can be left alone. Yet walls are a vital, three-dimensional part of your home's structure, not just its décor. They give shape to rooms, and contain beams and structural members that literally keep your house standing. Fitted with insulation, walls keep your house warm in the winter, cool in the summer. With proper vapor barriers, which we'll look at in depth, they will also remain structurally sound. By taking a look at the different layers inside your walls, we can begin to understand the forces that affect them—which will help you maintain them for the ages.

What's in a Wall?

Houses are built with two distinct types of framing. Masonry buildings are made of solid material—stone, brick, cinder block, or some combination of the three. Wood-framed houses, which are a truly American style of construction and account for nine out of every ten houses built in this country, are made of lumber. These can be sided with everything from wood to brick and stone veneer. Since they represent the vast majority of homes both old and new in the United States, I'll concentrate on them.

The walls in wood-framed houses contain thin pieces of lumber called studs. These can be 2-by-4s or (more likely if your house has been built within the last decade), 2-by-6s, and they're spaced vertically every 16 or 24 inches—the closer the better. The studs in the wall have to rise up right to the roof, and in homes a hundred years old or older this was accomplished using enormous studs as long as 24 feet. This type of construction was called balloon framing and was possible because there were enough giant trees around to cut studs of this length. Nowadays, however, the typical tree is only about thirty years old when it's cut, and you sure can't create a stud that long. Combined with this, carpenters have developed a better building technique called platform construction that creates a more rigid house. Instead of rising the full height of the wall, the individual studs rise only the height of a single floor—about 10 feet at the most. When they reach the top of that floor, they connect to a horizontal piece of wood called a plate. This acts as a supporting beam to stabilize the studs and also to hold the joists that create both the ceiling and the floor above it. When platform construction is done well, the lumber used to create that top plate is doubled up—creating what is called a double top plate above, as well as a sole plate below. This is a very durable way to build a wall.

Walls can be divided into two separate types according to their function. First, there are load-bearing walls, which do what their name suggests— they carry the weight of the house above them—and are one of your home's principal structural elements. Think of Atlas holding up the earth and you'll have a perfect idea of what these walls do in your home. Next come partition walls, which have a far easier life. Rather than holding up weight, these serve to divide up space. They're used, for instance, to divide the upstairs into bedrooms and to cordon off closets. Atlas they're not. In fact, these are more like the Vanna White of the framing world—their job is simply to look nice and doesn't involve any heavy lifting.

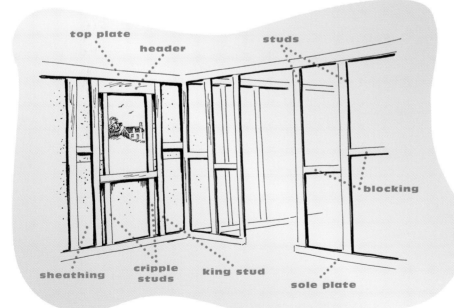

Don't Forget to Wash Behind Your Eaves

We wash our cars, why not the outside of our houses? They get just as dirty, when you think of it, with the accumulation of everything from dust to cobwebs. Mix up a little cleaning solution (the liquid they sell as a car wash is great) and get to work. Here's how: Work from the foundation up, to avoid streaks on dry surfaces that would form if you work from the roofline down. Choose one section at a time; hose off the dirt with a garden hose, then gently scrub it with a clean brush. Rinse the soaped-up area frequently as you work, to keep it from drying. If you wash your house once a year—spring is a good time for this—and if your home is painted, you may get an extra two or three years out of your paint job. Tempting as a pressure washer is, however, avoid using it on the exterior of your house. The high pressure can blast wood and vinyl to pieces, and it can easily send water up and under boards, soaking the sheathing behind it.

Partition walls are the simplest to work with. Doors and windows can be placed in them with no problem, and they can easily be knocked down or repositioned without causing any threat to the structure of your house. Load-bearing walls—which by definition include all exterior walls—present an altogether different problem, because they are indeed holding up your house. If windows and doors are added to them without thought, the entire weight of the house above would press down on them and crush them, and the walls might even give way. To keep this from happening, doors and windows in load-bearing walls require special framing. Above them, a small beam called a header spans the top of the opening and bridges the gap between the studs. Below them, they contain a sill, which helps to stabilize the framing. The headers and sills are supported in place by shorter pieces of lumber known as cripple studs—not the kindest name, to be sure, but one that has been around as long as the oldest house.

Inevitably, when planning an addition or a renovation, every homeowner fantasizes about moving a wall or two, whether it's to create a larger kitchen or build a walk-in closet. If you want to move a partition wall, the task couldn't be easier. All your contractor has to do is remove any wiring and plumbing, rip the structure down, and reassemble it where you want. Don't fret; load-bearing walls can be moved as well. In this case, however, the contractor first needs to install a beam to hold the weight above and transfer it to the adjacent load-bearing walls. Once this is done, the wall in question can be removed safely.

Believe me, you want to know for sure whether a wall is load-bearing or not before you start ripping it down. I once worked with a crew on an enormous old house where this had not been the case. The new home-owners wanted us to try to straighten a mysterious bow in the first-floor ceiling, and when we busted through the plaster we were shocked by what we found. A previous owner had removed a load-bearing wall and simply nailed the unsupported floor joists together. Those spindly little nails, rather than a solid beam, were all that was holding the second floor up. It was amazing that the entire house hadn't fallen down. Don't take these sorts of chances. A carpenter—or, better yet, a structural engi-neer—will be able to tell you in an instant whether a wall is load-bearing. And if it is, they'll also be able to calculate the exact dimensions of the supporting beam you'll need in its place.

Understanding Insulation

Walls are like sandwiches—albeit inedible ones—with drywall or plaster on the inside, siding on the outside, and layers of different materials between the two. Let's start with the insulation at the center and work our way first inside, then outside to examine these components piece by piece.

In terms of your overall comfort, the insulation inside walls and ceil-ings is crucial. The wood structure, for instance, may be able to block wind and rain, but the air gaps within it need to be stuffed with insula-tion to block the transfer of hot or cold air. Years ago, homes were built with no insulation—which is why the typical image of eighteenth- and

Giving Mildew the Brush-Off

Mildew doesn't just grow in the basement— it can also flourish on the outside of a house, especially where the sun doesn't shine, such as on the north side or behind foundation plantings. While mildew isn't necessarily destructive, it looks terrible. And if it occurs on wood siding and you paint over it, it will simply show through the paint and soon start to flourish again. Your solution lies in a bottle of chlorine bleach. Make a mixture of half water and half bleach and spray it on the mildew to kill it. Then wash it off, and the mildew will disappear. Done once a year, this can extend the life of the paint on your house. Be careful not to slop it around too much, however, or it could damage the plants beneath it.

nineteenth century life includes everyone huddled around the fire. The addition of insulation has single-handedly made homes more comfortable. There are many types of insulation, all of which work relatively the same way. No matter what the material—fiberglass, ground-up cellulose, or spray foams—they all trap air and slow down the movement of heat from the indoors to the outdoors in the winter, and from the outdoors to the indoors the summer. Wherever you live, from the cold North to the balmy South, your home can benefit from insulation.

Insulation is a lot like blankets on your bed. If you have one blanket, you'll be warm. If you put five blankets on, you'll be really warm, because the heat of your body can't escape. That's kind of the premise behind insulation. Insulation is measured by its effectiveness in restricting the heat flow, which is something called an R-value.

An R-value of 0 would be the equivalent of standing outside naked— no protection whatsoever. Glass, as we've seen in Chapter 4, can range from an R-value of 1 to an R-value of 9 or so. And a well-insulated wall built of 2-by-6 studs can easily achieve a value of R-22. Hot air rises, so there's a limit to the effectiveness of insulating the walls, since most of the heat that you're likely to lose goes up rather than out. Instead, the attic ceiling should have the thickest insulation, since this is where most heat is lost in the winter and most heat is gained in the summer. The federal Department of Energy recommends an R-value of 30, 40, or even 50 here, depending on what part of the country you live in, to add to your overall comfort and your home's energy efficiency. This can mean laying on an insulating layer 2 feet thick or more, which is something you wouldn't want to do in a wall.

As comfortable as insulation may make you feel, too much can create problems of a different sort. By creating a tight box, it also creates poor air quality indoors, which forces you to breathe everything from mold and mildew spores to dangerous carbon monoxide fumes from furnaces. Compounding this is an accumulation of humidity that results from daily activities such as taking showers and boiling water. If you're going to add more insulation to your house and go crazy with weatherstripping and caulking, you'll need to address these issues first. Remedying them would include things such as adding an outside air supply to the furnace or boiler as well as the fireplace, installing proper ventilation in the form of exhaust fans for the kitchen and bathrooms, and possibly considering an air exchanger that brings fresh air into the house continuously. These are the kinds of technology used in commercial buildings, and they're exactly the sorts of thing that people who live in well-insulated houses need to consider. A good contractor will be able to help you sort out the options. But the bottom line is, I would rather live in a drafty house than in one plugged up so tightly that the air inside it constitutes a health hazard.

Vapor Barriers Demystified

Home ownership is a never-ending process of discovering that things you never heard of suddenly matter a great deal. Take vapor barriers, for instance. To the uninitiated—say, about 95 percent of the population—these sound like they belong on a spaceship. But in fact they're inside your home and form a critical barrier to moisture that not only keeps your walls from rotting but keeps your insulation from turning into a soggy mess.

A vapor barrier is a water-impermeable layer positioned on the inside walls and ceilings, just over the layer of insulation. It prevents moisture from moving from the inside of the house and condensing in the wall. Now, in old houses there were no vapor barriers—but there was no insulation, either. In these homes, hot, humid air inside moved unimpeded through the walls and condensed on the outside of the house. But when a house is insulated, this humid air has a different trajectory. Instead, it condenses when it meets a cold surface—which just happens to be the layer of insulation within the walls. Once it condenses, it tends to stay there, causing everything from mildew to rot. When the weather heats up, the water eventually vaporizes and can rip off the exterior paint as it moves unseen through the walls.

Many things block water vapor at least partially and are technically components of the vapor barrier—including the drywall or plaster, which we'll get to in a moment, as well as the paint and wallpaper spread on top of the wall itself. Moisture can still penetrate these things, however, and something more is needed to block it effectively. Vapor barriers come in three distinct varieties. The backing of certain types of fiberglass insulation is covered with a water-impermeable kraft paper that has plastic fiber woven into it. This will work just fine as a vapor barrier. Another type of vapor barrier is a heavy plastic sheet, which is about as thick as a heavy-duty garbage

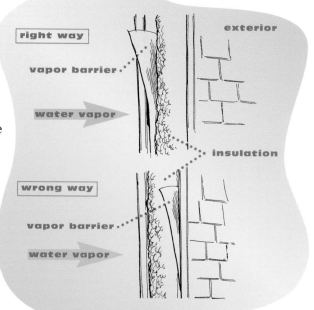

Some Pointers for Repointing

Brick houses may seem like they're maintenance-free—but guess again. The bricks hold the strength, but the mortar between them is expandable. It's a give-and-take, and as brick expands and contracts and gets soaked with water, it's the mortar that's supposed to take the stress. Eventually it starts to disintegrate and needs to be replaced. The process of putting a new layer of mortar along the edge is called repointing or tuckpointing. Whenever the mortar has lost a1/4-inch of its original depth, it's time to hire someone who will get out the chisel. To do this right, a mason will rake the mortar-filled gaps (joints) between the bricks to a depth of twice the width. Never try to stuff new mortar in without first chiseling or grinding out the old mortar in this channel. That would leave a weak connection between the bricks and makes joints susceptible to water infiltration.

One key point: Make sure the mortar is softer or brittler than the brick. If not, the brick, not the mortar, will yield and start to deteriorate over time—which is a common problem in houses built with soft brick before the 1920s if shoddy masons try to tuckpoint with pure portland cement. If you have an old house and your mason doesn't know about this, find a different mason. The damage that can be done to your home by repointing with the wrong mortar is incalculable.

bag. This comes in rolls that are unfurled and stapled to the studs in big sheets, and the seams are then taped together. A third type consists of foam insulation that is sprayed into the cavities between the wall studs. The bubbles in the foam seal off the transmission of air, so this acts as both a vapor barrier and insulation all in one.

Vapor barriers should go on every wall as well as on the ceilings in cold climates—although this last step is not necessary where winters remain mild. No matter where you live, however, there is one crucial rule about vapor barriers: They have to be installed on the warm side of the wall, which is closest to the inside of the house—because that's where the vapor comes from. Put it on the far side of the insulation, closest to the exterior siding, and you won't be creating a vapor barrier but a vapor dam that traps moisture in the wall. That would be every bit as dopey as laying sod with the green side down, and it will turn your insulation into a big sponge in no time.

If you live in a house with no vapor barrier—and you should assume that you don't have one if your house is more than sixty or seventy years old—I wouldn't necessarily recommend spending the money to have one installed. That would involve ripping down plaster or drywall and wouldn't be worth the expense and the mess. But if you plan to reinsulate an old house or renovate a portion of it, then you should insist on having your contractor install a vapor barrier, or use foam or paper-backed fiberglass insulation that doubles as one.

Covering the Interior

Fascinating as these structural elements of a wall are, the only thing we want to see in a home is a smooth, unbroken surface that we can paint or paper. In old houses, this was achieved with plaster slathered onto thin strips of wood called lath. But a century ago, an entrepreneur named Augustine Sackett cast plaster in a larger rectangular mold and reinforced it with layers of felt paper to create a rigid board that could be attached to the wall easily. First used as a base for plaster, this metamorphosed into what we now call drywall. Most houses since World War II have been built using drywall, which is a layer of gypsum plaster sandwiched between two layers of paper. The heavy drywall sheets are screwed to the wall studs to create an instant finished surface. The seams between the boards are taped and smoothed with joint compound, and

What A Steel!

While wood is by far the most popular material to frame a house, another product has the potential to change forever the way homes are constructed— steel. Long used in commercial construction, steel framing is increasingly finding its way into homes. Steel has some fundamental advantages over wood. For one thing, steel doesn't warp, and there is no variation in dimensions among different pieces. This takes the guesswork out of framing a house. Also, walls and ceilings built with steel studs, plates, and floor joists tend to be truer than those built from wood. They run flatter and straighter and are sturdier. One other advantage: Steel is fireproof. While we're not at the end of the lumber era just yet, I think you'll be seeing a lot more metal appearing inside walls.

voilà, a wall is born. The process of drywalling a house is exceptionally fast, and it's not uncommon for a crew of workers to finish the entire process in a single day.

While the basic ingredients of drywall remain similar from brand to brand, the thicknesses vary greatly. For instance, you can buy veneer drywall that's only 1/8 inch thick. Many times, people buy this to install over an old cracked plaster wall in the hope that it will save them the trouble of scraping and replastering. Unfortunately, they usually end up with a wall or a ceiling that has a wavy look to it, almost like the ocean. This is always a mistake. Better for this and all tasks are thicker sheets, ranging from 5/8 to 3/4 inch. My advice: Always upgrade to the best, thickest drywall you can get. It gives you a more solid wall, cuts down on sound transmission from room to room, and gives you a flatter wall. For a marginal cost increase over thinner products, you get a vastly better product.

And what's become of plaster? Well, it hasn't entirely disappeared— partly because everyone loves it so much. Paint tends to flow smoother on plaster walls, and wallpaper can be both applied and removed more easily. Plaster also is a better sound barrier than drywall, which means you don't hear noises so much from room to room. But, of course, plaster is also a lot more expensive than drywall. Still, it's possible to have the benefits of plaster walls at a cost not much higher than drywall using veneer plaster instead of the old plaster-over-lath method. In plaster veneer, the plaster is spread to a depth of between 1/4 and 3/8 inch over special drywall filled with plaster, which is commonly called gypsum.

If a wall gets soaked, both drywall and plaster veneer will disintegrate. This makes them entirely unsuitable for use in the wet areas of bathrooms. Put plaster or drywall in a shower stall or around a bathtub, and the tiles will soon fall off. For humid and slightly damp areas, I recommend using greenboard. Like regular drywall, greenboard has a gypsum core—but its exterior is water-resistant. Bear in mind that greenboard is not waterproof, and it will break down over time if penetrated by water. This makes it okay for bathrooms in general but not good for the shower

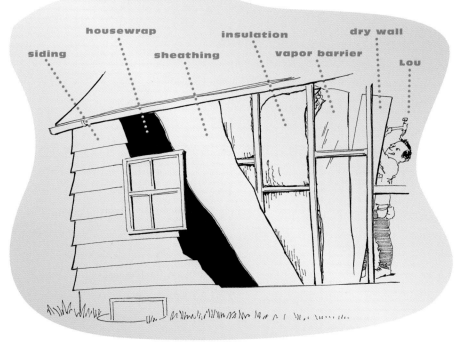

An Rx for Popping Nails

When a house settles, the wood framing shrinks over time—and the odd screw holding in the drywall can occasionally loosen a tiny bit. When it does, the little bit of joint compound covering the screw hole goes flying into the room like a champagne cork on New Year's Eve. You can try patching the screw hole again, but I guarantee you'll have the same problem. What's the remedy? Remove the screw altogether and patch the hole. To do this, install two additional screws a couple of inches above and below the troublesome one to hold the drywall in place. Then remove the jinxed screw and fill all three holes with joint compound. Problem solved.

or other constantly wet areas. For that, I'd recommend concrete board—which is literally made out of concrete. Concrete can stay wet all day and not disintegrate, which is why the Golden Gate Bridge, among other things, is still standing. These boards are basically impervious to water, will hold tiles indefinitely, and will keep the wall studs behind them free of rot.

On a side note, just know that the fasteners used to hold the drywall in humid and damp areas in place must be as waterproof as the wallboard itself. If you're using standard steel drywall screws in a wet location, you run the risk of having them bleed through, because those screws can rust. It's essential to use a corrosion-resistant or stainless-steel screw designed for wet locations. This represents a minimal increase in price, and yields a great deal of extra protection.

Covering the Exterior

So far, we have worked through a wall toward the inside of the house. Now let's move toward the outside.

On the exterior, the insulation between the studs is covered by a layer of wood sheathing. As with subfloors, this used to consist of 1-inch-thick planks nailed together, but it tends to be made of 5/8-inch-thick plywood in houses built since World War II. The sheathing does more than just

How to Find a Stud

No, I'm not talking about *The Dating Game*. But you need to find studs—those pieces of lumber running vertically in a wall—whenever you are hanging pictures, putting up a new set of shelves, or getting ready to build an addition. Nails or screws driven into the studs are much stronger than those driven into flimsy wallboard. To find a stud, you can tap with your knuckles until you hear a solid sound, but this is an inexact way to do it—especially if the wall is insulated, which makes all thuds sound the same. Instead, use a handheld battery-operated stud finder. These inexpensive devices (as little as $10) slide along the wall and beep when they hit a stud. You'll amaze your friends, and your pictures will stay hanging on the wall.

cover up the studs and the insulation. It adds a lot of stability to the walls. Without it, the studs would rock from side to side, and the wall wouldn't remain square and true. Studs alone simply can't support the weight of a home. Again, as with subfloors, some carpenters use the slightly cheaper oriented-strand board (OSB) instead of plywood, but I'd avoid this at all cost. Since OSB is made of wood mulch rather than thin sheets of wood sandwiched together, it tends to weaken and lose its strength if it gets wet during the construction process. And I've never yet seen a house or addition being built that doesn't get doused with rain. Sheathing is a major structural part of the home and gives walls their solidity. Scrimp here only at your own peril.

Years ago, the exterior siding—whether wood clapboard, shingles or even brick veneer—was attached directly to the sheathing. This created a problem because rainwater could seep through it and saturate the sheathing as well as the wall behind it. We're talking mold, mildew, and rot as a result. The first attempt to stop this came with the addition of a layer of tar paper between the sheathing and the siding. Tar paper is completely impermeable to moisture, so it did indeed block

Working with Fiberglass Insultation

Installing insulation, like so many other jobs around the house, is best left to a professional. But this is one area that many homeowners try to tackle themselves—and their product of choice is inevitably fiberglass. Tucking insulation into the bays between studs isn't rocket science, but I'm always amazed at how many people do it wrong. They try to jam-pack it into the spaces and around doors and window, under the mistaken belief that more insulation is better. Wrong. You want to fill up every gap, true. But if you compress it, you actually decrease the R-value by squeezing out the very air spaces that make it an insulating material to begin with. Instead, do what the pros do and keep it loose. Keep in mind also that fiberglass insulation can be a misery to work with, because it can irritate your skin and lungs. To protect yourself, always wear long-sleeved shirts and pants, as well as gloves that extend over the sleeves. You'll need a respirator as well, so that you won't breathe in all those airborne fiberglass particles.

water from passing through the siding. Unfortunately, with superinsulated houses, this had a sometimes disastrous side effect. Any moisture from inside the house that passed through the vapor barrier and into the insulation became trapped there permanently by the tar paper and created a great deal of structural rot in a short time—often in as little as five years.

One of the great inventions of the last twenty-five years are tar paper substitutes known as house wraps. These are remarkable because they selectively block water. Giant drops, such as those beating from a driving rain, are repelled by the house wrap. But at the same time, they allow the transmission of vaporized water molecules. If you hold a piece of house wrap over a cup of coffee, the steam from the coffee will penetrate right through it. This allows any moisture that builds up in the walls to evaporate, keeping the walls dry and rot-free. In addition, house wraps

What Goes on the Outside?

I love wood siding—and as much as everyone says it's a lot of work to maintain, keep in mind there really isn't any such thing as a maintenance-free exterior. That's as elusive in its way as fat-free ice cream, which will surely make you fat, if you eat it by the quart. Here are some of the pros and cons of the most popular siding materials.

Wood. This versatile material comes in many styles from clapboards to shingles and thick, hand-split shingles called shakes. Wood deteriorates not just from water, but from the sun itself, which destroys the natural material called lignin that holds the cellulose fibers. Properly stained, painted, and cared for, however, wood siding can easily last a hundred years or longer.

Vinyl. While this is marketed as the quintes-sential maintenance-free material, it is not. Vinyl planks can break just as wooden ones do—such as when a tree limb falls. And when they do, you may have a hard time matching the color to make repairs. Beyond that, the sun and the rain dull the surface over time. If you get twenty years out of vinyl siding, you're getting a lot.

Cement board. There are many varia-tions, including shingles and clapboard, some of which look just like natural wood. The advantage: No trees are cut down, and they'll never rot. While the cost of the material is somewhat less than wood, the installation is twice as high. Maintenance is sim-ilar to wood, however, since they have to be painted regularly.

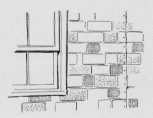

Stucco: This is a type of mortar that is spread over the walls of a house. Stucco is prone to cracking if moisture seeps behind it, so good installation is essential to its survival. And make sure you paint stucco with latex rather than oil-based paint. Latex breathes and is less likely to trap crack-provoking moisture behind the walls.

Brick or stone: These materials can be used in two ways. Masonry houses are built with solid brick, stone, or masonry block walls—involving no wood framing at all. In frame construction, the brick or stone is added as a thin veneer on the exterior of the walls—which is the far cheaper way to go. Either way, the exterior will have to be cleaned regularly and the mortar occasionally replaced.

also act as a wind barrier that will make your home much warmer in the wintertime by cutting down on drafts.

Proper installation of house wrap is the key to good performance. The seams need to be taped after the rolls of house wrap are stapled up, and the perforations around doors and windows need extra attention to help cut down on drafts. Install house wrap without proper taping and you'll be wasting your money. The one other thing that drives me crazy is when people install this with the brand name upside down. Sure, there's no difference in the performance of the material, and in any event it all gets covered up by siding. But to me it shows an overt sloppiness that hints of worse mistakes to come. I have made my work crews take entire walls of house wrap off and do it over, simply because

Blasted Sandblasting

Old brick houses have often been painted on the outside—and it's every homeowner's dream to strip the paint and reveal the beautiful surface beneath. That's a fine goal, but never, ever have the exterior of a house sandblasted to achieve this. First, most of the old paint on a house probably contains lead, which you would be sending into the atmosphere in one giant toxic plume. Beyond this, sandblasting can cause irreparable damage. Bricks—especially old ones—resemble a loaf of bread: They have a hard crust on the outside and a softer inside. If you sandblast the brick, you vaporize the hard face and expose the soft interior, which quickly erodes and deteriorates. Go ahead and have the paint stripped—but find instead a contractor who uses an environmentally-friendly chemical stripping process.

that upside-down lettering looked just plain unprofessional.

On top of the sheathing and the house wrap comes—at last—the exterior siding. Here, there's a myriad of choices. There's vinyl, aluminum, brick or stone veneer, wood (everything from red cedar to white pine), and even composite materials made with concrete. Any one of them will work well if installed properly, because the actual type of siding is almost incidental to the long-term performance of the walls.

Instead, if the insides contain what they should—from vapor barriers to insulation and house wrap—you can be sure that, unlike Jericho, your walls won't ever come tumbling down.

chapter**EIGHT**

A View from Below
Basements can be scary places—unless you know how to tame them

The call came in the middle of the night—and through the sobs I figured out what had gone wrong.

It was the wife of a friend. She and her husband had fallen in love with a house at the bottom of a sloping hill, and even though I warned them about the inevitable drainage problems that would come with this, they went ahead and bought the place. With only a crawl space, there turned out to be no real water problems to worry about—at least not at first. My friends went ahead and built a family room addition, and at the same time they excavated a full-sized basement beneath the house. Like everyone else, they prized this additional space. They carpeted it, put up paneling and an acoustic-tile ceiling, and turned it into a rec room with a bar and even a new refrigerator. Then came the rainstorm. In just a few hours, the deluge drained from all their neighbors' yards and driveways, ran down the slope, and funneled right into the basement. Not just a little, but a lot. My friend's wife (who was seven months pregnant, by the way) moaned into the phone, "There's five and a half feet of water in the basement, and everything's ruined!" By the time I got there, the new refrigera-

basements

tor was bobbing in the water like some forlorn lifeboat in a sea of trouble.

For many people, basements represent the worst a house has to offer. Damp, dark, with foul air, hard concrete floors, and low ceilings dripping with wires and plumbing, they can make you yearn for a high-rise rental rather than a place of your own. It's no surprise that one of the scariest scenes in the movie *Psycho*, for instance, involves someone mistakenly trying to seek refuge in Anthony Perkins's basement. Yet at the same time, we look at this underbelly of the home with covetous eyes. It is, after all, usually identical in area to the entire first floor of our house. And as though it were some bit of Oklahoma frontier, we greedily want to grab a piece of it for our own use. We dream of filling this expanse with a playroom, storage area, and laundry room, workshop, or clubhouse-style bar, perhaps—complete with a 1950s-style jukebox to entertain our friends.

Turning the average basement, which usually amounts to little more than a dank hole in the ground, into this subterranean fantasy requires far more than nailing drywall to the walls and laying down carpeting. Let's work through the major steps—which include keeping the basement dry, tackling basic design problems, maintaining mechanical systems, and controlling the house-destroying insects and rodents that thrive down here. Taking care of all this will make the difference between a basement that seems like a dungeon and a one that becomes a viable and inviting part of your house.

Keeping Things Dry

To homeowners, few things can match the aggravation caused by a wet basement. My friends found this out with heightened drama, perhaps, but many people suffer problems on a smaller yet no less irritating scale. Water is a remarkable substance in this way; it can torture you whether it's blasted from a hose or limited to an achingly slow seep. With water troubles, there's no comfort in company, either. According to the American Society of Home Inspectors, 60 percent of all houses in the nation have foundation leaks, and the number climbs to 90 percent for houses built with foundations made of cinder block.

Water is a home's greatest enemy. When it accumulates in the basement, even in tiny amounts, it can warp the upstairs floorboards, rust the life out of appliances and utilities, and turn finished rooms into mildewed grottos. Even crawl spaces and slab foundations that aren't technically basements at all can trap moisture if drained improperly. Hidden from view, the problem is easy to ignore—until it's too late. One home inspector I talked to remembers slogging around on his belly in a wet crawl space to discover that he could grab the beams above in his hand and squeeze them like a sponge. They were that far gone, just from being suspended above water.

There is another real problem caused by water in the basement, and that involves insurance claims. Many companies protect themselves from wet-basement claims by limiting their liability to, say, $5,000, or by denying coverage altogether. That means that if there's a flood, they may not be liable for much—-even if you lose your furniture, carpeting, furnace or boiler, hot-water heater, and laundry room. A tab to replace that much equipment could easily run to $20,000 or more, which you would have to pay out of your own pocket. It is up to you to take steps to prevent a disaster like that before it happens.

There's an additional benefit in making sure your basement is watertight. Not only will you be able to weather a storm without fearing a flood, you can also expect a direct increase in the value of your house when you go to sell it. No one wants to buy a house that smells mildewy or has water in the basement. But they will surely be interested in one that is guaranteed to be dry, and may even be willing to overlook

Cracking Up?

We somehow imagine that a solid foundation has to be crack-free, but nothing could be further from the truth. Over time, narrow cracks are natural and normal to see, both in the walls and in the poured concrete floor. For the most part, they're a sign that a house is settling, not falling down. Typically, if they're 1/8 inch thick or less, you've got nothing to worry about. If they're wider than that, however, you may want to bring in a home inspector to have a look. Far worse than any crack, however, is a bowed or leaning wall. This is caused by pressure from the earth bearing against the foundation and could literally cause the house to collapse. To solve this, consult an inspector—and quick!

some other flaws to buy it. In terms of resale value of your home, this is the best place to spend your money, without question.

Before going over some fixes, let's figure out why basements fill with water in the first place. The answer is partly obvious: They are literally holes dug into the damp ground. In this respect, they've got a lot in common with a sailboat hull floating on the ocean. The hull will stay dry—but if there are any small leaks, it will quickly fill with water and sink. The only way to keep the boat afloat is to plug the holes or bail out the water with a pump. And the same is true of your basement. Water from the out-

Mechanical Abilities

While we're in the basement, let's have a word about maintenance. The average house has a life-support system that includes thousands of dollars' worth of equipment, including a furnace and boiler, a blower system for air-conditioning and heating, a water heater, and a water softener—most of which ends up tucked away down here. As is always the risk, once it's out of sight it's out of mind. All too often, we tend to forget that these items are machines and, like all machines, need to be tended to or they will fail. No one would dream of driving their car 40,000 miles without several oil changes, a tune-up, and a new air filter or two. Yet that is exactly how many people treat their heating and cooling systems. As a result, these systems burn a lot more fuel than they need to, which costs you money. They can also belch toxic air into the basement as well as the rest of the house, which could cost you far more. The remedy is annual maintenance by a qualified service contractor. Ignoring it can threaten not just your comfort but your health and even your very life.

side will seep through cracks in the walls and floors and cause a chronic problem unless you seal the cracks and install a pump to drain it. Even if you don't have outright leaks, you may have serious dampness problems. Foundations, whether they're concrete or stone or cinder block, are porous. They act like a big sponge drawing in water to the inside, which no dehumidifier alone can tackle.

The first line of defense against moisture is to damp-proof foundations whenever a new house or addition is being built. At the most basic level, this involves coating the exterior foundation wall with tar. While this will provide a moisture barrier, it hardly makes the foundation waterproof, since any cracks that form in the walls will split right through the tar coating as well. A far better technology involves stretching a plastic membrane that's four or five times thicker than a heavy-duty trash bag on top of the tar. Imagine swathing your body in clear plastic wrap and running out into the rain; you wouldn't get wet, and this same principle applies here. The foundation membrane creates something much closer to a watertight structure, since it generally stays intact despite small cracks in the foundation it covers. While this is becoming standard practice for new construction, it can also be applied to an existing foundation—although it involves expensive and very messy excavation to make it happen.

As frustrating as basement and crawl space leaks can be, many can be fixed with minor effort, and some of the repairs can actually take place outside the house. There's one fundamental rule of physics that you cannot ignore: Water runs downhill. This means that if the ground slopes toward your basement rather than away from it, water will run toward the house and pool against the foundation wall. When it does that, it will inevitably find small cracks it can infiltrate. As a test, put a 4-foot level on the ground next to the foundation. If you see that the ground is pitched away from your home, the slope is fine. If not, you've got potential trouble.

Here's where to start: You'll have to clear away plantings and gently build up the soil to slope away from the foundation, with a grade of at least 1 inch for every 4 feet. To protect against rot and insects, however, you've got to keep soil at least 4 inches away from wood siding. In places where sidewalks or driveways press close to the house, the same rule applies about making sure they slope away from the house—but the repairs can be far costlier.

Downspouts can also be a source of trouble. Some end right at the foundation, where during rainstorms water runs from the roof to the gutters to the downspouts. When the water hits the ground, it accumulates into a giant pool that seeps through the walls. Simply rerouting the water by extending the downspout a few feet away from the house can help. And don't forget to clean the gutters. If water is spilling out of them, it's probably splashing right next to the foundation—and therefore undermines the entire point of having gutters in the first place.

Some homes still have downspouts that run into the town sewage system. If you have this type, make sure that the lines that lead into the ground are clear. These can get clogged with leaves and debris—and during heavy downpours they can back up, leading to potential leaks into your basement.

As in my friends' case, sometimes the volume of water bearing down on a foundation is simply too great to be altered just by adding a little fill around the foundation or extending the downspouts. The first line of attack in this case is analogous to the boy with his finger in the dike: You have to plug up the holes. You can seal small cracks in walls or floors, for instance, with a concrete epoxy kit available from a hardware store. If you have some slight seepage, there's a pretty good chance this will stop it, especially if you follow the directions and chisel out a small section around the crack so the epoxy has something to stick to.

Unfortunately, you may have bigger problems. At certain times of the year, for instance, rising groundwater can literally force itself into basements through a phenomenon known as hydrostatic pressure, which nothing can stop. In its most severe form, I've actually seen water squirting up and into the air through cracks in the basement floor, like a miniature version of Old Faithful.

Common wisdom used to be that the only way to deal with leakage is to stop the water from getting into the house—and that often involved excavating around the entire perimeter of the house, waterproofing the outside walls, and then laying pipes called drain tile at the bottom of the trench before filling it all back up again. This is very effective, but it involves ripping out all the landscaping, as well as any decks or patios and the front and back steps—and effectively turns the house into a construction site for weeks if not months. We now reserve that approach for only the most extreme cases, or cases in which the homeowner wants the most effective solution, all other considerations aside.

Now, the thinking on most water issues is that some leakage coming into the basement is acceptable as long as we channel it and route it out of the house—just like that boat floating in the sea with the pump working. This keeps the water from causing any damage. The way to do this is to have a perimeter drain installed just beneath the concrete floor around the edge of the basement. The concrete is chipped away, perforated pipe is laid down in a trough, and then the pipe is covered with gravel and more concrete. The pipes flow to a 3-foot-diameter hole in the floor, in which a sump pump is positioned that then forces the water up and out of the basement. Your problem is gone. Installing a system such as this is a major project, as it no doubt sounds, and involves people coming in, busting up the concrete, and carrying the rubble out by the bucketful. It might cost a few thousand dollars, but it will make it possible to save many thousands of dollars more in damages from flooding or moisture rot.

A Design in Mind

When you redo the living room or the kitchen or bedroom in a house, it's often a straightforward affair. You can pretty much choose your color scheme or renovation projects and get to work. With a basement, however, you have to slow down and address some basic issues first. Remember: In turning the basement into usable space, you're basically trying to renovate a cave. The first thing to be aware of is the temperature of the space. Many people think that just because the upstairs part of their house has the right heating and cooling that the basement will be comfortable, too—but this is a big mistake. In some instances, the basement heating is limited to a single duct branching off the forced-air system. Or it may be that the only heat in the basement comes from the glow of the boiler. Don't expect either one to keep you warm, especially since your feet will be in contact with an earth-chilled concrete slab floor that is likely to be a toe-numbing 55 degrees year-round.

Physics also affects basement heating systems, since hot air—as we all

Saving the Sump Pump

With the steadiness of a heartbeat, your sump pump works to keep your basement dry. Do it a simple favor in return, one that will put a lot less wear and tear on it. Each year, clean out the pit that holds the pump, where silt and debris inevitably accumulate. To do this, just unplug the pump, disconnect the discharge pipe that flows out of your basement, and lift the pump out of its hole. Then scoop out any water with a small container into a bucket. Don't worry, this is mostly groundwater—not yucky water from the sewer. Suck the rest of it out with a wet/dry vac if you have one, then when you hit the bottom, scoop out any debris. If you pull out the silt, pebbles, and leaves, the sump pump won't have to work so hard in order to do its job—which will lengthen its life span by years.

know—rises. What this means in practice, which you may not know, is that the staircase climbing up to the first floor actually acts as a giant vent, sucking all the hot air out of the basement and sending it upstairs, making the basement even colder. When you're in a space that's freezing cold, it's hard to appreciate the ancillary creature comforts, like that terrific sofa you spent a couple of thousand dollars on, or the great media center, or the state-of-the-art sound system. No one will care, because they're going to be distracted by their own feelings of misery.

A Sump Pump Test

Sump pumps switch on only when there's water in the basement. No water, no pumping. So if it's off, how can you be sure it will actually be working when you need it? One way is to take a bucket of water, pour it into the sump pump pit, and keep filling until the pump switches on. If it doesn't switch on, you could have a bad switch, which can easily be fixed. More seriously, you could have a failed motor that would require replacing the entire unit. It's a good idea to do this test a couple of times a year—and especially before heading off on a long vacation. That way, you can be sure your basement's being protected while you're away.

What can you do? That depends on your house—but the important thing is to think about it. If your furnace or boiler is big enough, a qualified heating contractor can add some additional vents to bring the basement temperature into line with the rest of the house. Or you can even add a separate heating zone and a separate thermostat that lets you control the heat in the basement separately from the rest of the house, which not only overcomes the variation caused by the different base temperature of the underground floor but saves you money by giving you the option of turning the heat down when you're not using the basement. You may also want to add an insulated door to the top of the basement staircase, which will keep the warm air down where you want it.

Keeping a basement cool in the summer presents another problem altogether. Basements are notably cooler than the rest of the house—again, because physics is at work allowing all of the cooler air to sink down into the basement. While this might seem like an asset, air-conditioning that makes the rest of the house comfortable can quickly turn a typical basement playroom into something that feels like a walk-in freezer. The solution will depend on how your house is set up—but the important thing is to pay attention to it and have a heating and cooling contractor come up with a plan before you start your basement renovation. You don't want to find out when it's too late that the only solution lies in running a new duct across the ceiling and through the walls—the very ceiling and walls that you've just spent a lot of time and money having installed.

Unlike upstairs rooms, basements present a design problem in terms of their very shape. In most cases, there's a good reason basements are hidden below ground. Instead of being conventional rooms conceived by an architect or an intelligent builder, the basement is most likely a vast, uncarved space in which the "finish carpentry" was more or less executed by a guy pushing around a wheelbarrow filled with wet cement. From this, you need to conceive a usable living space—and this is especially hard, since most people somehow imagine they can do this entirely on their own, without the input of a professional.

What you need to do is take a realistic look at what you have to work with, and this will usually involve the assistance of a creative carpenter at the very least. A normal ceiling height is 8 feet or more; in basements, it tends to be somewhat less than that. By the time you add a drop ceiling, that height shrinks further. And if you plan to make a floor that's comfortable to walk on—such as a plywood subfloor, or even a floor raised on wooden joists that can then be insulated for extra comfort—you've taken more space still and might end up with something that's only 6 feet high. Sound inviting? No? Then change your plans to what you have, either by scaling things down to a more reasonable level or making the extra effort to change the space to fit your needs.

No matter what you do, you will inevitably encounter extraordinary

The Best Flood Insurance of All

If you're looking for a foolproof way to prevent your basement from flooding, invest in not one but two sump pumps to keep things dry. Most people go for the cheapest units they can buy, which amount to little more than a 12-volt bilge pump best suited for a small boat. While these might be adequate, you hardly want to stake your $10,000 basement renovation on them. I recommend buying the sturdiest model you can find, and then also installing a second pump in the same hole to serve as a backup if the first one fails. This second one should be connected to a self-charging 12-volt battery, so that it will switch on if the first unit fails or if there is a power blackout. Unless you're experienced in setting these things up, this makes a great job for a plumber.

building challenges, ranging from ill-positioned ducts and concrete-filled columns to circuit breaker boxes and plumbing connections that can't just be plastered over. While some of these can be concealed with a little creative carpentry, others may perpetually annoy you. Who's going to find anything likable about that box-paneled column in the middle of the room, for instance, if it blocks their view of the TV or hits their elbow every time they're about to make a winning pool shot?

As a remedy, try to be clear early on about what you intend to do down here. If you want just a rustic space for a workshop or laundry room, then everything will probably be fine as it is. But if you plan to carve out an area that will be like any other room in your house—tasteful and comfortable, a place where guests won't scream and turn tail—then you've got to be willing to make some big changes, and pay for them. Staircases can be rebuilt, ducts can be moved, and columns can be repositioned. People hear the phrase "load-bearing wall" and panic, as if there's nothing they can do about it. But the space within a house—and in basements in particular—is infinitely malleable. All you need to do is hire a contractor or a structural engineer who can determine the best way to do it.

A Cure for Dampness

Even if water isn't squishing between your toes when you step into your basement, dampness can still cause you trouble. Since water in the air is heavy, it tends to settle at the lowest parts of your house. That's what causes basements and crawl spaces to smell musty and can turn them into habitats more suited to nesting bats than to humans. Dehumidifers do wonders to stop this. Another possibility is to install a simple exhaust fan, such as those used in bathrooms, that vents through the side wall and blows moisture-laden air outside. This fan can be attached to a device called a humidistat, which switches the fan on and off as moisture in the air rises and falls. I've found that these work even better than dehumidifiers at keeping things dry and fresh-smelling—and you never have to worry about remembering to empty the drainage bucket.

It will cost you money—but the end result will be a room that works, rather than something cramped and distorted, a space so ungainly and uncomfortable that people can't wait to get back upstairs. Approach it the way you would approach buying a new car. You might save a few hundred dollars by skipping the power windows—but you're going to kick yourself every time you see a friend on the opposite side of the street and have to stop, lean over, and hand-crank the windows down just to say hello. Pretty soon you'll hate your car, and you'll surely hate your hastily redone basement. Instead, spend the money up front to create the space you want; it'll save you the frustration of not being able to do anything about it later.

Creature Discomforts

The things we hate about basements—their dampness, their darkness, their location deep in the ground—are exactly the things that insects and rodents love about them. You can close your eyes to these invasions from the outside, but by doing that you risk learning firsthand just how adept many of these creatures are at destroying houses. Consider it another way. In this

HOW IT WORKS: The Foundation

Much as we like to curse them, basements and crawl spaces are crucial to maintaining the health of your house. First, the concrete or masonry in the walls separates the damp soil from the wood frame—which would otherwise decay and quickly turn your home into an insect condo. Even more important, these foundation walls literally shoulder the weight of your house and hold up the entire structure. Whether made of concrete, brick, stone, or cinder block, the walls take the weight of a fully loaded house—which can easily top 100 tons, give or take a grand piano—and transfer it effortlessly to the ground below. What gives the walls this amazing strength is their shape. The base of the wall, which is buried in the ground beneath the floor, widens to a 16-inch poured-concrete block called a footing. These footings distribute the weight of the house over a broader area than the walls alone would, and by doing so prevent settling or movement of the structure above.

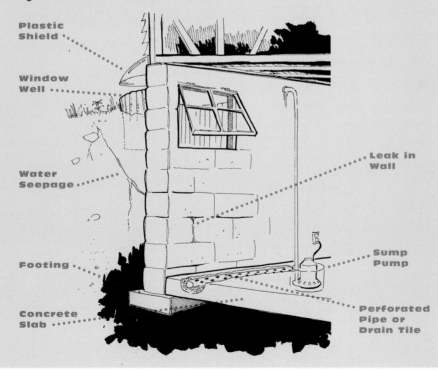

Plastic Shield

Window Well

Water Seepage

Footing

Concrete Slab

Leak in Wall

Sump Pump

Perforated Pipe or Drain Tile

security-conscious era, we think nothing of spending thousands of dollars on alarm systems to defend us against an attack by a robber. Yet all too often we fail to throw up some basic defenses against minute invaders that will leave behind the TV and the stereo but will steal instead the entire structure of your home.

Older homes, of course, are susceptible to the worst problems. Years of basement dampness inevitably create rot. And having a basement filled with this softened structural wood is like leaving milk and cookies out for Santa Claus on Christmas Eve: It becomes an irresistible snack. Only in this case you'll be inviting everything from powderpost beetles and termites to wood borers and carpenter ants. These creatures travel through wood that touches the soil outside, arrive through cracks in foundation walls, and fly in through open basement doors and windows. These creatures can create so much damage that your home's main structural supports start to give away. In that case, you'll be looking not at an exterminator bill of a few hundred dollars but at a massive structural repair bill from a contractor that will run you tens of thousands. Look for signs of damp, softened wood in your basement, and especially for tiny piles of sawdust that seem to accumulate once you clean them up. If you find them, act quickly—because these insects sure will. Formosan termites, for example, which are a non-native species found in southern coastal areas and in Hawaii, form huge colonies that can cause significant damage to a house in just ninety days.

Not all invaders have wings. Those cute little squirrels and chipmunks, for example, can all but ransack a house in a matter of days. But the most common pest is the lowly mouse. While a single one scuttling across the floor may kindle fond memories of your mother reading *Goodnight Moon*, there is little that's cute about them. A female mouse can, in one year, have as many as ten litters, with as many as nine mice in each litter. Let's do the math: That's ninety mice from a single mouse—each of which claws and scratches its way through your walls and does its best to create a family of its own. Not only are there justifiable fears of disease, but the damage that can be done by a mouse infestation is astounding. I've even seen cases in which they have started fires by gnawing through the plastic insulation of electrical wiring in the walls.

The best defense lies in the basement, especially in that area above ground where the foundation walls meet the main structure of the house. Here, any cracks or holes, such as those near the dryer vent outlet or where the electric cables enter the house, serve as a front door to these fuzzy vermin. Their 1/4-inch-wide skulls can squeeze through holes smaller than your pinkie. The best remedy is to seal up these tiny holes. Outside, stuff wads of copper mesh into the holes, since mice can't chew through this, then cover up the holes with siliconized acrylic caulk. Inside, use the same mesh and cover it with squirts of pressurized foam, which is easier to apply but deteriorates in sunlight. And make sure you have screens on your basement windows and doors. If you don't, you might as well put out a welcome mat for everything hungry in your local animal kingdom.

An Encouraging Word

So, as much as we may like to avoid it, the basement is one of the most important parts of the house—a place where you should spend quite a bit of time figuring things out and learning how to spot trouble. Since those foundation walls are holding up the entire place, you owe it to your home's future to make sure things stay dry as well as insect-free. Making the basement less inviting for insects will also go a long way toward making it more inviting for people. And once you've solved these issues, you can happily start making plans for what to do with all of this great, uncolonized space that lies just below the first floor. In fact, I'm now planning on building a family room of my own down in the basement. With the recent arrival of my fourth child, I'm in a rush to think about how to do the walls and the ceiling, what color carpeting to buy, and what furniture might look good. Maybe it's even time for a DVD player. Fortunately, my wife has followed my work enough through the years to be able to slow me down and remind me of what our priorities really should be. "All of that will be great," she told me, "after we put in drain tile and a sump pump."

The friends I told you about at the start of this chapter found out the need for this the hard way. After their flood receded, they ended up having to buy a new furnace, a new water heater, and new just about everything else. Fortunately, they didn't just give in to the relentless flow of water, or pack up and move. Instead, they added drain tile to the basement and took it a step further with a major drainage channel sculpted into their lawn that redirects water from the hillside before it even gets near the basement. The repairs cost them $20,000, much of which could have been avoided, but it made their house livable again. During the last major rainstorm, they called me up again. I got a little worried when I heard my friend's voice, but this time the news was excellent. "It's been pouring for days, and guess what? There's not a drop of water inside!" he cheered. Now, that's something that every homeowner would love to be able to say.

chapter NINE

A View from Above

Like a shingled umbrella, a roof protects your home from the elements;
here's how it works—and what you'll
need to know to maintain it

I know I'm not always right when I make suggestions about what people should do with their homes—but this was one time I had no doubts at all.

A couple contracted me to add a new roof to their old Arts and Crafts home, just down the street from Frank Lloyd Wright's place in Oak Park. The old one was black asphalt, which is the roofing equivalent of the Model T. Instead, they wanted "to liven things up a little," as the woman said. She went to a roofing supply store and found just the color she was looking for, nailed to a 3-foot-by-6-foot sample. It was a pale green, with a hint of blue. The supplier warned her about choosing a color based just on the sample—and anyone who has painted a room with a color that looked like tan on a paint chip but turned out pink on the walls knows the risks. He suggested she buy a few bundles of shingles, enough for a 10 foot-by-10-foot section on the roof, and have me lay them up on the roof without nailing them in place for her to look at. "It would be better

roofs

Anatomy of a Roof

There's more to roofs than mere shingles, as anyone knows who has ever talked to a roofing contractor. Let Mr. Fix-It show you all about eaves—not to mention fascias and rakes.

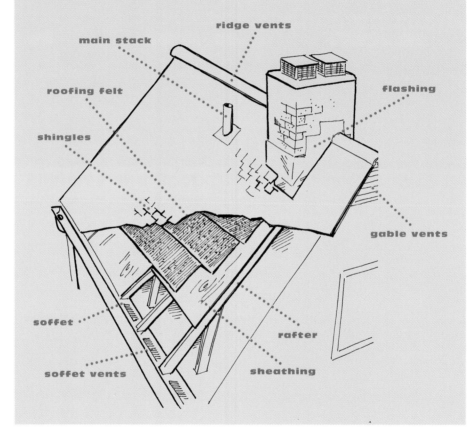

to know if you like it in advance," he told her, "rather than find out you hate it later."

I completely agreed, and the three sample bundles would have cost a total of about $75—which is a pretty good price to pay to be sure you like something as major as the color of your roof. The couple declined, however. They didn't want to spend the money and told me to hurry along with the roof. So while they were gone for a long weekend, my work crew and I ripped off the old shingles, checked the sheathing beneath it to make sure there was no rot or leaks, and nailed up the new shingles. A job well done, I thought. That is, until the homeowners arrived home late Sunday afternoon, a few hours after we had finished. "It's blue!" the woman yelled at me on the phone, and started to cry. "It's not green at all, it's *blue*! I hate it! I hate it!" And I had to admit, when I stopped by to console her in the cool evening light, it did indeed look as blue as a blueberry.

Our desire to turn a roof into a décor statement often obscures our view of the roof for what it is. Specifically, it is the first line of defense in protecting a home from the elements. In the summer, the relentless sun can easily raise the temperature of the roof to 125 degrees or more, which is an environment you'd more likely expect to find in the Sonoran Desert. In the winter, piles of snow and ice can accumulate on it and saddle it with literally tons of extra weight. And let's not forget water. No matter how much rainwater lands on a roof or how much it is driven in between the shingles by whipping winds, we expect the roof to keep us perfectly dry below. Beyond acting as a sort of shingled umbrella, however, the roof provides the upward structure to a home, in the form of rafters that literally hold the walls together. In addition, it creates a space that serves not just as an attic but as a buffer between the indoors and the outdoors—one that preserves the life of the roof and can help keep you more comfortable inside. Let's take our cue from the Drifters and head up on the roof to see for ourselves what's there.

What's Up There?

As with floors and walls, we tend to pay attention only to the finished surface of a roof, which would be the shingles. A well-built roof has much more going on beneath it, however, and it is these details that will make the difference between a nice dry canopy over your home, and one that's riddled with leaks.

How to Make a Roof Last

Your roof is up there—now what? Leave it untended, and you're in for some trouble. The worst thing that can happen to a roof is tree branches rubbing against it. While you may admire that cottage-in-the-woodland look, steady swipes from even the smallest twig blowing in the wind will soon scrape away even the toughest shingles. Start with a pruning, and keep any branches a good 5 feet away from shingles—farther if possible.

To begin, we'll start with the shape of the roof itself. A typical roof rises to a peak, and the wooden structural members that slant beneath it are called the rafters. These anchor the roof to the walls and transfer its weight so that it can be carried through the walls to the founda- tion. The top piece of wood that connects the rafters is called the ridge or roof beam. In older houses, this beam often starts to sag and sway like some wayward camel.

On top of the rafters lie several surfaces that culminate in the shingles. First comes the sheathing, which is a layer of plywood sheets nailed together to form a smooth surface to which the rest of the roof can be nailed. (In older homes, built before plywood was invented, you'll find the sheathing is most likely made from 1-by-6 planks.) The plywood sheathing gives a roof its strength and for this reason should be as thick as possible—certainly no less than 5/8 inch thick, although some local building codes will even require 3/4 inch. Anything less than that is a recipe for disaster and will almost certainly result in a wavy-looking roof as the thin sheathing bows between the rafters.

Strong as sheathing may be, it is not at all waterproof. Instead, this comes from laying a layer of tar paper, which is also known as roofing felt, on top. As we saw in Chapter 7, tar paper used to be used on walls just beneath the exterior siding, but though it prevented moisture from seeping into walls, it also trapped moisture that migrated there from the humid indoors. This is not a problem in roofs, since this humid air is

Gather No Moss

Another common danger to roofs is moss—which sounds as innocuous as it gets. But growing on a roof, moss traps and holds moisture, which can seep through singles and rot the structure beneath in as little as a few years. When you see that telltale greenish fuzz forming on shingles, it's time to take action. Using equal parts chlorine bleach and water, spray it to kill the moss, then scrub it gently with a soft brush—the same type you'd use on your car. This is wet, slippery work, to be sure; unless you know what you're doing, hire someone to do it for you. Repeat this every four or five years or as needed.

vented in other ways that I'll discuss shortly. It is for this reason that you never use a breathable house wrap on top of a roof. It's more expensive than tar paper and ultimately not as repellent to water.

After the sheathing and the tar paper come the shingles themselves. These give a roof its strength to endure the elements, like the armor of a turtle shell. Made from small, overlapping pieces, shingles form a waterproof surface by forcing raindrops to cascade off of them. Early American houses, especially in the East, were built with shingles split from cedar trees, as well as slate and even tin. The roofing industry was revolutionized more than a century ago, however, by the introduction of the asphalt shingle, which is a shingle coated with tar and sprinkled with tiny bits of stone to give it color. It may not be the most beautiful surface, to be sure, but asphalt shingles are amazingly easy to install and very inexpensive. Most asphalt shingles are known as "three-tab," because each long strip is actually notched to give the appearance of three separate shingles the same size as wooden ones—but even Mr. Magoo would be able to see the difference in color and texture.

Nowadays, there a bewildering variety of shingles, and trying to narrow down the choices for your roof can be nerve-wracking enough to *give* you a case of shingles. In addition to the old asphalt shingles, there

Pitching In

Call up roofing contractors and they'll instantly start talking about the pitch of your roof—and tossing out numbers like 9-to-12 or 10-to-12. This sounds more like the hours for their coffee break than anything remotely having to do with your roof. What's going on? Quite simply, this is the way they measure the steepness (what is properly called the pitch) of a roof. They calculate this by measuring the number of inches the roof rises for every foot it extends across. For example, a roof that rises 6 inches for every 12 inches of horizontal run has a 6-to-12 pitch; one that rises 10 inches for every 12 inches of horizontal run has a 10-to-12 pitch.

are now architectural shingles, which are thicker versions with a deeper texture and more color. These have a fiberglass rather than asphalt base and tend to be much heavier—which makes them more durable. You can easily find architectural shingles that have a thirty year warranty, compared to an asphalt shingle that might only be guaranteed for fifteen. Plus, since these look so good, your roof suddenly becomes an aesthetic focal point of your house instead of something you want to look away from. You can even find some that have a passable resemblance to wood.

Before talking about pricing, I need to explain how shingles are measured. If you go to a roofing supply store, all you'll hear anyone talk about is the cost of shingles "per square." No, they're not referring to Pat Boone; this is simply the way roofing materials are sold. A square refers to 100 square feet. So a square of shingles would be a patch of shingles needed to cover a 10-by-10-foot section of a roof. Let's extend this to a larger example. The average roof on a 2,000-square-foot house might cover a total of 3,000 square feet, which would amount to thirty squares of shingles.

When you price shingles, you will invariably be comparing the price per square. My advice, which by now should come as no surprise, is to buy the best shingles you can afford, since the real cost comes in the installation. You'll find ads in your local paper for home centers that have dirt-cheap sales on shingles—as cheap sometimes as $25 a square, when the going rate for good asphalt shingles is more like $70 a square for material only and rises to $90 or more for decent architectural shingles. While that might sound like a bargain, you'd be better off spending your money on a camping tarp and stringing it over your roof, because it will probably do a better job of keeping your roof waterproof. I mean, these shingles might be okay to use if you're shingling a doghouse—but then you probably don't have a lot of respect for your dog. They simply don't hold up.

While three-tab and architectural shingles account for about 90 percent of all shingles sold, let's take a quick look at some of the alternatives. Cedar shake roofs are very popular, particularly in the Northeast and Midwest. They're also pricey, at about $200 a square plus the installation. The misconception about cedar shake roofs is that they're maintenance-free, but this isn't the case at all. Cedar is wood. It expands and contracts, and it's porous—so it's more susceptible than asphalt to the growth of moss and mold and the accumulation of leaves and debris. With this sort of roof, you need regular maintenance. This includes having the roof professionally cleaned and preserved probably every three or five years with a linseed-oil-based preservative. The sun just beats the heck out of cedar shake roofs, so these shingles typically have a UV block on them to limit the damage. Just for some comparison, the typical roof on a 2,000-square-foot house might cost about $3,000 including installation to cover with asphalt, and architectural shingles may be twice that. But that can easily rise six or seven times that amount for cedar shingles.

Profiles in Roofing

Like a person's haircut, a roof gives a home character.
Here are the major styles.

Gable roof.

Two pitched roofs, joined back to
back, form a classic roof. Nothing
says "house" more than this.

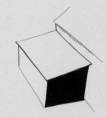

Shed roof.

A single sloping plane, this is often
attached to the back of a house to
expand space.

Saltbox roof.

The Colonial classic, this is a shed
roof built onto a gable roof at the
same pitch.

Flat roof. Formed from a single
plane, this is pitched at an impercepti-
ble angle to drain rainwater.

Hip roof. A modified gable
roof, this has the gable ends brought
together at the same pitch as the rest
of the roof.

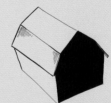

Gambrel roof. Popular
with early Dutch settlers, this is a
modified gable roof with breaks in the
planes.

These days, there are many new types of tiles to choose from that are very much worth a look—especially since they're attractive, as cedar shingle roofs are, but cost much less and require less fussing. You can find a high-quality slate lookalike that is made with shredded automobile tires, of all things, or a low-cost concrete tile that also mimics the look of natural stone. Concrete tile roofs are extremely heavy—about 1,000 pounds per square. While this might sound like a roof crushing burden, any well built roof can easily hold this weight. Plus, in high-wind areas such as the Florida coast, where hurricanes abound, or the earthquake-prone areas of California, these tile roofs hold up very well. The reason lies in the installation. Rather than being attached directly to the roof sheathing with nails the way shingles are, they lie loosely on top of the sheathing and are held in place by wood battens. If the house shakes when wind strikes or the earth moves, the shingles move slightly without falling off. The cost, amazingly, is very low—about $50 to $80 a square for the materials, which is even less than the cost of a good asphalt shingle.

Fun With Flashing

Cover a roof with shingles and tar paper alone, and it will still leak. That's because water sometimes defies gravity and manages to seep horizontally as it falls, especially when it reaches the edges of a roof. This can lead to leaks in the rooms below, and eventually decay of the roof structure. The key to a waterproof roof, then, lies in flashing—and no, I'm not talking about those weird old guys in the trench coats. Flashing is the strips of metal—aluminum and copper being the most common—that are positioned along edges of the roof, or wherever the roof meets an angled portion of a dormer, or any protrusions from the roof such as a chimney, plumbing exhaust vents or skylights. Shingles simply can't be installed to form a watertight seal around these areas, and you sure don't want to start squirting a giant tube of caulk around. That would not hold up to the elements. Instead, flashing endures. It works something like a bucket brigade, taking drops of water and

Gutter Life

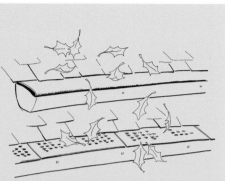

In most parts of the country, gutters are an evil necessity. They're evil because they can look fairly ugly and frequently clog with leaves and muck. But they're a necessity, because without them, rainwater draining from your roof dumps right alongside your house, which is practically a recipe for a leaky basement. If you live in, say, New Mexico, you're in luck. You get so little rainfall over the course of a year, you can happily do without gutters. But the rest of us have to learn how to manage them.

The number one thing to keep in mind is that gutters need to be cleaned out, especially if you have trees near your home that drop leaves on your roof. If these stay in the gutter, the gutter can't drain. Water then overflows and collects by the foundation, as I mentioned. But other than that, the constant dampness and spilling water can begin to rot the fascia board, which is the piece of wood on your house just behind the gutters. Worse still, it can even start to work on the ends of the rafters, resulting in major structural damage.

To avoid this, gutters should be cleaned out once or twice a year, depending on how filled with debris they get. There's no fancy way to do this. You have to hike up a ladder with a plastic bucket and muck the stuff out with your hands. It's a good idea to flush the gutter out with a garden hose when you're done, just to get rid of little bits of junk that could clog the downspout. If you don't feel safe climbing up a ladder, by all means hire someone to do it for you.

As an alternative, consider installing so-called leafless gutters. These have a trough just like a regular gutter but are covered with a curved rooflike plate that deflects leaves even as it allows water to drip inside. They're far better than traditional gutter screens, which never seem to stay in place. And although leafless gutters might cost $10 to $20 per foot (compared to just $4 to $7 for ordinary gutters), they'll let you appreciate the beauty of fall foliage—rather than curse it.

dumping them directly to the next piece of flashing, or to the roof shingles, so that they eventually fall to the ground.

Flashing is one of those parts of a house that few people other than roofing contractors know much about. But once you know what you're looking for, you'll find it just about everywhere on your roof. Small sheets of it, called step flashing, are tucked along the edge of the chimney, which keeps water dripping away from the joint between the chimney and the roof rather than draining right into it. Longer pieces, called continuous flashing, form what is known as a drip edge along the bottom row of shingles, right near the gutter. This piece may seem pointless, but it is actually crucial. Without it, water would seep back under the overhanging part of the roof, called the eaves, and begin to rot the wood structure. Similarly, flashing rises along the rafter edge of the roof, called the rake, where it performs the same service. Flashing can be found around plumbing vents that stick through the roof, and around skylights. Any time two shingled angles join together to form what is known as a valley, that joint is first lined with flashing before the shingles are laid on top. In places such as these, flashing is far better than shingles at diverting water.

Why should you care about flashing? Because about 90 percent of all roof leaks have nothing to do with shingles and everything to do with flashing that has pulled loose or been improperly installed. If you have leaks in your home, you may be able to solve them with a few simple repairs to the flashing rather than a $6,000 reroofing job.

Flashing problems can be notoriously difficult to pinpoint, however. You can't usually see them, the way you can something as obvious as a missing shingle. And since water can sometimes travel 10, 15, or even 20 feet before it drips inside, you can't assume that the problem lies directly over the affected spot inside. Good roofing contractors, however, will use what is known as a hose test to scout them out. On a clear day, they'll hop up on your roof with a hose while you're inside, and squirt water at different angles until the drips begin to flow inside. This method is all but guaranteed to work.

Ladder Madness

Did you ever fall off a ladder? I have, several times, and I can tell you it is not fun. Nor am I unique. Last year, there were an estimated 171,000 ladder-related accidents in the United States, according to the American Ladder Institute, which is an astounding number. Climbing up a ladder is probably the single riskiest thing you can do as a homeowner. Part of the problem is that we take little time or care to make sure we're safe as we haul ourselves skyward. With extension ladders, we think nothing of using old, rickety ones that were handed down to us from our parents, broken rungs and all. And with stepladders, we practically make a habit of perching on that step they tell us not to stand on, because we're too lazy to get a ladder sized correctly for the job. It's time to put this foolishness to an end. Here are a few ladder dos and don'ts:

• Do position extension ladders correctly. For stability, a ladder has to be planted with its feet one-quarter of its extended length away from the house. This is not as tricky to calculate as it sounds. If it's a 12-foot ladder, that means the base has to be positioned 3 feet from the house. For a 16-foot ladder, make it 4 feet.

• Don't carry an extension ladder upright as you move it. This is a maneuver best saved for the clowns at the circus. You could easily lose control of it in this position, smashing windows and gutters along the way and knocking into power lines. Instead, lower it and carry it parallel to the ground.

• Do make sure the ladder is positioned on a level surface. Don't try to use rocks or bricks to prop up one side of it; those will surely pop out as you're climbing up.

• Don't ever work alone. A helper can keep you from making stupid mistakes, such as having the ladder fall down while you're stuck up alone on the roof.

If there's one guiding principle with respect to ladders, it's this: If you feel squeamish, don't go up. Period. This is all you need to know as far as I'm concerned. No matter what the chore is, it's a lot cheaper to hire someone to climb up for you than it is to head to the hospital.

Venting a Roof

If you insulated a roof just like a wall, you would create enormous problems. In the summer, penetrating heat would build up beneath it. This would shorten the life span of the roof and make the upstairs rooms all but unbearable to live in. In cold weather in places where snow accumulates, the troubles would turn even worse. Heated, humid air rising from inside the house would accumulate in the attic and melt the snow off the roof. As this melted snow dripped, it would then refreeze when it reached the overhanging edges of the roofing, forming gigantic icicles—turning your home into something resembling a Bavarian ski chalet. While romantic-looking, these icicles form a dam that traps melting snow behind them. The accumulating water on the roof then seeps beneath the shingles, until it inevitably leaks through the sheathing. Ice dams, as they are called, can create the most destructive leaks of all. Repair bills in a severe winter can easily top $20,000, and some home insurance companies don't even offer protection against them unless you buy special policies.

To survive, the roof needs to be separated from the house through ventilation—which is something that simply is not done for walls. By whisking air away through natural circulation, ventilation in the summer keeps heated air in the winter from melting the snow on the roof, and in the summer keeps the air under the roof from reaching shingle-buckling temperatures. Ideally, the temperature just beneath the roof should be as close to possible as the outdoor air temperature. This requires a combination of good insulation and some special ventilation.

The first line of defense in protecting the roof is insulation. Obviously, you need a thicker layer in the attic than in any other part of the house because warm air rises. Just how thick, however, depends on what part of the country you live in. The amount recommended by the federal Department of Energy, for instance, can range from about 8 inches in the South to as much as 2 feet or more in the far North. No matter how much insulation you put up there, however, warm air can still rise through it in

The Trouble with Chimneys

We think of chimneys as the most solid, stable part of the house—but actually they're quite fragile, especially where water is concerned. Most leaks around chimneys involve a flashing detail that's come loose. Flashing details are pieces of metal attached to the brick that shed water directly to the roof shingles. Another possibility is a crack in the crown, which covers the top of the chimney. Usually made of poured concrete, the crown acts like a lid that keeps water out—with a vent that lets the smoke out. A crack might not be visible from the ground, but it allows water to drip into the chimney. Masonry and brick act like a gigantic sponge and absorb this water. As the chimney heats up from ordinary sunlight, this water vaporizes and is drawn outside, leaving a telltale salty efflorescence on the brick. As things worsen, you'll see pieces of the brick flake off due to excessive moisture, a condition known as spalling. If you see efflorescence or spalling, call a mason immediately.

cold weather, and the attic will still fill with superheated air in the summertime from the sun. To alleviate both of these things, your roof needs to be ventilated.

When we think of ventilation, we normally think of whirling electric fans, but what we're talking about here is natural ventilation. This involves the spontaneous upward flow of hot air. To keep things moving underneath the roof, this requires creating vents for hot air to escape. Sometimes these are louvered vents in the gable, known as gable vents. There can also be a vent hidden under a row of shingles along the entire ridge of the house, which is known as continuous ridge vents. And sometimes vents can sprout along the back of the roof, which are commonly known as mushroom vents. No matter what the style, all vents accomplish the same task. They release hot air that accumulates in both summer and winter, and keep the temperature of the roof more or less equal to the outdoor temperature.

Vents alone, however, do not guarantee a flow of air. In order for hot air to flow out of the attic, cooler air has to be drawn in from somewhere down below. It would be pointless to draw air from directly inside the house; nothing could be more inefficient in terms of your heating and cooling comfort and monthly fuel bills. Instead, in an ingenious solution, the cool air is drawn in through vents positioned under the eaves that extend from the edge of the roof. The underside of an eave is sometimes called the soffit, and these are usually known as soffit vents. In order for air to flow, these soffit vents have to be connected to the roof vents— which they are through the gaps, or what are more properly called bays, between the rafters. As hot air flows out of the attic vents above, cooler air is drawn in through these soffit vents and pulled up between the rafters. It is an efficient system that uses no added energy.

Insulation and ventilation can work together to create the perfect environment for a stable roof. If it's done badly, however, insulation can actually interfere with ventilation and create more problems than it solves. If

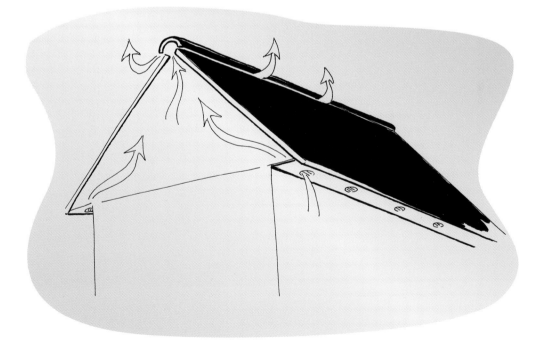

A Leak-Free Window to the Sky

Skylights can be among the best additions to a home. They bring in light, add openness and a sense of drama to rooms, and can help with ventilation if you install the kind that can be opened and closed. Many people have an aversion to skylights, however, because they fear they'll leak—which is justifiable, considering you have to cut a hole in the roof to install one. The key to a leak-free skylight lies in choosing the right one. In short, you can't get a good one cheaply. Expect to spend at least $300 and probably much more. This will guarantee that yours has the proper flashing to shed water and the proper sealing to hold the glass tight to the frame. Good installation is also essential. Here, the cost can range from another $300 to $1,000 or more, depending on the positioning in the roof and the amount of drywalling needed inside to finish it off. When you hire contractors, make sure they have plenty of experience installing skylights. You sure don't want anyone experimenting on your roof.

attic insulation is pressed tightly against the underside of the roof, for instance, then there is no channel for the air to be drawn in through the soffits. It acts like a cork. If there's no channel, then there's no flow of air— and no adequate ventilation out the top. These points where the insulation presses against the roof then become a breeding ground for moisture, mildew, leaks, and decay. If you have an uninsulated attic, where only the floor is insulated to keep the rooms below comfortable, then there is little risk of this sort of condition. In many ways, this is the ideal attic to have. But if you have a finished attic, or a cathedral ceiling where the insulation rises with the roof, there has to be a channel for air to flow beneath the insulation and the underside of the roof sheathing. This is easier to accomplish than it might sound. Contractors staple up a small channel made out of plastic foam to the back of the sheathing, and then gently tuck the insulation into place on top of it. This seems like a minor step, but without it, the entire ventilation of the attic and roof will fail.

Natural ventilation is a marvelous thing, but I also like some electrical assistance—in the form of a roof fan, which is connected to a thermostat. These are basically exhaust fans that poke through the roof to mechanically force the warm air out, and make a great add-on to any home. I have one in my own house, and I make a point of installing one on every home that I build or renovate. To operate these fans, I usually set the thermostat to 90 degrees. Whenever the temperature exceeds that, the fan automatically turns on and exhausts all that hot air.

Time to Get a New Roof?

Installed correctly, you won't have any unexpected roof troubles. But depending on the material, all roofs have a natural life span and begin to wear out. Slate and clay tile can last for a hundred years or more with minor repairs, but anything else—particularly asphalt or architectural shingles—will eventually need replacement. If your roof is fifteen years old, it may be time to think about a new one. If it's twenty years old, you're on borrowed time. How can you tell for sure? If you see shingles that appear to be curling, or if shingles regularly blow off in the wind, or (obviously) if you are experiencing leaks, it's time to have a roofer come out and take a look at it.

There's one rule I have when replacing an old roof, and that is never, ever place the new shingles on top of the old ones. When you're reroofing you get the opportunity to inspect the sheathing and make sure there is no damage; if there is, you can replace the material. Your roof could have leaks that you don't know about, which have started to rot the sheathing and the rafters. The only way you're going to find out and be able to fix it is by tearing the shingles and tar paper off completely and inspecting what's under there. Otherwise, you're just covering up trouble—and wasting your money. While complete tear-offs cost more than simply laying new shingles on top of old ones, they definitely add value to your house when it comes time to sell it.

This is especially true in cold areas, where ice damming is a problem.

Each time you put on a new roof, it's important to lay down new tar paper, and in cold climates you should also add a waterproof membrane—a rubber sheeting that extends in a band 30 inches wide across the gutter edge of the roof and folds into the gutter. I'd actually recommend a double coursing of this material, for a full 60 inches of protection. Do this, and you will never have to worry about an ice dam again.

Shingles All the Way

Oh, and in case you're wondering about my Oak Park friends from the beginning of this chapter, they tried to get used to their colorful roof, and it gave them nothing but the blues. After a year of staring at it, and no doubt enduring taunts from their neighbors, they called me up again to lay a new layer of shingles. To save them money, I broke my own rule and laid it right on top of the blue ones—but only because I knew the condition of the sheathing firsthand. Rather than trying for that just-so shade of green, they played it safe with an earth-tone blend. They even let me lay out a couple of bundles of shingles in advance, just to be sure.

A few days of work, and their house was reborn. The bad news is that it cost them an extra $4,000. The good news is that they have a really thick roof now—one that I'm doubly sure won't leak.

chapter TEN

Specialty of the House

More than just a place to cook, the kitchen has become the focal point of the household

Crazy as it sounds, I have an idea that I am sure could make me millions.

Someday I am going to build an entire community of houses in which the whole first floor is devoted entirely to the kitchen. There won't be a dining room, or a living room, or even a family room—just one enormous area that encompasses all of these things, along with a stove and refrigerator.

Scoff if you will, but there's great merit in this. I have built or renovated more than 125 homes in the last decade and a half, but no matter how nice the place is, the same thing inevitably happens: The homeowners end up spending all their time sitting in the kitchen. They cook there, entertain there, watch TV there, help their kids with their homework there, pay their bills there, and even squabble there. One such person is my friend Mike, whom I helped build a house a few years ago. His place has a giant combination kitchen and great room with the two areas separated by a granite-topped peninsula. Every time I go there with my family, we all end up crowded around that peninsula. Mike and I laugh

kitchens

because we thought the great room would be a way to keep everybody out of the kitchen. Yet there we stand or sit on stools, leaving the great room with its beautiful couches untouched.

No doubt about it, the kitchen is the magnet of every household, my own included. Maybe it's the convenient location, usually with a door to the outside, a door to the garage, and a connection to the dining room and living room. This makes it a sort of crossroads of a home—in the way that Times Square is the crossroads of the world. Maybe it's because this room, by definition, is designed to withstand messes and also to be eminently cleanable. We can be comfortable in the kitchen without worrying that we're going to ruin anything. Or maybe it's because we simply love food.

Whatever the case, the kitchen is truly the centerpiece of a home. Because of that, it has become the number one spot for renovation and redecoration. Spending money here will yield you the single highest return on your investment should you ever decide to sell your home. By far, it will also end up being the most expensive room in the house. The average cost of a renovation—according to the National Kitchen and Bath Association—tops $26,000. This average somehow masks the reality of the cost for a complete overhaul. An acquaintance of mine, for instance, recently spent $150,000 on a kitchen but didn't move one wall. If you're going to be spending this sort of money, you want to make sure you get the recipe right. Just what might the ingredients to the perfect kitchen include? Many things—from the right layout to the best-quality cabinetry and countertops and a ventilation system that works. To find out how to blend it all together, let's take a cook's tour of this all-important room.

Looking Beyond the Triangle

Back in the 1950s, when everyone believed they had an answer for everything, home designers came up with the perfect plan for kitchens. The refrigerator, sink, and stove—where women obviously wanted to position themselves all day long—were supposed to be placed in a triangle, at least 4 feet apart from one another. The entire perimeter of the triangle connecting the three was never to exceed 26 feet. Somehow, this Stalinesque layout was intended to create the most efficient plan possible.

Fortunately, we've all gotten a little more enlightened in our thinking. While the triangle may not have disappeared altogether, you can now happily design your kitchen according to what works best for you. You may have a big family or no family. You may be a relentless

A Water Filter that Works

We're all fairly obsessed about the quality of water we drink. Just look at the proliferation of all the bottled water you can buy in the supermarket. While most tap water is perfectly fit to drink, many of us—including Mrs. Fix-It—have gotten it into our heads that the stuff is toxic. How else to explain the aisles filled with water at the supermarket? Bottled water goes for about $1 for 32 ounces, which is more expensive than gasoline at the pump. Bottling companies are making money hand over fist by taking ordinary tap water and purifying it by running it through a filter, which is something you can easily have installed in your own kitchen.

When my family's bill for supermarket water topped $50 a month, I knew I had to do something. I bought a filter that installs beneath the kitchen sink and contains a separate spigot located next to the main faucet. It can pump out 1,500 gallons before needing a $20 filter change—which lasts my family about a year. The water tastes fresher and chlorine-free, and we use the spigot to make coffee, fill water bottles and ice cube trays, and even fill pots of water for cooking. The spigot makes the filtered-water supply instantly available, which is far more efficient than those pitcher filtration systems that you have to remember to fill.

The best part of this is the cost. The system I bought cost about $200, and I paid a plumber another $150 to install it. While that does add up to $350, it was cheaper than the cost of a year's supply of water from our local supermarket. And we'll never have to embarrass ourselves by shopping for water again.

cook or a master of the art of thawing and reheating. You may entertain a lot or never at all. And your kitchen should be allowed to reflect that.

Don't underestimate the change that can occur in your home just by redoing the kitchen. How should you start? Head to a kitchen design store. Most of them will offer design advice for free, and the designers have a lot of experience about the latest trends and possibilities for awkward spaces. If you show up with the exact dimensions of your kitchen, they can really help you put this together. Keep in mind, however, that the design is really a personal thing, and your kitchen will probably end up becoming the most individual room in your home. Some people like islands and peninsulas; others prefer the space-saving layout of a galley kitchen. Some people want giant stoves and double ovens; others could make do with a toaster oven. No matter what you choose, there isn't a place where the quality of the materials you choose could be more important than the kitchen. That's because this room gets so much abuse and because you're destined to spend so much time here.

Inevitably, there are designers to this day who will tell you that you have to adhere to the triangle in order to have an efficient kitchen. That's hogwash. You should be free to design your kitchen the way you want it. In my house, we have a separate cooktop and oven. We use the cooktop constantly, so it makes sense to have it right in the middle of the kitchen. But we use the oven less often, so I put it at the other end of the kitchen, to free up some cabinet space near the cooktop. I happened to have a designer come over a while ago, and he took one look at this arrangement and said, "Good lord, I can't believe you put the oven over there!" I objected. When you put something in the oven, you leave it there for a while. It's not like a pot that you have to stand next to and stir. My wife's cookies stay in for ten minutes, my lasagna for forty-five. So what if you have to walk four extra steps when it's time to put them in and take them out? The point is that our layout freed up space for other cabinets and makes a lot of sense to my wife and me—which, in a kitchen, is all that counts.

A Cabinet Meeting

What's the single most expensive item in your home? The kitchen cabinets. Of the $26,000 the average homeowner spends on a kitchen overhaul, according to the National Kitchen and Bath Association, some 50 percent— or more than $13,000—goes for the cabinets alone. These wooden wonders can also take a disproportionate bite out of a bathroom renovation budget as well. So what do you get for all this money? A great deal at a good price, if you know what to look for—but very often homeowners don't.

When it comes to cabinets, doors are everything. You can have great-looking doors attached to great cabinet boxes, as they're called and you end up with great cabinets. Or you can have great looking doors attached to solid but not quite superior cabinet boxes, and guess what—you still end up with great cabinets. The point is, it's the doors that matter, not the boxes. And what people don't realize is that most of the doors sold by the finest cabinet manufacturers all come from smaller companies that are in the business of making doors alone. Search for a high-quality but less-expensive brand, and in many cases you could actually be getting doors identical to those from a pricier manufacturer.

Let's take a look at how this works. I have a friend who is in the cabinetmaking business, and he, too, buys his doors from these companies. The cabinets he produces look terrific, but they're a lot less expensive than what you'd pay for cabinets from a company that advertises in a fancy magazine. One of his recent customers was a woman redoing a fancy kitchen who'd gotten a price quote of an astounding $58,000 for cabinets alone from a name-brand company. While she thought this a fair price, her husband objected. She happened to hear me talking about my friend's cabinetry on my radio show and stopped by in order to maintain domestic peace. He gave her a quote of $28,000 for the same cabi-

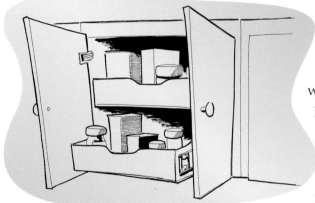

nets—and even upgraded the interiors to all wood, rather than wood laminate, to match the quality of the original bid in every way. Well, the woman couldn't believe this. "There must be something wrong," she told him skeptically. "That extra $30,000 has to be going for *something*."

The Dirty Truth About Garbage Disposals

In the kitchen, there's probably nothing more convenient than a garbage disposal. You flick a switch and everything disappears down the drain. Convenient, yes, but I also happen to think there is nothing sloppier, more wasteful, and more offensive to any sort of environmental standards.

Let's start with the problem. Food goes in the garbage disposal, and a series of blades grind it up. The resulting slurry is washed down the drain with water. From a technical standpoint, this works great. But from any other standpoint, this is awful! Garbage disposals allow people to turn their drains into garbage cans. And garbage cans and drains do not mix. All that pureed corn and potato peels and remnants of macaroni and cheese can clog up your sewage system, especially if you have a septic system. If you're connected to a municipal sewage system, you're adding needlessly to the burden of creating clean water by overloading it with all this slop.

So what's the alternative? The sink strainer. This is a low-tech device that's 99 percent effective at catching debris before it goes down the drain. Then you simply scoop it out and empty it in the trash or, better yet, on the compost heap. That's what I do, and that's why there will never be a garbage disposal in Mr. Fix-It's house.

It was going for something, actually. It was going to waste.

The lesson is that you need to search for cabinets and do a lot of price shopping so you don't waste this sort of money yourself. What should you search for? I can't help you with style and taste, but I can help you with quality. The first thing to do is to look at setups of cabinets themselves, and start opening and closing the drawers and doors—so much, in fact, that you practically make a nuisance of yourself. You'll feel it when you hit upon a well-made cabinet. Drawers glide open smoothly

Preventing Fires

Much as we love kitchens, they can be dangerous places. According to statistics kept by the U.S. Fire Administration, some 23.5 percent of all house fires start in the kitchen, and the number jumps to 46.1 percent for apartments. How can you cut the risk? Here are a few tips:

● Tend to your cooking. A watched pot may never boil, but an unwatched one is surely a fire hazard—since an untended stove is the leading cause of home cooking fires.

● Keep a potholder and lid handy. Never pour water on a grease fire, which can end up splattering burning grease around the kitchen and actually spread rather than extinguish the flames. If a small fire starts in a pan, smother the flames instead by sliding a lid over it.

● Close the oven door. For fires in the oven and microwave, turn off the heat, unplug the appliance if it is electric, and keep the door closed to starve the fire of oxygen. Don't open the door again until the flames are extinguished and the oven has cooled down.

● Keep a fire extinguisher designed for kitchen use on hand. These might cost all of $30 but can save your home by helping you extinguish small fires before they get out of hand. Know that fire extinguishers, like batteries, have a definite lifespan. Check the date on yours, and make sure you replace it when it expires, usually in about three years.

Above all, be aware of your limitations. If a blaze gets out of control, save your family and yourself rather than trying to play the hero by fighting it.

and ease shut without wiggling. Doors swing open effortlessly and have a solid sound when they close. Whether you're buying top-of-the-line cabinets or those that you have to assemble yourself and stain or paint, you should expect this sort of excellence. If the drawer and door action annoys you after a half hour in the store, just think how annoying it will become when you try to live with it in your kitchen.

A lot of fuss is made over whether the cabinet boxes are all wood or made from laminates or composites—with the bias for the more expensive all-wood construction. But I think this makes no difference at all. For one thing, laminates and composites these days are often stronger and more durable than ordinary wood, which sure seems preferable to me. For another thing, the boxes are covered by the doors, which means you'll never really see inside them unless you get in there on your hands and knees with a flashlight to make a close inspection. Instead, focus on the hardware—the door hinges and drawer glides that actually make your cabinets function. Here there is one guiding principle: Get the best you can. You can usually choose to upgrade the basic hardware, and it's worth your money to do so. Another upgrade that makes good sense is to get drawers made from solid wood with seams that are dovetailed, which means that they're notched and glued tightly together for extra strength. This might cost you 20 to 25 percent more per drawer, but it's money well spent. Nothing drives me crazier than rickety drawers, and part of the problem is that the integrity of the drawer system isn't very good. There's little you can do to fix it—except to get the right drawers in the first place.

There's also a great deal of snob appeal in having cabinets that are "custom-made." For some reason homeowners like to brag about this, but I think it's foolish to assume handmade cabinets are necessarily better than factory-made stock ones. Is a BMW, for instance, any less desirable simply because it rolls out of a factory? No, and neither is the average cabinet. You're looking for quality, period; however a manufacturer arrives at that should be of no concern. Some people resort to expensive

Unsinkable Sinks

Think of a kitchen sink, and your mind immediately goes to cast-iron enamel. These may have a classic look, but they aren't my favorites. For one thing, the enamel can easily chip if hit with a pot or frying pan—and they require constant cleaning to avoid stains. While this obviously doesn't pose much of a problem in a bathroom, the kitchen clearly calls for more rugged material.

Solid surface. These excellent, long-lasting sinks are made from the same high-quality materials found in solid-surface countertops. While expensive—a good sink might cost you as much as $700—they're easy to clean and durable. In fact, I'd call them indestructible. They're nonporous, which makes them impossible to stain, and any gouges can be sanded away. These sinks can be paired with any countertop or integrated seamlessly into a solid-surface one.

Stainless steel. These sinks can be long-lasting and easy to maintain—as long as you buy a sturdy one. Good ones, which might cost you $300 and up, are made with a thick gauge of steel and have a higher nickel content, ranging from 5 to 8 percent, that forms an impervious finish. If you try to pick up a $50 sink at the home center, you might as well forget it. It won't hold up at all. Look for 18 gauge steel or less; the lower the gauge, the thicker the metal.

custom-made cabinetry because they think it's the only way they can have flexibility in their kitchen design, but even this is a fallacy. With the right thinking, stock cabinetry can be given a custom look. Standard units can be grouped together in interesting ways, and moldings ordered from manufacturers can be pieced together to create bold designs that lend an air of originality. If the cabinet manufacturer you're looking at offers only a limited supply of these add-ons, then move to a better line of cabinets and look for one with a wider selection of components.

This takes extra time, I know. But it's worth fighting very hard to find great cabinets at good prices. As my friend's client discovered, the money you save doing this could cover many months' worth of mortgage payments—and will do a world of good to preserve a marriage.

Counter Culture

What's the second most expensive item in your home? Very possibly the countertops. These also rank as one of the most abused surfaces in your home, with knives slicing into them, pots and pans banging on them, and a steady rain of food and spills. Yet we expect them to return to a neat, shiny, and antiseptic condition with a simple swipe from a sponge. Talk about a tall order!

If an existing kitchen is starting to look worn out and tired, replacing the countertops often ranks as a great improvement project. It can radically change the look of things without running up the massive bill that a whole-kitchen renovation involves. There's a huge assortment of materials to choose from for countertops, ranging from the classic maple butcher block and natural stone to synthetic solid-surface materials that are probably the most popular of all. With these possibilities come price tags that vary wildly. For a stretch of countertop 10 feet long, the price can range from $300 for lowly laminate all the way up to $3,000 and more for the finest stone. Keep in mind that more expensive doesn't always mean better, however. High-end countertops such as granite can require more fussing and be far more delicate than you'd ever believe. And the low-end materials can often work perfectly well and even suit you better.

Let's start on the low-end of the scale—that being laminate tops, which are sold under a number of different brand names. These are basically a thin plastic veneer glued over particleboard. While some people are biased against laminates—after all, what screams the 1970s more than, say, a slab of orange or white Formica?—they've come a long way in terms of colors and style that mimic the look of natural stone. The great thing about laminates, of course, is their cost. Countertops are sold by the linear or running foot (as opposed to the square foot), and the cost of these materials probably starts at about $20 a foot. These aren't particu-

Getting a Handle on Faucets

A trip down the faucet aisle in the typical home improvement store can be as bewildering as shopping for a telephone. The number of gadgets, designs, and styles boggles the mind. Yet faucets, whether for the kitchen or bath, can be grouped into two major categories—those in which the hot and cold water turn on with separate handles, and those in which one central lever controls both. Here's what you should look for with each variety:

Two-handled faucets. Older faucets as well as inexpensive new ones contain rubber washers to control the flow of water, which deteriorate over time. When they do, they leak and have to be repaired. Who wants more work, especially when it involves plumbing? Instead, look for faucets that have washerless construction. In these, the water is controlled by two ceramic plates hidden in the faucet that slide on top of one another and act as floodgates. These long-lasting components are indestructible and virtually leakproof—and make the best value for any sink or tub in your home. How do you tell whether you have a faucet with rubber washers or a washerless one? Try turning the handle. If it makes a complete 360-degree rotation, you've got a rubber washer in there; better brush up on the art of replacing it. If you can only turn it a quarter turn, or 90 degrees, then you can be certain that you've got long-lasting ceramic disks.

Single-lever faucets. While some of these also contain ceramic disks to control water flow, most single-lever faucets contain either a rotating ball or a perforated cartridge that performs the same task. These can be made from either plastic or metal—but only the metal ones will hold up over time.

Regardless of what type of faucet construction you want, always choose those that are built from solid brass rather than cheap metal or plastic. This doesn't mean the faucet will look brass-colored, since they can be finished in chrome or zinc or nickel or anything else you may want. But the only way those finishes will hold up is if they're coated over a solid brass core. Anything else will begin to deteriorate very quickly.

larly durable; they'll scratch if you try to chop on them, and scorch if you touch them with a hot pot. But the great thing about laminates is that since they're inexpensive, you can easily afford to replace them again in seven or eight years when they start to wear out. If you burn or scratch your laminate countertops I can recommend a quick fix. Go get some nail polish in a color that matches the countertop, and touch it up. The nail polish should last for a couple of months, before it needs retouching. It's not permanent, but it works.

Laminates may be popular, but what has revolutionized kitchen countertops are solid-surface materials. I am huge fan of these. Sold under a number of brand names including Avonite and DuPont Corian, these are not a thin laminate at all. Instead, they're solid, as their name says, and the color goes all the way through. The material was originally invented for use in artificial hips, which should give you an idea of how sturdy it is. As a result, they resist scratches, nicks, and burns. You can sand away any imperfections, and the countertop pieces can be "welded" together using liquid versions of the material to create long stretches that look virtually seamless. If it's done right—and this is where you want professional installation, not a do-it-yourself job—you'll never spot the seams at all. Beyond this, solid-surface materials are nonporous, which no natural surface, even granite or slate, can claim to be. They won't absorb any bacteria from, say, raw chicken. Wipe them clean, and they're 100 percent clean. If you're a serious cook, this is the countertop for you.

I'd probably feel strongly about solid-surface materials even if they only came in orange and white, like the old laminates. But fortunately there's a great assortment of colors to choose from. New versions even have bits of quartz mixed into the material, which mimics the look of stone by creating a depth of color that has not been available before. No matter what you choose, you should expect to pay a great deal for solid-surface countertops. You might pay upward of $200 a foot, which is about ten times more expensive than laminates and often even more expensive than some types of natural stone. While this is indeed costly,

Good Cabinet Habits

Great kitchen cabinets are the equivalent of fine furniture, but no coffee table or bureau has ever had to put up with the sort of abuse these workhorses endure every day. Food and water regularly drip on them, grease accumulates, and pots and pans bang in and out of them. To keep cabinets looking fresh, you have to come up with a plan for their maintenance. Start by making a point of wiping up any spills as they happen—with a damp cloth, followed by a dry one. For bigger jobs, try a mild solution of soap and water, still followed with a dry cloth. For smudges that build up around door and drawer pulls, try cleaning them with furniture wax remover, followed up with furniture polish—but not paste wax, which can cause yellowing over some urethane finishes and can gunk up crevices. To hide dings and scratches, fill them with colored paste wax that is sold in little tubes like lipstick. Pick the right color, and the marks will disappear.

these countertops come with something that natural stone does not: a warranty, usually ten years or longer, that covers both labor and materials. It's a nice bit of reassurance that lets you know your money is being well spent.

Now we come to natural stone. Stone is beautiful, of course—and for sheer snob appeal, nothing can compare. Telling someone you have granite countertops is like boasting that your daughter goes to Harvard. As a result, the more expensive the kitchen, the higher the likelihood that it will contain granite, bluestone, marble, or even something exotic like fossilized volcanic ash. In my opinion, these create truly the most beautiful surfaces in the kitchen. But even if you choose a hard stone such as granite, you need to consider careful maintenance. While stone is durable, it is also fragile. I know this may seem like a paradox; the stuff, after all, is rock itself. But fragile it is. For one thing, the edges can chip fairly easily—such as if you accidentally tap the edge around your undermounted sink with a cast-iron pot. Beyond this, natural stone prod-

A Counter Offensive

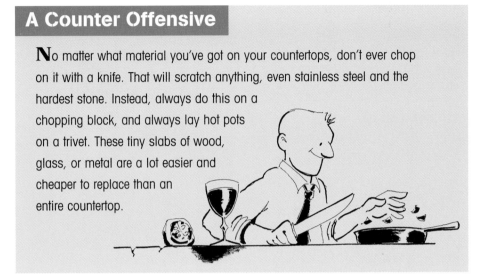

No matter what material you've got on your countertops, don't ever chop on it with a knife. That will scratch anything, even stainless steel and the hardest stone. Instead, always do this on a chopping block, and always lay hot pots on a trivet. These tiny slabs of wood, glass, or metal are a lot easier and cheaper to replace than an entire countertop.

ucts are porous and hence absorb stains. This seems implausible, but it's true. Leave a glass dripping with grape juice or red wine on a stone counter for a few hours, and when you go to wipe it off the ring will still be there. Even something as innocuous as a dripping candle can leave a spot.

I found this out the hard way. I worked on a new home some years ago with a granite countertop that I can only describe as "cookies and cream"—a stone with a white background swirled in brown. Not my taste, to be sure, but that's what it was. In any event, we were days away from the closing when the developer came by and had lunch. By accident, he left a bag containing his salad—dripping with olive oil and red vinegar—on the island countertop, and when I moved it the next day I discovered to my horror that it had left a big stain in the middle of this $6,000 granite slab. Uh-oh. I quickly tried to wipe it off with a sponge, but no luck. Fortunately, I discovered a marvelous product called marble poultice. They say caulk is the carpenter's best friend, because it helps cover up all of our mistakes. Well, marble poultice, I suppose, is the tile guy's best friend. I mixed it with mineral spirits to create a thick paste, spread it over the stain on the counter, and covered it overnight with plastic wrap. To my relief, it actually sucked the stain right out of the stone. I wiped everything up the next day, and the new homeowner was none the wiser.

If you have natural stone countertops, you can do yourself a favor by hiring someone to maintain it once a year. This person will come to your home, clean the stone with chemicals that extract stains, then seal it with stone sealer. This will probably cost you about $150 or $200 a year. That may sound like a lot, but hey, if you enjoy the beauty of granite, you should be more than willing to pay for its upkeep. Know that yearly professional maintenance is the only way to keep it looking good for years and years.

Blowing off Steam

Simmering vapors from pots and pans in the kitchen may smell tasty, but they can create big problems in the form of humidity. All that moisture, let alone stale-smelling odors, needs to be vented with mechanical fans rather than simply left to accumulate. Too much moisture, as we've seen, can condense in the walls and breed mold and mildew—hardly an appetizing situation.

Beyond this, the kitchen poses enormous challenges for keeping the temperature of your home comfortable in warm weather. You have giant appliances in here, from the obvious stoves and ovens to dishwashers and even refrigerators, all of which spew out heat. In fact, the only other place in your home that comes close to this heat overload is the furnace or boiler room in your basement. While this might seem like a bonus in the wintertime, much of this generated heat contains a high degree of humidity. Just look at the plume of steam, for instance, that rises the next time you open up the dishwasher or cook a pot of soup. In the summer, however, this excess heat is even more of a concern. It can make a kitchen that's not air-conditioned oppressively hot—so hot, in fact, that you'll probably prefer eating nothing but cold cuts to avoid turning on

the stove. If you have an air-conditioned house, this heat overload in the kitchen will force your system to work overtime—which will cost you more money to cool things down.

What can you do about it? Whether you live in a house or an apartment, you need to plan the right ventilation system. If you've got an enormous kitchen, a tiny little exhaust fan hovering over a six-burner stove isn't going to give you nearly the exhaust capacity you'll need to keep things comfortable. Talk to a good contractor to get the right system. The solution might involve a more powerful exhaust fan as well as an extra duct or two to bring in air-conditioning if you have it, and maybe even a ceiling fan—which is a low-cost way of moving air quickly and an ideal accessory above the kitchen table.

One more thing: With exhaust fans, you have to remember to turn them on when you're cooking or they will do you no good whatsoever.

As obvious as it may seem, this is something that drives me crazy because people don't use them. Whenever I remodel kitchens, homeowners always want me to put in great big exhaust fans—but then they never seem to turn them on! It's partly because they dislike the noise and partly forgetfulness. But either way, the accumulation of heat, moisture, and cooking odors can shave years off the life of this major investment.

Turn the fan on when you cook, and you'll be doing the most important thing you can to make your kitchen more palatable.

chapter ELEVEN

Bathing Beauties

Want an inviting bathroom? First take care of mold, mildew, leaks, and foul air

When I began renovating one of my first bathrooms in the mid-1980s, neither the homeowners nor I had any idea that they would end up taking a bath—financially, that is.

The bathroom in question was on the third floor of a big stuccoed Victorian. Because the out-of-the-way room was used only by the homeowners' children, they didn't want a fancy makeover. "Just a little sprucing up," they told me, with some new fixtures, a new tile floor, and a fresh coat of paint. Which sounded like a $5,000 job, and that was exactly what I quoted them. All looked pretty good—until my partner and I removed the tile and took a good look at the subfloor.

Actually, to call it a subfloor would be an exaggeration. It was really no floor at all. The joists holding everything up had been saturated from leaks over the years and were completely rotten and spongy. I could literally stick a pencil through some of them, which is not what you look for in a structural member. To make things worse, I also noticed a few squishy areas in the tile wall in the shower. With the homeowner's consent, I removed a few and

bathrooms

Slow the Water Flow

Everyone wants to conserve water—but how best can you do it? By targeting the bathroom. Between showering, flushing the toilet, taking baths, and running water at the sink, the bathroom accounts for the heaviest water use in a household. If you reduce the flow here, you can save a tremendous amount of water. Low-flow shower heads, for instance, have dropped water use from about 8 gallons per minute to just 2.5. A toilet now uses just 1.6 gallons per flush, compared to between 3 and 5 gallons in previous decades and simply turning off the faucet while brushing teeth or shaving can save additional gallons every day. Don't overlook plain old faucet maintenance, either. A faucet that leaks at the rate of five drops per second—which is certainly not uncommon—can waste 43 gallons of water a day, for an astounding total of 15,000 gallons of water per year. Fixing problems such as these may be the easiest and most effective way to save water.

found something that made the floor look sturdy by contrast. A leak from a dormer in the bathroom had obviously been draining into the wall since around the time of the Battle of Bull Run and left the studs not just spongy but completely decayed. The only thing holding up the wall was apathy. When we removed the tile on the inside, the stucco on the outside gave way and crashed to the ground outside. "Uh, we seem to have run into a snag," I told the homeowners, with an understated delivery worthy of an Oscar. In the end, their $5,000 bathroom spruce-up wound up costing them a total of—yikes!—$35,000.

Even if you're not planning a renovation, your bathroom is a room to watch closely in order to maintain what you've got. We've all got fantasies of a candle-and-plant filled oasis, with a fluffy bathrobe, slippers, and towels poised for the moment we step from the bath or shower. Yet this happy scene often clashes with reality. Because of constant humidity, bathrooms probably share more in common with a greenhouse than with the living room. As a result, we all battle mildew that sprouts between the tiles, bathtubs that pull away from the walls and create leaks to the floors below, and chronically clogged bathtubs, toilets, and sinks. I can't tell you how many times I've been called in to spruce up a bathroom only to end up ripping everything out to make essential structural repairs. Most of this decay could have been prevented if homeowners knew how to spot signs of trouble. Let's take a look at some various aspects of a bathroom, from overall design to essential details such as caulking, to help manage things.

Big Plans, Small Spaces

When I was growing up, a bathroom meant something modest—usually a 5-by-7-foot room in which were lined up a Pepto-Bismol-pink sink, toilet, and bathtub. Good-looking? No. Functional? To be sure, and in many households that single bathroom sufficed for everyone, including the guests. Things have changed since then, and not just because we now have multiple bathrooms and guest lavatories. The actual size of these rooms has grown as well—and with that have grown the demands on how to take care of them.

You can still find a 5-by-7-foot bathroom, but master bathrooms in particular have transformed themselves into something more than a room in which you take a shower or take care of business, then leave. Instead, they've also become a place to relax. We dream of walk-in closets and dressing rooms, a raised tub with a tiled deck around it, perhaps a chair for reading, and all within reach of a telephone, a TV, and perhaps even a stereo. For busy couples, the master bathroom is second only to the bedroom as an intimate and private space. Even strictly functional bathrooms have evolved as well. Because of families' hectic schedules—more often than not, Mom and Dad are getting ready for work at the

Keep the Toilet Tidy

Sometimes life can be distilled to a series of little clichés: Eat your vegetables, don't forget to wash behind your ears—and never store anything on top of the toilet. The lid covering the water closet is not a shelf, which may come as a surprise to the many people who use it as one. It slopes, for one thing, and jiggles when a toilet is put to use. As a result, things fall off when they're placed on it and invariably land right in the toilet, where they tend to cause plunger-defying clogs. I have seen lost engagement rings, bracelets, children's plastic squeaky toys, and even alarm clocks pulled from the toilet's depths. To spare yourself an embarrassing encounter with a plumber, leave the lid empty.

same time as the kids are getting ready for school—bathrooms operate according to a rush-hour schedule all their own. To accommodate this, they've grown larger; double sinks are common, as are showers and toilets set off in separate compartments so that more people can be in the bathroom at the same time.

With all of these changes, the price of a renovated bathroom has risen dramatically. I've installed bathrooms recently that easily top $25,000 for a room that I did not consider particularly extravagant—and, unlike my friends' bathroom at the start of this chapter, this was for a room that needed no structural work at all. The bathroom, in fact, has become the second most expensive room to renovate after the kitchen. And on a square-foot basis, it probably ranks as the most expensive of all. You may wonder how a little-bitty room can end up costing so much money. Well, the drywall and 2-by-4s are the cheap part. More expensive are the whirlpool tubs, brass fixtures, tiled shower surrounds, leaded glass medicine cabinets, and "luxury" toilets (truly one of the great oxymorons in the construction trade). Add up the cost of these materials alone, and you can easily reach $10,000. Then factor in the work needed to install everything—the plumber, the electrician, the drywall taper, the tile setter, the painter—and you're looking at practically the same roster that would be needed to build an entire house. That's why everything gets so expensive so quickly.

Fortunately, renovating a bathroom at any cost ranks as a worthwhile project that can truly increase the value of your home. With an investment of this size, however, I think it's crucial to make sure you get what you want—not what some designer thinks you should have. You'll still find a lot of 5-by-7-foot bathrooms these days—mostly because the 5-foot dimension exactly corresponds to the width of a tub. If you want more space, don't be shy about colonizing it from adjacent areas. Maybe there's an adjoining closet that can be absorbed into your new configuration to create a shower stall or even a 6-foot tub. You'd be amazed at how much bigger that extra foot can make a bathroom feel. Or maybe a portion of a large bedroom can be turned over to create a space for a whirlpool tub and spa.

As we saw in our discussion in Chapter 7, don't let the current configuration of walls prevent you from creating the bathroom layout of your dreams.

Venting the Humidity

In our rush to get on with the task of laying pretty tiles and installing new fixtures, we often overlook the single most important aspect of any bathroom: ventilation.

Ventilation has only a little to do with clearing the bathroom of what I will tactfully describe as the unwelcome odors associated with daily life. More critical, however, is the use of fans to clear the humidity that builds up in bathrooms, especially those with a shower. Whether you live in a house or an apartment, you absolutely need a mechanical exhaust fan, or you risk laying waste to that $25,000 investment in quick order. I have seen bathrooms where poor ventilation has deteriorated things so rapidly that in as little as five years of ordinary use they need gut renovations. Don't let this happen to yours. You might think cracking open a window will accomplish the same thing —but it won't. Windows do only

a portion of the job that a mechanical fan does. To understand the scope of the problem, let's look at what happens in a bathroom in terms of moisture.

The average family of four generates about four gallons of moisture a day, and most of that comes from bathing and showering. Steam pours out into the room, and anyone who has a teenager or two in the family knows that they can stay in the shower practically forever—generating even more moisture. (In this last case, a timer on the shower may make good sense.) Imagine what would happen if you squirted your living room with a gallon-sized spray bottle filled with water every day; it would turn into a disaster. The same thing happens in your bathroom, only we somehow seem to accept it. This daily dose of water leads to mold and mildew, swelling of doors, and even a rotting structure. In the winter, moisture accumulates and beads up on the windows, which can eventually rot them from their sills.

If you're renovating a bathroom, by all means talk to your contractor and figure out an adequate exhaust system that will vent directly out of the home—not just into the attic, where dumping all that moisture would create even more problems. Engineers have this figured out to a science, and a good rule of thumb is that you need a fan that can move at least 90 cubic feet of air every minute—blowing all the air out of a 5-by-7-foot bathroom in about three minutes. For larger rooms, my rule of thumb is to have a fan that moves at least 1 cubic foot of air per square foot of bathroom space per minute. And if your fan is bigger, that's great; this is one of the few instances where bigger really is better. Fans have to be sized correctly, or even the fanciest, most lavish bathroom will turn into a grotto in no time.

Having a fan is essential, but so is turning it on. Amazingly, people misuse these fans terribly. They diligently switch the fan on when they step into the bathroom, take a shower, and turn it off a few minutes later when they're done. Not surprisingly, the moisture doesn't just follow you out the door when you're finished; it sits there. You need to leave the fan on for a full half hour after you're done in order to properly reduce the humidity.

You can nag everyone in your household to remember this, but that can be a bothersome chore—especially since turning the fan off doesn't rank high on anyone's to-do list. To get around this, some manufacturers have created timers that you switch on when you walk into a bathroom, which removes the guesswork. Even better are fans connected to motion sensors that don't require switching on at all. They flick on automatically the moment you walk into the bathroom. In addition, they contain a humidistat, which

measures moisture and keeps the fan on until the humidity drops to an acceptable level, somewhere between 15 and 20 percent.

Good exhaust fans and control devices such as these might cost $300 and can easily be added to existing bathrooms. This is probably the single most important thing you can add to ensure the longevity of your bathroom. And when you're talking about an investment of $25,000 or more in a single room, you'll appreciate all the peace of mind you can get.

Putting It Together

As always, the components of a bathroom that you choose are subject to taste, budget, and what's available. I can, however, explain the features about tubs and toilets that I think matter most.

Bathtubs have come a long way since ancient Greece, where the Spartan warriors considered it unmanly to take a heated bath. Instead, they stood in a tub while servants doused them with cold water. Nowadays, a good bathtub—with hot water, fortunately—can become a focal point of a bathroom. But no matter the size or style, I happen to think the only type of tub you should consider is a cast-iron enameled one. I like them because of the way they feel when you sit or stand in

them. They feel substantial rather than like something that's about to give way. You can find cheaper fiberglass, acrylic, and even steel tub alternatives, but these often feel springy to me—which is not what I look for when I'm standing in a bath or a shower. One way to improve these units is to make sure that the plumber sets them into a solid mud base during installation. When this hardens, it will make the tub or shower feel as solid as cast iron. Beyond the feel of things, cast iron finishes hold up better than anything else, which is one more reason I prefer them. Of course, your plumbers may gripe as they carry a 300-pound tub up to a second-floor bathroom to install it, but it's you—not they—who will have to live with it every day.

There's no such materials option with a toilet, since all are made from a hard type of porcelain called vitreous china. This is clay that is fired at ultrahigh temperatures, and becomes completely waterproof. Toilets are basically giant china bowls and have a great and colorful history. Believe it or not, the ancient Minoans on the island of Crete are credited with inventing the first indoor version of the toilet, all the way back in 1,500 B.C. And who could forget the contribution of the inimitable Thomas Crapper, a 19th-century English plumber, whose production of the valve-and-siphon combination made modern flush toilets possible?

Whether you spend $75 or $750 for a toilet, the essential design never varies. The toilet contains a P-trap, which—if you remember from Chapter 2—is the water-filled curve in the drain that keeps foul-smelling gases from belching back into the house. This is located within the toilet itself, and the outline of it can be seen bulging from the sides of the toilet. With a good deal of imagination, it can look something like a swan's neck. When you flush the toilet, water from the tank above falls by gravity into the bowl below and washes everything down the P-trap.

The only major adjustment in

A Field Guide to Tiles

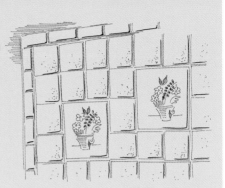

Few things come in as much variety as tiles. They range from nonvitreous, which absorb water and are used only on walls, to vitreous, which are impervious to water and can be used in shower stalls. Beyond that, tiles come in three distinct types. Learn these, and you'll impress any tile setter you ever happen to encounter:

Field tiles. No, these don't have pictures of meadows painted into them; instead, they are set in the main portion of the tiling installation. Think of them as the background to whatever accents you're doing.

Trim tiles. These have a shaped edge and are used to provide a border around the field tiles. Bull-nose tiles have a curve that can form a gentle edge—perfect to run around the deck of a bathtub.

Decorative tiles. These are used as accents to a wall of field tiles. They can be handmade or feature raised-relief shapes. One good idea: If you've got some damaged field tiles and no replacements for them, consider removing some and peppering decorative tiles over the wall to disguise the patch.

recent years has been the shift beginning in 1982 to low-flow toilets, which use just 1.6 gallons of water instead of the 3 to 5 gallons previously required. Since this is a third or less the amount of water involved, the flushing action is sometimes—how shall I put this?—incomplete. For this reason, I would recommend going with name-brand toilet manufacturers only, since they seem to be the ones who have best figured out this particular design challenge. Nevertheless, people are fond of griping about

A Sure Sign of Trouble

Do you want to get a quick idea of what structural shape a bathroom is in? Take your hands and press firmly against a tiled wall in the shower or near the bathtub. If it's solid, you're in luck; the wooden structure hidden beneath is most likely in good shape. But if the wall feels loose and squishy, you may have major problems. This is a clear indication that water has penetrated into the wall and will surely have saturated and begun to rot the studs.

low-flush toilets, claiming that they don't work or that you sometimes have to flush twice to get everything down. But you can't argue with the savings in water, which is substantial even if you have to occasionally flick the lever twice. If you have a regular toilet in your home dating from before 1982, you're not required by law to change it—but I think you should. It's your civic duty to help conserve water.

Tiles, Mortar, and Grout

Tiles and bathrooms belong together like Antony and Cleopatra, Abbott and Costello, or maybe even hamburgers and hot dogs. They form a match made in heaven.

Tiles are waterproof, easy to clean, and have a beauty that no piece of vinyl ever will. Whether natural stone or fired clay, tiles can be used on walls and floors, as well as to line shower or bathtub enclosures effectively. While this last task can be done less expensively with fiberglass surrounds, as they're called, I always prefer tile. To me, tile or stone adds a warmth and a value to a bathroom that you just don't get

Ventilation: A Quiet Alternative

Crucial as ventilation in a bathroom is, we don't always like the way it sounds. What's cozy and charming, after all, about the rattling whir of a fan? It's no wonder that many homeowners prefer leaving the fan off altogether. A far better option, however, is to have a remote ventilation fan installed in the attic. The fan is attached to the rafters. One end is attached by a dryer hose to a vent in the roof; the other end connects by the same type of hose running in the walls to a vent in the bathroom. Flip a switch on, the fan goes on and all you hear is a quiet, distant whir. If that seems like too much work to have installed, you can find a quiet conventional fan. Just make sure to check what is called the sone rating. The lower the sone number, the quieter (and more expensive) the fan will be. Always try to get one with a sone rating below 3.0.

from a plain-looking, prefabricated surround. Plus, they come in a limitless variety, from natural slate, marble, and granite, to handmade enameled tiles and even the clean, appealing look of manufactured ones.

As far as tiles are concerned, it's not what you put on the wall or floor that matters—it's how you put them on. The first step is to prepare the surface itself. As we saw in Chapter 6, you can't install tile on top of ordinary drywall in an area, such as a shower, that becomes constantly wet. Inevitably, the drywall will become saturated, and when it does, it will start to disintegrate. Instead, tile should be mounted on concrete wallboard, a material that's about as impervious to water as anything could be. For other areas, you can simply mount the tiles on top of ordinary drywall or on top of a clean, solid subfloor.

Now come the tiles. Some people attach tiles using special glues, but I am not a fan of this at all because the adhesives tend to expand and contract excessively with the seasons. As a result, you may find the tiles loosen up over time, which is annoying. Instead, I prefer using what is called a thinset mortar, which dates back all the way to ancient Rome and is still the best option today. Tile setters— or especially handy home- owners—attach the tile by spreading the thin-set, then combing it out with a notched trowel. This cre- ates a good, level base that will hold tile or stone tight for ages.

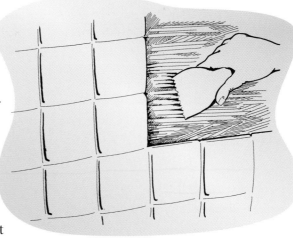

Tile isn't complete without grouting, however. This softer mortar comes in many colors and fills the gaps between the tiles to create a smooth, attractive appearance. If tiles are set close together, pure grout can be used to fill the narrow gaps. If tiles are set farther apart—say, 1/4 inch or more—sand has to be mixed into the grout to give it more strength. In general, you'll find regular grout on walls, since the tiles here tend to be smaller and spaced close together, and sanded grout on floors, where the tiles tend to be larger and therefore spaced farther apart.

In wet areas, grout can lead to trouble. Because it absorbs water slightly, it can serve as the perfect environment for mold and mildew to grow. One alternative is a new kind of epoxy-based grout. Like all epox- ies, it is formed by combining two chemicals that harden once they're mixed together and is a little like putting glue in between your tiles. While it may look like grout and comes in as many colors as grout, epoxy grout has one distinct advantage over the real thing—it does not absorb any water at all. That makes it as resistant to mildew as the face of a tile.

Why haven't we heard more about epoxy grouts? Because they're mostly used by commercial contractors in industrial sites. Epoxy grouts have to be put down quickly, and you have to be careful to wipe any

Unclogging the Tub

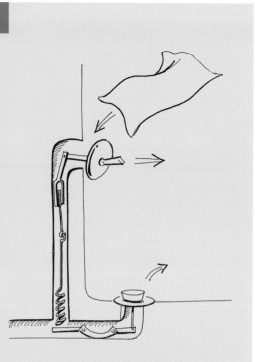

About 90 percent of all clogged bathtubs result from gunk—that's a technical term, of course—getting trapped right where the drain pipe curves and enters the wall. This should be a simple clog to clear with a plunger, but for one thing: The overflow drain, usually located just beneath the bathtub spout, is connected directly to this same drain pipe. As a result, you can plunge away until you sweat, but the clog won't budge because the pulse of air will instead vent out of the overflow drain.

In order to plunge a clogged bathtub, you first have to plug up the overflow drain. To do this, unscrew the overflow cover, then stuff the hole with a wet rag to temporarily seal it up. Fill the tub with about 2 inches or so of water, just deep enough to cover the plunger, then get to work. When you're done, remove the wet rag, replace the overflow drain cover, and you're ready for a bath. This method is far more effective—and a whole lot safer for you and your environment—than relying on caustic chemical drain openers. And unless you know what you're doing, don't ever try using a snake on a clogged bathtub. Because of the intricacies in the way the plumbing is set up, it's very easy to break a pipe.

excess off the tiles or it will create a permanent smudge. You certainly wouldn't want to practice using epoxy grout on your own bathroom tiles, but it's worth talking to your tile setter about it. Trust me, you'll never have to use spray cleaners to remove mildew again.

Unclogging the Toilet

All right, so everybody thinks they know how to use a plunger on a toilet. Yet, surprisingly, there's a right way and a wrong way to do it—and most people do it wrong! The most common way is to stick the plunger in and push down with all your might to force water into drain. But because of the way a toilet is designed, this is just as likely to com-pact the clog as it is to clear it, which would make your problem worse than when you started. The right way to use a plunger in a toilet is to compress it slowly, then pull it vigorously toward you on the upstroke. This draws the clog upward and is far more effective at elimi-nating it.

Don't Balk at Caulk

Mortar, grout, and tile can work wonders to keep water from seeping through into a bathroom wall. But these still leave an unprotected area along joints where sinks, bathtubs, and shower stalls press against tile walls and floors. An additional sealer is needed, and this is usually applied in the form of pure silicone caulk—which is the same material that's used to seal the inside of a fish tank. Caulk comes in a broad range of colors to match just about any grout or tile color, and if applied correctly, it can make things look neat and finished.

That's a big if, I realize, because few contractors and even fewer do-it-yourself homeowners ever seem to get the knack for how to apply caulk neatly. More often, things ends up looking like they tried to decorate a cake, and the blotchy surface they leave behind ends up trap-

A Safety Device Everyone Needs

We've all been in this situation before: You're standing in the shower when someone in your house flushes the toilet. Before you know it, that stream of warm water pulsing over your body turns so hot it could literally scald you.

The problem results from changes in water pressure within your plumbing supply system. The best way to defend against this is to have a plumber install an antiscald valve in the shower and bathtub faucets. Also known as pressure-balancing valves, these simple devices detect sudden changes in pressure in either the hot or cold water and immediately compensate for it by reducing the overall water flow through the faucet to ensure an even temperature. So while your shower may suddenly dip to a trickle for a moment, you'll be spared the pain of a hot-water dousing.

These valves are required by building codes in new homes. But if you live in a place built before 1988, it makes great sense to have them installed anyway, especially in families with young children or the elderly. If everyone had them, you'd never hear of anyone being scalded again

ping water and soap scum, becoming an active medium for mold and mildew to grow. Even if a caulking job is done well, however, caulk doesn't last forever. After four or five years it begins to discolor and lose its grip. At that point it's time to redo it—otherwise water can begin to work its way beneath the tiles and start to damage the walls and floors underneath.

To begin a good caulking job, you have to first remove the old caulking completely. If you don't, the new caulking simply won't bond well to the deteriorated layer. Plus you'll never be able to clean up the old layer adequately, so the dirt and mildew will inevitably show through to the new layer. It would be like putting a new Band-Aid on top of an old one; you never want to be this sloppy. The best way to remove the old caulk is to cut it out carefully with a sharp utility knife, then scrub out any residue with a plastic scouring pad like you'd use on a frying pan in the kitchen.

When the gap dries, it's time for the new caulk. You can use any color you want, from white to black and every color in between—just as long as it's pure silicone, which is the only type that's 100 percent waterproof. The mistake people make is when they squirt the caulk out of the tube like a line of toothpaste, and just leave it there. What a way to ruin the look of a bathroom! Instead, you have to work the surface of the caulk to create a nice finish, which is a process called tooling. To do this, first squirt a bead of caulk in place, then run your fingertip over it to create a nice concave shape. That way, any water that hits the caulk after it dries will simply drain away instead of pooling there.

The hardest part about caulking, however, is forming a neat line along the edges of the tile and the tub or sink. You'll frequently see caulk smeared all over, which is about as unprofessional as it gets. To do it the right way, you'll need a roll of painter's masking tape, which is easy to remove once you stick it on something. After removing the old caulk, you peel a piece of tape and run a line on the wall about 1/8 inch away from the gap to be caulked, and a second line about an eighth of an inch onto the tub or sink on the other side. Then you squirt the caulk into the quarter-inch gap that remains and tool it with your fingertips. Wait five minutes, then carefully strip the painter's tape away. The result will be a caulk line done to mathematical perfection. You'll come off looking like a pro.

In the rush to have a grand bathroom, things such as caulking, grout, and ventilation probably don't rank high on every-

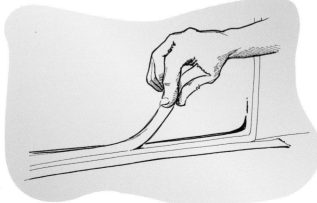

one's wish list. But it's exactly these sorts of mundane details—rather than a whirlpool tub or some hand-painted tiles or custom-made shower door—that will help you create a fresh-feeling room that lasts.

chapter TWELVE

Rooms to Live In
What you need to know about setting up rooms—from décor and lighting to closets that work

We have one rule in my household that has done more than anything to preserve domestic peace. It is simply this: My wife is responsible for everything inside the rooms, and I am responsible for everything inside the walls.

Happily, this makes me the guardian of the wiring, plumbing, heating and cooling, and insulation. Fortunately, I have also kept my ears open enough to understand the difficult task of setting up the living areas of a home. While this has nothing to do with structure, it has everything to do with comfort. What is the point, after all, of ending up with a house that will last for ages if it is ugly and unbearable to live in? I so often talk about the need to focus on what's beneath the surface of the walls and floors, but that is to emphasize the need to take care of business there first. Once things are structurally solid, it's time to think about setting up a comfortable place to live. More times than I can count, I have seen wonderful houses overrun with a hodgepodge of furniture, organized in ways that makes no sense at all, and finished off with tasteless décor and bad lighting. The result is gloomy chaos.

rooms

I don't want this to happen to you. Although I can't advise you on what sorts of draperies might look best with your Turkish carpet, I can offer a few useful guidelines about what your priorities should be. By creating a master plan and sticking with it, you'll end up with a house that looks great and functions smoothly—and inspires you to live, relax, and even work at home.

The Art of the Plan

As a builder, there are two little words that used to fill me with dread: interior decorator. These were people, I wrongly thought, whose sole purpose in life was to inspire homeowners to rip apart and change everything inside a house after it was already built. So I was skeptical when my wife said she wanted to use a decorator to help redo our living room—although the experience would ultimately prove a valuable one.

Whenever people renovate their homes, it's important to create a master plan before touching anything. That way, you won't have to undo mistakes you've made. And the same is true with décor, our decorator informed me. You don't want to randomly start buying furniture or painting walls in offbeat colors in the hopes of stumbling on the right note. Instead, this is something good decorators achieve by taking a broader view of the whole house. The first question they ask is, "What's your lifestyle?" If you have kids (as I do) who want to eat cookies and milk in the living room (as I surely do), then this would suggest a more casual state of affairs. If you want a museum-quality living room where there are no crumbs, by all means go for it.

You can have little corners filled with fragile and priceless treasures, but keep them confined to a few areas. That way, you'll be able to live in your home as well as look at it. If you want to keep on the cutting edge of décor, you'll have to explore places other than the major retail chains. By the time these places take notice of things, they're no longer trends. You'll be better off looking at home décor magazines and choosing what fits into your lifestyle. Don't fall into the trap of thinking you need to buy

Décor Is No Chore

Daunted by household decorating? I know I am. I am far happier with, say, a bucket of plaster and a spackling knife than I am with swatches of fabric. Fortunately, I have paid attention to those around me concerned with such things when I work on homes. Whether your taste ranges from Victorian frilly to neo-minimalist, here are a few tips from the pros that will help you end up with a livable, lavish interior that people will love.

- Avoid overwhelming tones on walls and in rugs. Instead, bring color into your home by accessorizing—whether it's that magenta lampshade on the end table or those electric-blue vases on the mantelpiece.
- Look to nature as a guide for how to decorate home. When you look outside, the colors go from dark to light—and they should do the same in your home. White ceilings make rooms look taller and more open, as do light-colored walls. A darker carpet will make things feel grounded.
- Limit those "don't touch" areas. A few eye-pleasing antiques or tables filled with precious tchotchkes can be wonderful. But by confining them to a nook here or a corner there, you'll actually be able to live in your house rather than just look at it.
- Avoid adding too much—or too little—to a room. Clutter can be unbearable, which is why we hate our attics and basements. But too little furniture can leave a home feeling unfinished.

everything from one place or one manufacturer. Rooms can be tied together through accessories—and that's the fun and the challenge of decorating.

I have to say I don't always have mainstream taste. When building a house for *The Today Show* last year, in which TV viewers were able to vote on décor, I was amazed at how plain and practical most people are. For the corner of a living room, one possibility was a wild Medusa lamp

A Decorative Option

I'll admit it, I had been skeptical of interior decorating as a profession since, oh, about 1984, when I first went into business for myself. After all, where's the challenge in going to a store, buying a couch, a few chairs, and a rug and calling it a living room? I've since realized the hard way that creating a look for an entire house is actually an enormous task, and one in which you can waste a lot of money by buying the wrong things. Decorators can be of great help, and the best part about it is that they may not end up costing you anything. Here's how: Most make their money by collecting commissions from furniture that you buy. Let's say you go out and buy a couch at a store, which costs you $2,000. Hire a designer and you'll still pay $2,000—but stores sell to professionals at a discount of about 10 to 20 percent. You end up with the same couch at the same price, but the decorators get to pocket the difference. In other words, it's like getting their services for free. This sounds like a bargain to me. If it does to you, too, find a decorator by heading to the Web site of the American Society of Interior Designers (www.asid.org).

and Medusa chair that I happened to like. Luckily, my voice was in the minority on that one; the viewers went instead for practicality and chose a couch that could turn into a sleeping area. In general, you can get very far by avoiding bizarre things such as snake-themed furniture, overwhelming colors for walls, and rugs that dominate the interior landscape. Instead, go slightly simpler for the overall scheme—and add those charming, offbeat, or eclectic items as accessories. In my own house, the decorator didn't suggest Ming Dynasty antiques or cashmere draperies, as I feared. Instead, it's a more relaxed setting with themes that we were able to carry throughout the whole house. And it gives us plenty of places to display a few wild things of our own, such as my wife's treasured collection of Polish figurines that once belonged to her grandmother. We've also got some red couches with matching red pillows, but we have

Smoke Detectors

Everyone knows a home has to have smoke detectors. They're required by every building code, and you literally cannot buy or sell a home or apartment without having them installed. But what everyone does not know is that these smoke detectors wear out—even if they're not buzzing every morning while you're burning the toast. After about fifteen years, according to one safety study, the chances are worse than fifty-fifty that the smoke detector will not operate properly. This is true whether you have battery-operated smoke detectors or those that are hard-wired to your electrical system. To guard against this, the National Fire Protection Association recommends that every smoke detector be replaced after ten years. If you can't remember the last time that you replaced the smoke detectors, err on the side of safety and buy new ones. Make sure you or your electrician puts them on every floor in your home—typically near the kitchen, at the top of the stairs, and at the top of the basement stairs.

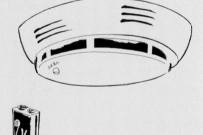

a few fancier pillows in contrasting fabric that we tuck away and enjoy bringing out for parties.

As a general rule, always buy the highest-quality items you can afford. This will guarantee the best long-term value for your money. But allow yourself some fun, too. My living room, for instance, contains a fabric-

Carbon Monoxide

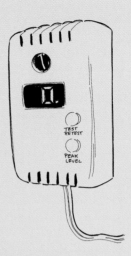

We all fear smoke, but something else we should be wary of is carbon monoxide. This gas results from combustion of fuels in furnaces and boilers, as well as wood in fireplaces. If these are vented properly, the carbon monoxide exits your home harmlessly. If there's a flaw in the ventilation, however, your home can fill up with these deadly—and odorless—fumes. An important safety device to protect against this is a carbon monoxide sensor. This is very sensitive and makes a loud chirping or buzzing sound (similar to a smoke detector) when it goes off. If you hear this, open a few windows and leave the house. Carbon monoxide sensors can sometimes be combined with smoke detectors. I think they should be on every floor of the house—but especially near the heating equipment in the basement, and near the fireplace or woodstove if you have one. Install them, and you'll have one more reason to sleep soundly.

covered pedestal table that I built out of plywood. It looks pretty good, I have to say—and makes a great spot for a plateful of cookies.

Lights Up

A room's mood depends on more than just what it looks like and how it's furnished. It also depends on lighting. We all love light, and I think the more of it you can get into a room, the happier you'll be. You can accomplish this through natural lighting and electric lighting; let's take a look at each.

There's a strange home I know of on a lake in Wisconsin, near where my family spends summer vacations. The house is set in a beautiful loca-

Sprinkler Systems

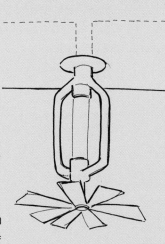

We keep coming up with new, innovative ways to avoid fires and loss of life, and sprinkler systems top this list. Most people are familiar with these only in schools and high-rise buildings, but they are becoming increasingly common in homes as well. In these systems, sprinkler heads fit inconspicuously into the ceiling of a room and are connected to a hidden network of pipes. When exposed to heat from a flame, each head can send a spray of between 8 and 18 gallons of water per minute into the room. Although this may sound like a lot of water, it's far less destructive than the deluge from a firefighter's hose. And only the head that is exposed to the heat is triggered, so it's not as if your whole house ends up drenched. Many cities and towns are already starting to require sprinkler systems in new construction and major renovations, and I think over the next decade they'll become standard everywhere. Sprinkler systems can be expensive, easily costing $12,000 to $20,000 for an average-sized house. They all but eliminate the risk of fire, however, which brings a peace of mind that you have to agree is priceless.

tion that faces the water, but it has just two narrow windows that look toward it. That to me makes no sense at all. Windows help create an open, airy feeling in a way that nothing else can achieve. Good natural lighting can make even the smallest home seem twice as big. If you don't have enough, consider adding more. As a construction project, this does not rank as a tremendous task. Even so, it's easy to overdo it on windows if you add them haphazardly to an existing home. There's a balance you have to achieve between bringing in as much light as you can and having adequate wall space for furniture, bookcases, and pictures.

Mechanical lighting is obviously essential, yet this is something to which people often give too little thought. I'm sure most of us grew up in houses where the guiding principle of lighting seemed to be to hang one ceiling fixture in the center of a room and milk it for all its watts. This creates all the charm of a room at Motel 6. We've gotten more experienced, I'm happy to report, to the point that there are even lighting designers who do nothing but think about the possibilities of illumination. Rather than approaching lighting as just something that turns either on or off, experts group it into three major categories—ambient lighting, task lighting, and accent lighting.

Ambient lighting provides overall illumination, sort of like that single fixture in the center of the ceiling. But this can also be accomplished with lamps, wall-mounted fixtures, recessed lighting, and track lighting. Regardless of the source, the point is that the glow from the bulbs spreads out and fills up a whole room, making everything brighter.

Pantry Pride

So often, we find the solutions to our current problems by looking to the past. In the homes I build and renovate, for instance, I'm on a one-man crusade to bring back the walk-in kitchen pantry. These were last popular somewhere before World War II, but they make a lot of sense even today. They're like giant kitchen closets for food, as well as brooms and buckets and cleaners. And they free up your cabinet space so that you have more room for dishes and glasses. The pantry is something that everyone I know appreciates—even if they aren't exactly sure what it is at first. In fact, I recently gave some prospective homeowners a tour of a house I just built. As they walked through the kitchen, they gave me a "So what is this?" look when they spotted the pantry. They bought the place, and when I checked back with them after they moved in, I discovered I had two new converts to my cause. Their favorite feature? Why, the pantry, of course.

Task lighting provides a more specific focus and supplies direct light for whatever it is you happen to be doing—whether cooking, reading, or playing the piano. Again, you can use any number of types of fixtures for this; it's just that the fixtures are pointed in a specific direction.

The final category is accent lighting, which breathes warmth and life into a home. These are usually lower-wattage bulbs—too small to read by, certainly—that provide decoration rather than overall illumination. You can find accent lights underneath cabinets, pointing upward to illuminate a wall or painting, and generally decorating things. Good designers use a combination of all three kinds of lighting, and arranging them has become an art in itself.

One of the most popular types of fixtures that has emerged in recent years is recessed lighting. Unlike chandeliers or track lighting, recessed lights have a low profile because they're flush with the ceiling. As a result, people have come to love them—sometimes to a fault. A mistake that I often see is a room so loaded up with these lights that it becomes ridiculous. In new homes particularly, I've seen ceilings filled with recessed lights positioned every two feet. The ceiling becomes so pockmarked with holes, it's like you're looking at a piece of Swiss cheese. The way to avoid this is to be smart about where you position these lights. You can't just place them willy-nilly. Instead, you need to follow the formula set out by manufacturers that shows how much light

Shelf Life

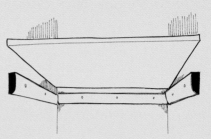

Do-it-yourself projects tend to have a lot in common with Martha Stewart's cake recipes. They may sound simple on paper, but the reality often turns into a fiasco. There is at least one great project, however, that is very easy to do, and that is to install additional closet shelves. This can greatly increase your storage capacity. And even if your first attempts are slightly botched, who's going to notice? The finished results will be *inside* a closet.

To begin, you have to create a continuous row of wooden supports called cleats along the sides and back of the closet. These are nailed to the walls to support the shelves. The best way to do this is to cut long strips of 3/4-by-4-inch pine (knots are okay). Then nail them securely into the studs with 2 1/2-inch finishing nails. These are the ones with the small heads. Now come the shelves themselves. For the wood, I'd go with paintable birch-veneered plywood rather than planks of solid wood such as pine. The plywood won't warp, and it's actually a lot stronger than most plain boards. Cut the shelves (or have them cut for you at the lumberyard) to fit, then slide them into place on top of the cleats. Instead of nailing them to the cleats, I'd attach the boards with a few 1 1/2-inch screws, after predrilling some holes. That way, if you ever want to rearrange the shelves, you can remove them easily.

these fixtures shed based on the height of the ceiling and how closely they should be positioned.

In addition to the lighting fixtures, the types of bulbs that go in them can affect the quality of light. The most popular are incandescent bulbs, which have a warm look to them. In commercial buildings, you'll frequently find fluorescent bulbs, which cast a somewhat colder look. These give you that kind of bright white look that you see in schools, but it's such a stark color that I discourage people from installing these bulbs in their homes. Halogen bulbs are a brighter and hotter looking alternative to incandescent bulbs, and rank as the most popular type of bulbs for recessed lights. The light from a halogen bulb is most nearly like sunlight—often a little *too* much so. To control this hyperwatt glow, I'd recommend installing dimmer switches. As a matter of fact, I'm a huge fan of putting dimmers on almost every fixture, no matter what type of bulb you use. The added cost is just a few dollars per switch, and you'll appreciate the control dimmers give you over the feel of a room.

Home Offices That Work

I clearly remember the setup of my first home office. Located in a windowless corner of the basement, it consisted of an almond-colored laminate countertop nailed to the wall with some track lights up above. Not the most desirable place to pay my bills or make phone calls to clients! Fortunately, we have all come to realize that working at home doesn't have to mean sentencing ourselves to miserable conditions—whether stuck down in the basement, or in a sweltering attic, or in a cramped and poorly heated space above the garage. With some forethought, you can create an amazingly comfortable and even inspiring workplace in your home.

Home offices have only recently gotten the attention they deserve. I remember that not even ten years ago, they were considered a waste of money as a home improvement. One study I saw reported that the investment return on a home office would be only 58 percent of the money you spent on it when you sold your house—which was hardly encouraging. Recently that number has risen dramatically, in part because the number of people working at home has also skyrocketed. According to one survey, there are now more than twenty-seven million people who work at home at least part-time. Into these ranks I would also add people who work in offices during the day, yet still spend some time working when they arrive home. We're working harder and longer than ever, and deserve a pleasant place to do it in.

Home offices will end up being as individual as the work you do. Even so, a few general guidelines can help you set up one that functions well, no matter what line of work you're in. First, whether the office is intended for full- or part-time work, or just as a place to organize records, pay the bills, and give the children Internet access, choosing the right spot is crucial to its success. Everybody assumes that all they need is a little corner of a room—but usually they end up spread all over the house. Instead, go for a room that measures at least 10 feet by 10 feet. The nature of the work to be done and the number of people using the office can also dictate its site and setup. A solo workspace may need less seating and desktop space than one the whole family will use. If clients will be coming for meetings or work sessions, a separate entrance might be useful to keep them from traipsing through the house. Visitors need their own chairs and perhaps a table, a place to hang their coat, and access to a guest bathroom, unless you want them to use a family bathroom and risk having them trip on your child's rubber ducky.

The key is to make this a place you want to work in. Remember, you're your own boss: So which character from *A Christmas Carol* are you going to act like, the wretched Scrooge or the benevolent Fezziwig? Be kind to yourself. If you're someone who likes music as you work, maybe you can put a nice sound system in your office instead of that old clock radio that has been kicking around since your college days. Or how about a little TV so you can catch the news or watch *Seinfeld* reruns when you want to take a break? Consider a couch for creative ruminations as well as the occasional nap—something that your boss at work surely would have frowned on. Whatever it is that makes you excited about a place to work, make sure you include it in your home office. That way, when it comes time to crunch some numbers, draft a report, tally up an expense account, or do whatever it is you do at home, you won't dread it because you'll be heading to an environment you love.

The wiring that goes in the home office is also important because of all the technology that we demand—from high-speed modems and Internet access to multiple phone lines. In my own home, I've run wires for phones and data that can handle just about anything the future might bring. We don't use it all, of course, but I want to be prepared for whatever comes along in ten years. If you're renovating a home, I think it's a great idea to run a spare conduit to your home office. This is basically an empty pipe running from the electrical service panel, through which an electrician can fish wires without ripping up walls. It allows you the flexibility to expand your electrical, telephone, and data possibilities as you need them. Whatever you do, however, spend the money to make sure that your office doesn't become a jerry-built collection of wires and extension cords. If there's no phone jack where you want to plug in the fax machine, for example, then hire an electrician to install one. It will be a lot better-looking—and a lot safer—than running the cord around the perimeter of the base trim or, worse, running it across the room and covering it with a rug where it can become frayed and dangerous.

Closet Desires

In my years of working with homeowners, I've never heard a client or a friend say to me, "Oh my gosh, I have too much closet space." In fact, I doubt such a person exists anywhere. Closet space, after all, is the one thing we all crave.

It wasn't always this way, of course. When I was growing up, my father's closet had just one thing in it—his Texaco uniform, which he would wear to his job at the gas station. But the days when a closet could be rigged out with a single metal pole are long gone. I take a look at my own closet, for instance, and find more baseball caps than a major league team might own. And my wardrobe is modest by today's standards. I recently built a closet for a client with a collection of four hundred sweaters, and another for one with two hundred pairs of shoes. Yet it's

Sounding Off

Much as we love them, our homes are not always oases of calm—especially if we live in apartments or multifamily dwellings. The noise we hear from neighbors or even our own family members clomping above us or through the walls can be extremely distracting. Sound is a vibration that passes through the solid structure of your home. Jump up and down upstairs, and the vibrations travel through the floor, subfloor, joists, drywall, and then out toward your ears. Laying carpeting on floors or putting cork tiles up on the walls can muffle the noise, but you'll still be able to hear it.

A more thorough way to deaden sound is to have a contractor sever the connection between the wall or ceiling and the noise on the other side. In the case of the ceiling, a contractor would create a drop ceiling that attaches to the adjacent walls rather than the joists above and leaves a gap of air that can be filled with sound-deadening insulation. This new ceiling is then finished with drywall and looks just like an ordinary ceiling—except that it will be quieter, since the sound vibrations won't travel through it as well.

Walls can be treated the same way, with a false wall built a few inches away from the actual wall. This also severs the structural connection to block sound vibrations but is strong enough to hold any electrical or plumbing systems you might need.

In either case, you'll be sacrificing 6 inches or so of ceiling height or floor space within a room. But if constant noise irritates you enough, I'm sure you'll be willing to make the compromise.

more than just the amount of clothes we have that's increasing. We store everything in our closets: sheets and towels, extra blankets, Christmas and holiday decorations, bicycles, golf clubs, coolers, even grills. The amount we accumulate has increased, and as a result, our closets have to hold more than ever.

Obviously, the simplest solution would be to build more closets. But this, as we all know, is not always practical. A better way is to make use of the space within a closet by segmenting the space with a variety of shelves, cubbyholes, and clothes rods set at different heights. Not only does this eliminate the wasted 3 or 4 feet below a dangling shirt, it makes it easier to see an entire wardrobe at a glance. Whether you have a big walk-in closet or a standard reach-in one, you want to be able to choose your clothes for the day and close the door in about two minutes rather than having to rip everything apart searching for something, then ending up with a mess all over the bedroom. Believe me, I speak from experience.

In order to intelligently divide the closet, professional designers begin by sorting through a person's wardrobe—a first step even for those heading to the local home improvement center to buy inexpensive shelving. There's no formula that works for everyone in terms of how many linear feet of rods or shelving you'll need, but by grouping like items of clothing together and seeing exactly what you have, you can pretty much figure out how to make any closet work. Believe it or not, there are professional closet organizers willing to do this for you. When they get to work, they organize your wardrobe into categories according to how much space they take up when hung from a rod. At 64 inches or more, long gowns, overcoats, and bathrobes use up the most. But few people own many of these, so you might be able to get away with a rod only a foot or two long that could be hung at eye level. Next come medium-length dresses and trousers hung by the cuff, which need 48 to 56 inches, followed by shirts, jackets, blazers, and folded pants, which, at 38 to 42 inches, require the least space. Rods holding these shorter-length clothes can be hung one above another, thereby layering more into the closet.

Some designers plunge feet first into the closet by counting shoes. These create sort of a limiting factor for how much can be stuffed into a closet. After all, you can squeeze shirts on thin wire hangers if you need more room, but you can't squeeze a pair of shoes. If you've got a dozen pairs of shoes or less, you can probably get away with a rack that fits on the floor below the clothes or shelves, and slides out so you can reach things. A greater collection—on the order of, say, Imelda Marcos's—requires cubbyholes that hold individual pairs or large sliding shelves that can store them two deep.

Toward the bottom, shelves can be added to store items such as sports gear and winter hats and gloves, while shelves at a more accessible height make good places for dress shirts and sweaters. You can stack them, but if you can't pull the bottom one out without toppling the entire pile, it's probably too tall. For sweaters, limit the pile to three or four; for shirts, five or six. Add a shelf across the top of the closet about a foot from the ceiling to store extra blankets, pillows, or other things that you might need only a few times a year.

Where do you get all of these dividers? You can go to a hardware store and spend about $25 on the most inexpensive organizer—and it really will make a difference. In about an hour, you can transform your closet and probably get 30 to 40 percent more items in it. The prices rise from here. You can get more elaborate systems from specialized stores, which might cost $300 or $400 per closet. These will give you things such as tie racks, drawers, and shelves to really customize your closet, which will make your life so much easier. Or you can hire a closet company to remake your closet, which might cost $2,500 or more. I've seen some of these custom-made closet organization systems that looked great. In fact, my kitchen cabinets aren't as nice as the cabinets some people have in their closets.

There is another solution, however, and that is to pare down what you own. People stockpile clothes, along with everything else. I'm not saying you have to limit yourself to one set of clothes, as my father did. But before you make adjustments to your closet, start by making some adjustments to your wardrobe. Purge first. You'll be amazed by the extra space you find.

chapterTHIRTEEN

An Eye for Detail

It's the little things—from paint to woodwork—that bring out the best in a home

If you're anything like me—tall, thin, and good-looking—nothing can make you feel less confident about your home than looking in a house magazine.

There you find lavish pictures of beautiful places, right down to the table settings done up with napkin rings, fresh flowers, and bowls of ripe fruit artfully arranged. Does your home look like this? Am I tall, thin, and good-looking? Probably not. Yet there's a reason these places in the magazines look so appealing—and one that can inspire us all rather than depressing us. It's because professional designers with an eye for detail have made sure that everything in the scene looks perfect.

We tend to judge a house by what we can see and feel—the paint job, the heft of the wood trim, and the well-done features that we find in it. No one's going to want to ogle your great insulation or magnificently up-to-code electrical and plumbing systems. These things are essential and worth bragging about, to be sure. But, unfortunately, we live with the finished surface, not the bones beneath it. As such, our eyes focus on the quality of the paint job,

Goodbye, Old Paint

Need to strip paint that has been gunked up for a few decades on intricate woodwork? Don't sand it or burn it off with a blowtorch. Not only are these time-consuming, but you can end up releasing toxic plumes of lead-tainted smoke and dust into your home from old paint. A better way by far is with a citrus-based stripper. There are natural and synthetic varieties, both far less caustic to work with than other chemical strippers. They come in either a gel-like form that you can paint on with a brush or an aerosol version that you can spray on. You apply this citrus stripper that smells something like Anita Bryant's basement, then let it sit for a half hour before peeling it away. While the chemical strippers can sometimes get down to the bare wood with one application depending on the layer of paint, you may have to apply two or three coats of the citrus stripper to get the same results. But it's a lot more pleasant to work with if you're doing the task yourself. Leave the more caustic strippers to the professionals.

the way the wallpaper meshes neatly on the wall, and the intricacy of the woodwork and crown moldings. These are the things that make a home seem special. They sure don't make up for any underlying structural flaws—anything but—but they do set a tone and mood for a house that give it character. You don't have to be rich or live in a mansion to have great detail, nor do you have to resort to napkin rings and bowls of fruit. You just need to make the effort to think about it. Let's take a look at some of the possibilities to see what you can do.

A Signature Look

There's a house painter I'm familiar with in Chicago whose specialty is those grand Victorian "painted ladies." These homes have an excess of detail on the outside, to be sure—from newel posts and columns to frieze boards and more gingerbread than you'll find at a holiday party. Not only does he do a brilliant job in his work, but he caps it off by adding a line of gold paint on the exterior. It's an extra bit of whimsy, and sort of like his signature. Whenever you see one of these homes, you can look for the gold line, and know that it was painted by a master.

I think there's room for a gold line or two in all of our homes. I'm not speaking literally, of course; unless you've got a gaudy Victorian color scheme, I'd certainly vote for restraint here. But you can focus on giving your home a signature all your own. Start by asking what's memorable about a house. Think about places you loved when you were younger, and what details in those places linger to this day. Maybe it was the built-in kitchen cupboard in a grandmother's house, or the ornate mantelpiece above the fireplace owned by a favorite aunt. Or even a wine rack in the kitchen or a staircase banister that goes beyond the ordinary. These are all wonderful details that capture the eye. By focusing on your own home, you can add a few of them for a modest cost and create a home that's truly your own.

The way to add these details is to plan them so that they make sense. You don't want to just stick them on. Whenever I build stairs to a deck or porch, for example, I make the treads extra deep—at least 18 inches, compared to the usual 10 or 11. There are two reasons for this. One is that I have small children, and I know how a slightly wider tread makes it easier for them to crawl or walk up the steps. The second is that older people also appreciate the extra space as they navigate the steps; it's like walking from landing to landing. Granted, this isn't a show-off detail that draws attention to itself. But it's something extra that makes living in a home that much more comfortable

In my home, I've always installed built-in bookcases rather than buying portable ones. When they're installed, trimmed, and painted, they look like they've always been a part of the house. You don't have to be a builder to do something like this. In fact, I had a friend build the bookcases for me. I'm also partial to screened-in porches. There's something about children, hot midwestern summers, and these porches that were made for one another. In each of my homes, at my wife's insistence, I've built one. We're now in our third home, and the screened-in porch has become a sort of family trademark, one that our friends and relatives look forward to spending time in.

There are lots of places to add details such as these in your home. The delight comes in adding these in unexpected places, so that something as simple as walking down a few steps to a patio or grabbing something from a bookshelf can become a pleasure.

Wood Trim

What makes old houses so special? It's sure not the structure. For the most part, we build things better today than ever. Yet older homes have something that you have to work very hard to get in newer ones: thick, ornate wooden trim around doors, windows, and baseboards. And don't overlook crown molding, where the ceiling meets the wall. This sort of detail jumps out at you the moment you enter one of these places. It makes a home seem elegant, solid, and permanent—the opposite of chintzy. Great woodwork is one of the reasons homes in old-line suburbs are sought after, and it's what makes classy prewar apartments in places like New York City so prized.

Molding and trim used to be a lot cheaper to buy, and so this was the first thing downgraded in the rush to build houses on a budget. Not only has the trim become thin-ner, but it has become plainer as well. You can find the same ho-hum Colonial casing on homes from Florida to Hawaii. Fortunately, you don't have to settle for the trim that happens to be on your home when you move in. With a little inge-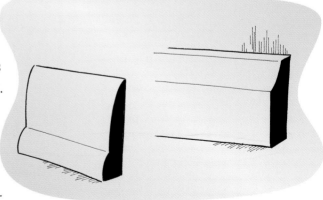

nuity and some slight expense, you can have a carpenter make some changes for the better by installing wider molding.

Cutting the wood requires a carpenter's skill, but as a home renovation project, this is far closer to, say, changing a light bulb than doing a gut renovation. The standard Colonial casing might range between 2 1⁄4 and 4 1⁄4 inches wide, but it is usually only 5⁄16 inch thick. This is not much thicker than a pancake. The trim used on houses built before World War II averaged 3⁄4 to 1 inch thick. Even if the molding is the same width, this extra thickness makes everything look more substantial. How much money would it cost to swap you for something thicker? It depends on the size and complexity of the room. You might spend $1,000 or more for the materials and labor to bring a large room to life. Compare that to the cost of draperies or carpeting, however, and the amount seems reasonable. If you can't afford to do your entire home, consider focusing on the main areas, whether that's the living room, the dining room, or the entry hall. Plus, you'll actually be improving the value of your home. I've seen this on the homes that I renovate myself: People will actually walk through and comment on how nice the trim looks. And if they're choosing among a number of similar homes in a particular neighborhood, guess which one they'll end up buying?

If you already have an old home, I would caution you to take extra care of your trim if you add a room or do some renovations. It can be hard to match trim styles, and so many homeowners give up and install whatever they happen to find at the local lumberyard. Don't take the lazy way out.

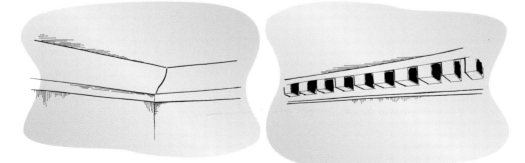

Oil Versus Latex?

Get a painter started on what is better, oil or latex, and it's like the Hatfields and the McCoys revisited. Everyone seems to have their preference—and so do I.

Everyone used to think that oil-based paints were superior to latex, and in many cases I think oil still makes the best choice. It's the most durable paint there is, which is why I like to use it on surfaces such as trim and doors that take a lot of abuse. It also levels better than latex paint, which means that there will be fewer visible brush strokes than with latex. With a glossy or semigloss paint, the results are much better. But latex paints have made remarkable advances in recent years—especially those that contain acrylic resins, which are more durable and flexible than the cheaper vinyl ones. They're easy to paint on, easy to clean up, and provide a lasting surface both for the interior and exterior of the house.

My preferred MO when I paint is to use them both. I use the more durable, smoother-finished oil paints for trim and doors. Then I follow up with latex on the walls. Typically, the wall finish is in a satin or eggshell finish. That little bit of sheen offers the best cleanabilty—far superior to just flat latex. This way, I get the best of both paint worlds.

Instead, take a piece of the old trim to a lumberyard or millwork shop that shapes wood and have them duplicate the trim for you. To do this, they take an impression of the wood and set a series of metal knives to cut new trim to match it exactly. You'll end up with what amounts to a photocopy that is indistinguishable from the original. The cost of setting up the knives might run about $200, and then you'll be charged for each foot of wood you order. It will cost you more than ready-made trim, but you'll be preserving one of the very things that made your home desirable in the first place.

One other thing to keep in mind about trim is the number of different types of wood you can find it in. Too often we choose pine because that's what most lumberyards stock. Pine is okay, but remember that it is a soft wood. If you have children, it's probably not the best choice because it can get banged up quite easily. A better choice is poplar, which is a harder wood, or hemlock. You may have to search around for these woods, but they are a far better wood for painting than ordinary pine. And if you're planning on staining your trim instead of painting it, oak has a beautiful grain that makes a great alternative to pine. Another thing to consider is price. Although it seems cheap, clear or knot-free pine is actually one of the most expensive woods around. In many places, the alternatives—even oak—may actually cost you less.

Brush with Success

Done correctly, a paint job is practically invisible. All you see are the clean lines of the wall and trim. Done sloppily, however, it can look like some Jackson Pollock experiment—a collage of drips and splatters, flecked with stray bristles that have pulled loose from the brush.

Painting is a job many inexperienced homeowners think they can simply tackle themselves. While that may be true, the task is far from simple. There are many things to keep in mind in order to keep your home looking crisp and fresh. There's a saying that a good paint job is 90 percent prep. That's contractor lingo for preparation, and I have to agree. If you start spreading paint on walls that are glopped up with five or six decades' worth of paint beneath it, you're going to end up with something that looks like a science experiment in sedimentary rock formation rather than a decent paint job. Whether you're doing the work yourself or hiring someone, there are some key steps to keep in mind that will guarantee good results.

The first step—which right away is one that most people skip—is to wash the walls and woodwork. We wash our floors, our countertops, our cabinets, even our windows. Yet it never occurs to anyone to actually wash the walls. Instead, we blithely paint over a decade or so of grime and dirt and hope the paint sticks to it. It will—but not for long. This is a

Types of Brushes

When we think of painting, we immediately imagine the paint itself—the color, the sheen, and whether it's latex or oil. But the real secret to a good paint job lies closer to hand: the paintbrush. There is no such thing as a one-size-fits-all brush. Instead, you need some variety. Good paintbrushes have bristles that are firmly attached to a metal holder, which is called a ferrule. The more expensive the brush, the more bristles it has—and the more tenaciously they'll stay in place. Buy the best you can, keep them clean when you're finished using them, and they'll stay with you for years.

Flat brush. For painting exterior siding, a 4-inch flat brush with either natural or synthetic bristles is the applicator of choice—it covers large areas quickly, yet is still light enough to maneuver easily. The best-quality brushes may cost $20 or more.

Trim brush. Ranging between 1 and 2 inches wide, trim brushes have bristles cut on an angle that makes it possible to paint crisp lines on trim, molding, and windows. Chisel trim brushes are angled on both sides for extra precision. Expect to pay $10 for a good 2-inch brush.

Stain brush. The bristles on these are shorter and wider than a paintbrush—which gives them less of a tendency to drip.

recipe for peeling and chipping. Instead, begin by mixing a solution of a good cleaner such as sodium triphosphate (sold in hardware stores as TSP) and warm water, and wash the grime off the walls and woodwork.

When the surfaces are clean, you should follow up with an old

Brushes: Natural Versus Synthetic

Paintbrushes come in two major varieties, natural-bristle and synthetic-bristle. Each one has a place in your toolbox.

Natural-fiber brushes. These brushes are made from animal hair—the most common being hog hair, which is labeled "China bristle." Use these with oil paint and solvent-thinned finishes only, since water-based paints will absorb into the bristles and leave them limp and moplike.

Synthetic-fiber brushes. The brush of choice for latex paint and water-based finishes, these contain fibers made of nylon or polyester. Generally less expensive than natural fibers, the fibers are hollow—which is why after cleaning they continue to leak paint-tinged liquid. Some brushes contain blends of both synthetic and natural fibers, which can be used with any type of paint.

painter's trick. Take a bright work light—for this, a halogen one is best—and hold it up close to the wall and at different angles to inspect for imperfections. This will reveal chips, dings, cracks, and bulges, all of which will detract from the finished job. To fix them, sand the ones that protrude and fill the indentations with spackling compound, followed by a gentle sanding and a little spot priming when it dries. If you don't prime, the paint won't cover consistently, because the spackling compound absorbs it, so you'll have lighter tones. Now comes the first coat of paint. And after this, good painters will bring out the halogen work light and go back over everything a second time before applying the second and final coat. This is the only foolproof method there is for walls as well as trim.

Another trick I can share with you is what to do if you're painting the walls a very dark color. My wife and I painted our dining room a dark navy blue, for instance. This sounds crazy, I know, but with white trim the

On a Roll

If you're painting a wall, a roller works much better than a paintbrush. Not only is it faster, but it leaves a smooth matte finish in its wake rather than a bunch of brush strokes. Rollers come in two styles based on their cores. Cheap ones contain a core made out of cardboard, which begins to compress and give way when it gets dampened from paint. Plus, the more you roll, the more the fibers glued to this core tend to pull out and stick to the wall. You can't win. Better by far are those with a hard core that does not yield. To make sure you're getting these, squeeze them in the hardware store: If it collapses when you compress it, that's not the roller for you. The good rollers cost more, but they have an extra advantage. They're completely cleanable, so you can get far more painting mileage out of them.

Also, when choosing rolling pans, make sure you get a sturdy metal one. The low price of plastic pans makes them seem appealing. But if you fill one with paint and try to pick it up, it invariably ends up bending and spilling the paint all over.

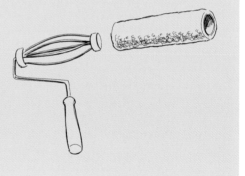

walls actually seem to recede and the whole room feels bigger. It's a look we love. Well, the thing about dark colors is that you can't even get close to covering a wall with two coats of paint. The lighter undercoating just continues to peek through. So what I did was apply a layer of primer that I had the paint store tint blue. It was more of a robin's egg than a navy blue, but it saved me from putting on a fourth coat. If you're going in the opposite direction with colors—say, to white instead of the navy blue those wacky previous homeowners used everywhere—you've got a different problem. That dark paint will continue to bleed through an endless number of coats of paint. The solution here is to use a shellac-based primer first. Shellac is a wonderful sealer, and it will block water stains, smoke damage, or any previous coat of dark paint. It's great if, for instance, the kids have used your walls as a canvas for permanent-marker art. A single coat of shellac primer will block dark colors from coming through. You may even be able to get away with a single coat of paint on top of it.

Does painting sound easy? It shouldn't, because it's not. Yet even if you plan to hire someone to do it for you, you still have to learn the basics so that you can check prep work they're doing. Knowing what's involved will also help you accept the fact that good painters charge a lot. The going rate runs anywhere from $2 per square foot of room space to as high as $5 or even $7. This can get very pricey, especially if you're having the entire interior of a house painted. Depending on the colors and the prep work, you might be looking at a bill of $15,000 to $25,000 for a whole-house makeover that's done to perfection.

The Wonder of Caulk

When I worked for a production builder—which is a fancy way to describe someone who churns out about five thousand houses a year—my foreman had the soul, as well as the aesthetics, of a drill sergeant. To speed us along, he used to bark out a simple order: "Beat it in, caulk it, paint it." That meant beat it with a hammer, caulk it to cover up the gaps and dents, then let the painters have at it. Amazingly, it worked. Caulk is truly a painter's ally, one that can create a smooth surface out of even the most unlikely hodgepodge of wallboard and trim.

We last encountered caulk in Chapter 11, where it was used to create a waterproof bead around

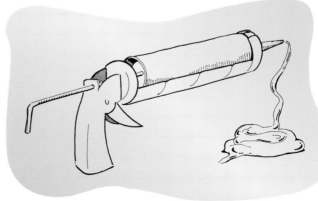

Got Lead?

There's only one approach when dealing with lead paint: Don't touch it. If there's lead in the paint, hire a licensed lead abatement specialist to deal with it. As a paint ingredient, powdered lead carbonate once seemed ideal. It gave durability and a self-leveling smoothness to paint that made application easy. But all this came at a cost. Some dried layers contain up to half their weight in lead, and ingesting paint chips or dust over time can cause learning disabilities, anemia, and other disorders. That's why lead paint was banned in 1978. If a house contains lead paint—and you can assume it does if it was built before, say, 1960—leave it alone. There's little hazard just from touching it and none at all if the lead is concealed beneath an intact layer of lead-free paint. But if renovation plans call for scraping, sanding, or heat-stripping, take care. If you have any concerns about the paint in your house, check it with a lead test kit or have a professional analysis done by a state-certified specialist.

sinks and bathtubs. Rather than making something waterproof, however, painter's caulk is designed to seal up small cracks and crevices that occur wherever baseboard, window, and door trim presses against a wall. This is one of those details that really gives a room a polished look. The result is a seamless connection that makes the trim and the wall look as if they were always meant to be together, rather than appearing as an unlikely union destined to fall apart. If the wall wavers a little away from the trim or if the joint between two pieces of molding is not exactly right, caulk fills the gap and makes it disappear. It's not uncommon for a good painter to use an entire case of caulk when painting the interior of a home.

The first step when caulking is to choose the right material—which can be a chore in itself, given the dozens of varieties for sale in the average hardware store. Waterproof varieties are made from 100 percent silicone caulk, but paint won't stick to these at all. Instead, you have to look

A Sticky Situation

Wallpaper is a tricky endeavor. Just think back to the old *I Love Lucy* episode where Lucy embarks on a decorating frenzy only to end up gluing herself to the wall. I've done wallpaper twice in my entire life and fared only slightly better. To me, wallpaper is time-consuming and tedious. You have to make sure the edges match up, the corners are neat, and no air bubbles are trapped beneath it. Don't let me stop you from trying this—just be sure to start simple. Begin with a border that's easy to figure out, rather than an entire bedroom or bathroom. And if you're not willing to spend the time learning how to do this correctly, then hire someone to do it for you. When I want a wallpapered room, that's the route I take.

for siliconized latex caulk, which is completely paintable. You'll find a great number of caulks, which sell for about $1.50 for an 8-ounce tube. I've even seen generic versions of this, which say nothing but "caulk" on the label in the same way some cans of food just say "beans." I'd avoid these and stick to a name brand instead. You'll pay a few dimes more per tube, which I think is a good investment in guaranteed quality.

With caulk, technique is everything. The first thing you need is a caulk gun. This is a metal contraption into which you insert the tube of caulk. You then cut the tip off the caulk tube at a slight angle and squeeze the trigger of the caulk gun, and out comes a delicate bead. By the way, that 79-cent caulk gun on sale at the clearance table at the hardware store isn't the one for you. You need to pay a few dollars more for what is called a dripless caulk gun. With cheap versions, the caulk will keep gushing out of the tube long after you take your finger off the trigger. What a mess! In dripless versions, the pressure against the tube relaxes when you remove your finger from the trigger, and the caulk stops flowing. This gives you a great deal more control and a far neater result.

Once you have the right gun, however, you can't just start squirting caulk into place like so much toothpaste. Caulking is an unsung art form. There are people who are really good at it. Then there are people who should be brought to trial before the International Paint Crimes Tribunal for the damage they perpetrate. The key lies in how the caulk is tooled after being applied. You have to take a finger or putty knife and work the surface to make it smooth. A wet rag can help in this task, as well as to wipe away any excess.

Fortunately, latex caulk is about the most forgiving material ever created. If you don't like what you've just done, you can take a paper towel, drench it with warm water, and wipe the caulk away. Then start over, comforted by the knowledge that in a home it's the smallest details—not the largest—that matter most.

chapter FOURTEEN

The Great Outdoors

Your home should be connected to the land that surrounds it; here's how to devise a plan

Say the word outdoors to a homeowner, and the first thing that comes to mind is a chore list. It's as if all we can think of is yard work—cutting the lawn, trimming the hedges, and the infernal raking of leaves.

I'd like to leave the lawn mowers and the bags of fertilizer aside for a moment, however, and take a look at the outside of your home not as an arena of endless work but as a vital part of what makes your home inviting. We spend a great deal of time sorting out the insides of our homes in terms of how the rooms flow from one to another, and how the décor and furniture work to create that put-together look. The same should be true on the outside of the home.

The way your home sits on the land creates a vital element to how your house looks, functions, and what it's like to live in it. I'm not talking about ethereal design aspects here, such as what brick pattern in your pathway will best highlight that Alberta spruce topiary. I'll leave that to the landscape designers. What I am talking about are some broader, practical considerations that will make the difference between a house that looks grounded and one that looks as if it fell from the sky and landed completely out of place— like Dorothy's high-flying Kansas home that ended up on the witch. In addition, these same ideas will actually help preserve the structure of your home by draining rainwater away from your foundation rather than toward it. Let's take an outdoor whirl, from decks and driveways to the basics of landscaping, to figure out how you can make the best—and most lasting—improvements to that strip of land around your home, whether it's a fifth of an acre or 50 acres.

Inside Out

We often wonder what makes a home look inviting from the outside. Surely it has a lot to do with its style and how well a place is maintained. Yet it also has to do with how a house is tied to its land.

One of the most challenging things to think about in working on your home is the transition between the inside and the outside. We all crave some sort of outdoor living space, whether it's a terrace, a deck, or a screened-in porch. These places for lounging and eating make a home feel grander and more permanent. Without them, a house can take on all the appeal of a parking lot.

People often try to accomplish this by simply building a raised deck and tacking it on to the back of the house. That sort of contraption doesn't really do much for the house, and it certainly doesn't do much for the surrounding landscape. It can look unfinished and, worse, can actually separate the yard from the house rather than connecting it. Sometimes a better solution is to add a raised terrace or patio. Elevated on a bed of sand and gravel, these can be finished in brick, slate, stone, or even colored concrete. They sit high enough to appear to be floating on the land, but not quite as high as a deck. There's nothing wrong with trying to achieve this effect with wood, of course. Just keep these same principles in mind: You don't want to separate yourself from the ground with a high deck and tall railing; instead, you want to try to link yourself to it.

Grading is important here, too. Your goal is to tie things together and make things flow, so that it's easy to move from one area of the yard to another. All too often, shrubbery is hauled in around a deck or patio and planted in a tight row. Not only does this look pinched, but it can create the equivalent of the Great Wall of China in the middle of your yard and completely seal off one area from another. A more effective (and cheaper) approach is to grade the site in a way that allows for interesting changes in contour and elevation. That way, the patio or deck can stand on its own, without a fortress of shrubbery. Also, think about the steps from the inside to the outside, especially those toward the back of the house. Rather than two quick steps down, think about elongating them so that they form one or two miniterraces that make you feel as if you're gliding from the indoors to the outdoors. You can pay a landscape designer or architect to help you come up with distinct plans. If they're good at what they do, this is what they will focus on.

A Shady Deal

In winter, few things feel cozier than a room filled with warm sunlight. But in summer, the sun can quickly turn from friend to foe. Old houses offer plenty of relief from the sun in the form of shaded verandas, covered porches, and over-hanging eaves. This is not always the case with newer houses, however, and a shadeless home can be misery to live in. What are your options? Well, you can wait twenty or thirty years for that row of shade trees you just planted to reach maturity. Or you can take quicker action. Cloth awnings look good with just about any style house and can greatly cool down a house by blocking direct sunlight from entering windows or spilling onto porches. Outdoors, you can build pergolas, which are a wood lattice structure that dapple a patio or deck with shade. Overhead, they can be fitted with canvas for more shade. Better still, add a few vines—such as grapes or wisteria—and you'll have a leafy cover that comes and goes with the seasons. Either way, you'll have it made in the shade.

Landscaping Basics

Mention landscaping, and everyone's mind quickly shifts to golf-course-quality lawns and pink and white azalea bushes. Not so fast. These are indeed elements of the landscape, but the first thing everyone has to consider is the land itself—specifically, where does it slope?

As we've seen, a great many drainage problems can be created by ill-planned slopes. No matter whether your home is brand-new or a century old, take a critical look at the grading all around. Is it mostly flat but with a slight pitch aimed directly toward your home? Is the soil compacted or composed mostly of clay, which creates long-lasting puddles or even ponds when it rains? Are there ditches formed by soil settling around the foundation that fill with water? If you answer yes to any of these, you'll seriously want to consider having the yard regraded so that water does not collect and splash up against the house during a rainstorm. After all, if you have a swamp in your yard, you will inevitably end up with a swamp in your basement. Be mindful of your close-by neighbors, however. The last thing you want to do is have your yard reconfigured only to end up drenching them. Cooperation, in a case such as this, is crucial.

Another thing to consider when looking at a landscape is how far into the ground a home is buried. It should be obvious—but often it is not—that the foundation has to rise out of the ground between 3 and 6 inches. If it's less than that, then what you have created is not so much a foundation but rather a bridge between the house-devouring creatures that live in the soil and the house itself. Nothing could be riskier! Regardless of these pitfalls, people seem to love the flush-with-the-ground look of a house. To this end, they often end up piling soil and mulch up against the siding of a house to hide the protruding foundation, which is an invitation to disaster. Not only does this give insects better access to a home, but moisture also ends up wicking into the structural frame of the house. Whether your home is sided with wood, vinyl, brick, or stone, you must leave a soil-free barrier all the way around the exterior.

As far as what you should plant in your yard, I can't tell you. From

Hit the Deck

After a deck is built and finished off with wood, people often do nothing to it. Then, in a year or two, they wonder why their deck looks awful. Those decks surfaced with pressure-treated wood begin to warp, crack, and turn dingy gray. Redwood and cedar may not warp, but they, too, turn gray. What's a harried deck owner to do? This may come as news, but you are supposed to coat your deck with a preservative every few years. Some people try using products sold as "deck sealers," but even though the name sounds promising, the product itself is useless. These sealers create a temporary water-repellent surface, but in a matter of months they will peel and look blotchy. I am at a loss to explain why anyone would ever buy these products, much less manufacture them. Instead, you need to use a penetrating preservative that contains a tinted stain. The ideal preservative should contain a linseed or rosewood oil base, which drives the stain deep into the wood. Your wood will indeed end up being stained—but that is the only way to block the sun's ultraviolet rays, which are what damages the wood fibers.

hemlock to bromeliads, there's room for just about anything depending on where you live. But I can tell you about mistakes I see. The single most common one involves homeowners losing a sense of scale and vision and forgetting that the little sapling they cart home from the nursery will soon grow up into a strapping tree. It's a little like buying a cute puppy, only to end up with Cujo galumphing through the living room. Or, in my case, a 115-pound shepherd-collie mix named Barney (we didn't yet know about the purple dinosaur). And so that cuddly rhododendron, which looks so forlorn in its ball of burlap, gets crowded close to a bunch of its buddies. This looks great for a year or two, but then it starts to resemble a woody thicket. Before you know it, you'll have to rip everything out and start over. The flip side of this, of course, is the Spartan look. People buy a few plants, then place them here and there at random.

Mr. Fix-It Plants a Tree

When planting trees and bushes, there's a simple rule to remember: Whatever the size of the root ball, the hole you dig should be twice as big around and one and a half times as deep. The key to success, however, is with what you fill this hole—and for this I will give you Mr. Fix-It's Surefire Soil Recipe. In a wheelbarrow, I mix equal parts of mushroom compost, peat moss, and black dirt. This gives the roots of new plantings the opportunity to flourish even in marginal soil and greatly enhances their survival rate. Mushroom compost is sold in bales at nurseries and is a nutrient-packed material that plants love. The peat moss holds moisture and guarantees that the plants won't dry out. And the black dirt or topsoil binds everything together. By the way, you don't ever want to remove the burlap from a tree or shrub before setting it into the ground. That would be like suddenly yanking the blanket off a sleeping baby. It comes as a needless shock to the roots, one that you would be better off avoiding. Instead, my soil recipe will give the plants the strength they need to eat through the decomposable burlap in no time. *Buon appetito!*

The result is like a bad hair-plug job. It sure doesn't appear natural, and the end results can be pretty unsettling.

What's the best approach? As always, to come up with a plan before you start wielding the spade. When you're working on your décor inside your home, you don't just buy pieces of furniture at random and fill the gaps haphazardly. The same is true outdoors. Good landscape designers will literally create a floor plan of the yard. They think about the size of plants and about how to group things together in logical clusters. Some plants may be added for their interesting texture or height, others for their colorful flowers or foliage. You can have large-leaved plants mixed with plumes of flowers, and maybe some tall prairie grasses behind it. The goal isn't to carpet-bomb the entire yard with shrubbery. Instead, it is to create small oases of flowers, bushes, and trees that work together—like a well-chosen couch, chair, and coffee table grouping in the living room. If it is done well, people will be drawn to these areas outdoors, and you can accomplish much more with much less landscaping. Not only does this cost you less, it ultimately means less yard work.

A Route to Success

Paths, terraces, and driveways provide surfaces to walk and drive on, and part of the challenge is to figure out exactly where they should go. But an even greater challenge is to figure out exactly how to construct them so that they don't end up pitching drainage water toward the foundation. A flat surface such as a driveway or walkway has to slope away from the foundation. You don't have to slant it so much that you feel like you're standing on the deck of the *Titanic*, but it has to tip enough for water to drain away—which can be accomplished with a pitch of about 1/8 inch per foot.

Another thing to watch out for with driveways in particular is the connection to the house. Usually, the area around a house is backfilled after the foundation is excavated, and it takes years or even decades for this soil to settle down. If you try to run a concrete or asphalt driveway over this former trench before it's fully settled, it will inevitably sag a small amount—enough to crack the surface and cause water to infiltrate. There's a simple method to prevent this, which involves attaching short steel sup-

port rods to the foundation. A con-tractor will use a masonry bit to drill holes into the founda-tion every 4 feet or so just below the soil level, then install rods so they jut out about 6 inches. Then the concrete or asphalt is spread on  top of this. A group of such metal pegs might cost you all of $50, but they will hugely assist in preventing cracks near the foundation. The pegs act a lot like toeholds in rock climb-ing—your driveway just needs a little something extra to hold on to so it can stay connected to your house.

For driveways, people have become accustomed to concrete and asphalt. But I prefer blocks called pavers. To me, the cobbled look is absolutely gorgeous and is quite durable as well. What's great about pavers is that they're practically self-healing. If there are any areas of set-tling in a driveway, all a homeowner has to do is pull a section of pavers out, add a little sand and tamp it in place, then put the pavers back. The driveway will look as good as new.

The best part about pavers is their cost. Once extremely expensive, they have become cheaper as their popularity has begun to climb. Let's do some comparison pricing. Asphalt ranks as the cheapest of all drive-way coverings, at about $4 a square foot. If you've got a 100-foot-long driveway, figure on spending about $4,800. Concrete comes in slightly higher at about $5 a foot, for a cost starting at $6,000. Neither of these driveways is permanent, of course; eventually they will need to be replaced. Pavers cost more than either of them, starting at about $7 a

Paving the Driveway

Asphalt and concrete rank as the two most common driveway surfaces, but they're far from trouble-free. Cracking, buckling, and—in the case of concrete—spalling can reduce an expensive driveway surface to rubble over time. To get the best results for each, follow these guidelines:

Asphalt. The key to a good driveway lies in the preparation. In particular, it's about the amount of compacted stone used as a base. The best recipe for an asphalt driveway is to use 6 inches of compacted stone, topped with at least 2 inches of compacted asphalt. To get that, a contractor will have to lay down at least 4 inches of asphalt before rolling it down and making it smooth. If the contractor tells you he's using 3 inches of asphalt, that's even better—so long as it's 3 inches of the compacted rather than uncompacted stuff. In cold climates, asphalt driveways need to be sealed every three years or so to prevent cracking.

Concrete. As with asphalt driveways, a 6-inch layer of compacted stone makes the best base for this material. On top of this, add 4 inches of concrete. There's one truth about concrete, however: It will crack no matter what. To accommodate this, it has to be stamped with expansion joints, which are designed to limit the cracking to specific areas. The worst thing that can happen to the concrete is that the surface blisters and spalls. This results from contractors using a stiff mix that sets faster than a wet mix. For the best results, tell your contractor to mix your concrete wet. This won't harden as quickly, so you'll need to spend the day in a lawn chair standing guard so that no one walks on it. You'll end up with a better job—and one free of footprints and graffiti.

square foot, or about $8,400 for this same hypothetical driveway. Yet once you spend the money, the driveway will last forever—not counting the need to reset the occasional brick. If you've ever taken a trip to Rome, you'll see what I mean. Some stretches of the Appian Way, which was built by the Romans a couple of thousand years ago, can still handle modern-day traffic (Now *that's* Italian!)

Finally, pavers go a long way toward enhancing the appeal of the exterior of your home. Give buyers two similar homes to choose from, and they'll take the one with the pavers on the driveway every time.

Getting Decked

What's the number one outdoor home improvement project? Building a deck, of course. Yet in our rush to get the barbecue set up, we often forget to pay close attention to the structure of the deck. Whether you build a deck yourself or have it built, remember: This is a part of your house, a structural part. Slipshod work here can be disastrous.

Go to a lumber yard, and you'll find lots of design help concerning how a deck looks. But I'm more concerned with how a deck works, because we tend to always overload them. Invite a big group of your rib-eating friends over for the afternoon, and you can easily end up with a few tons of people clomping around and swaying in unison. Talk about a live load! Decks can collapse under this sort of weight, which is a tragedy you can easily avoid. Make sure whoever designs your deck builds it to hold a weight load greater than the code requires. For the structural part of the deck, I like using pressure-treated lumber because of its ability to survive insects, rot, and decay. I always set the joists at 16 inches apart instead of 24 inches, which some building codes allow. Plain and simple, it gives you a stronger, wobble-free deck.

The span of the joists is also crucial. They need to be supported underneath by posts, and then the posts need to be connected well to the ground. There are two ways this can be done, according to building codes—but one is far better in my view. You can use the post-in-concrete

method, which means that you dig a hole, throw some concrete in it, then stuff the post in. This is a quick and cheap method, if you ask me, and not very strong. A far better way is to actually excavate the post hole like a foundation, which means below the frost level (if you're in a cold climate). Then you pour what is called a concrete pier that rises just above the ground. The post rests on top of this, and the result is an exceedingly strong structure. It costs a little more, but your deck will last for the ages.

One other thing to think about is the connection to the house. Often, the deck is connected with nails simply pounded in place. This is a disaster waiting to happen. Not only do the nails allow water to seep in and rot the structure of the wall, they don't hold very well. Get a group of people jumping around, and the whole thing can pull away from the wall and collapse. You can avoid this by insisting on a strong attachment. The deck should be bolted to the wall, never nailed. The bolt holes should be filled with silicone caulk to block water *before* the bolts are attached. And in most cases you'll need flashing so that water drips away from the connection to the house, rather than into it. Good contractors do this by instinct. Make sure yours does. And if you're planning on building a deck yourself—as many people do—make sure you understand these design elements before beginning.

With a good structure in place, it's time to think about surfacing. Everyone defaults to pressure-treated lumber, which is also used for the structure. This is a mistake, I believe. Pressure-treated lumber may not rot, but it does not hold up to weather very well. Even with applied preservatives, the wood tends to warp and crack in the sun, and it will need replacing within ten years easily. I prefer alternatives. Certainly

A Freezeproof Faucet

When water freezes in an outdoor faucet or hose bib, as it is often called, it expands and can put enough pressure on the pipe to split it open. This isn't the exciting part, however. The exciting part comes on that day when the pipe then thaws and sends a jet of water gushing into your basement. If you live where it freezes in the winter, you need to turn off the water supply to the outside faucet— using a valve that is usually located a few feet inside the house on a pipe leading to the faucet. Then you have to drain the faucet by opening the outside valve to let any water run out. A fail-safe alternative is to have a plumber install what is called a freezeproof faucet. This looks like an ordinary outdoor faucet on the outside, but the valve that opens and closes the pipe is actually located at the end of a long stem located about two feet inside the house. Since this portion of the pipe stays warm all winter, it will never freeze—and there's no need to shut off the supply. That means you'll be able to hose off all that road salt from your car whenever you want to.

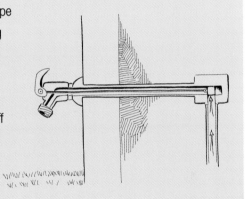

redwood and cedar are always a great choice and really add warmth and beauty. These both involve cutting old-growth trees, however. Fortunately, there's an even better alternative now with new synthetic woods. These are made out of sawdust and recycled plastic grocery bags. The performance of this material is amazing: It literally does not warp or crack, and you can cut, shape, and nail it just like wood. The material never has to be sealed or stained, either. Originally, synthetic woods came in just one color, which faded to a sort of battleship gray. But now it comes in many colors. The color is impregnated all the way through, so it holds up very well.

The prices and life spans of these various options fall in a wide range. Pressure-treated wood will probably only last about ten years before your deck begins to look tired. But you'll easily get twenty years out of cedar, redwood, and synthetic woods. As far as costs go, the materials in total to build and surface a 10-by-10-foot deck might amount to $1,000 if you use pressure-treated wood. For cedar or redwood that rises to $1,700, and for synthetic wood you'll be looking at a bill of $2,000. Still, by spending more money, you'll get a deck that lasts twice as long—and easily looks ten times better than pressure-treated wood.

Do Fence Me In

"Good fences make good neighbors," wrote Robert Frost in a memorable poem. That may be true—so long as your neighbors know about this proposed fence in advance. Think of a fence and the word spite no doubt comes to mind. While nothing can look more elegant around a yard than a fence, nothing can be more divisive in a neighborhood, either.

Before you construct a fence, you have to think about not just the neighbors but your local government as well. Many towns and cities require you to get a permit before you erect a fence, so it makes sense to check this before renting the post-hole digger for the weekend. These requirements may involve things such as setbacks from roadways and property lines, as well as the height of the fence. Although it may not be an actual rule in every municipality, it's certainly a prime point of etiquette that wherever you install a fence, you have to have the "good side" (if there is one) facing out toward your neighbors. That means the structural side—which is the ugly side—has to face in toward you. If you want to see the good side, too, then you have to erect a double fence.

Besides the actual permits, negotiations with the neighbors can be a little tricky. If you're on friendly terms, by all means tell them what you plan to do in advance. And if you're not on friendly terms, it's probably even more important to let them know what you're doing and why. The fact that you may need a secure play area for the kids or a dog run will

A Garage Full of Dreams

A garage forms a strange boundary in the universe of our homes. It's neither indoors nor outdoors, but rather a no-man's land between the two. For many of us, it becomes the de facto main entrance. It can also become the recycling center, a place to stockpile bins of stuff, a repository for everything from bicycles to rototillers, and even a workshop. And, oh yes, we occasionally even find a spot here to park our cars.

With all this activity going on, garages deserve a little extra attention—beginning with organization. As with closets, you can make more efficient use of space with garage organizers, tool holders, and storage cabinets. If you have the money, you can even hire a garage organizing company to do this for you. It can make the difference between a garage you curse and one you actually use.

Since garages are subjected to heavy abuse, they also require special care. In particular, garage floors take a beating, even if they *are* concrete. One complaint I hear from people who live in icy climates is that the concrete spalls; its surface begins to fleck away and become pockmarked. Much of this is caused by corrosive road salt tracked in by your car. You can protect the floor in two ways. First, coat the floor not with paint but with an epoxy sealer. This is the sort of no-nonsense finish that is used in warehouses, where people drive forklifts all day long on it. It's nonslippery but tough enough so that oil and salty water bead up on it and can be wiped off. You can also extend the life of your concrete floor with the help of an old-fashioned push broom. Simply sweep a couple of times a week and everything from salt to abrasive grit will be whisked away.

always serve as good excuses—just as long as you actually have kids or a dog (if not, may I suggest acquiring them?). No matter what, I don't like high fences because I think they're patently unneighborly. A 6-foot fence can seem like the old Berlin Wall. Something lower that you can still have a conversation over is far better, even if it doesn't give you 100 percent privacy. I know someone who thought they loved the look of wrought iron make the mistake of installing an 8-foot fence around their yard. The effect was disquieting, like Sing Sing in the suburbs. If you take that same fence and limit it to 42 or even 36 inches high, you'll find you get all the benefits of quaintness, elegance, and privacy, without the drawbacks.

Neighborly negotiations aside, it's easy to see the appeal of a fence. They're as American as Tom Sawyer, after all. A white picket fence makes a home look festive—like it's the Fourth of July every day. And nothing can match a simple cedar split-rail fence for rustic beauty. Beyond the look alone, fences offer a tactile pleasure as well. Who can deny the joy of opening up a gate on your way into your home? As for what the fence is built from, there's a huge choice. From iron or stone to chain link, you can get whatever look you want—from decorative to functional. I'm personally partial to ornamental iron, partly because one of my first jobs in the construction business was building them.

Wood fences can also add a charm and a beauty, but they require a lot of maintenance; whether you stain them or paint them, it can be a lot of work to upkeep them. Still, nothing looked quite as good—until the recent advent of vinyl fencing. I love authentic things, like lemonade with a few pits and Christmas trees with actual needles. But vinyl fencing is an amazingly good substitute for painted wood fences. They're extremely strong because they're reinforced with metal, and come in a big array of styles and colors. But the best part about vinyl is it doesn't weather. This means no painting, scraping, and otherwise watching your expensive fence rot into the ground. My last house had vinyl fencing that looked as good after six years, when I sold the place, as the day I installed it. It didn't show any signs of weathering at all, although my dog did manage to get it muddy when he jumped on it with his big paws.

Before guests ever came over, in fact, my job was to wash those paw-prints off the fence. As an outdoor chore, it was a bit tedious, to be sure. But it was a whole lot more entertaining than scraping and painting a wooden fence every year, only to watch it give way one day to inevitable rot.

chapter FIFTEEN

Sixty-Minute Inspection

Mr. Fix-It takes you on a tour of your home and helps you make a list of what to tackle first

A home can tell you a lot about itself—if you learn to listen to it.

A friend of mine discovered this a few years ago when she found a forty-year-old home for sale west of Chicago. She knew the place needed some work, but when the home inspector came to take a look the news couldn't have been worse. There was a major crack in the foundation wall, the heat exchanger in the boiler was cracked, and the electrical system was seriously out of date. Or so he said. This sounded serious, but before giving up on the house altogether she gave me a call. "Look, I'm really in love with this house," she said. "Would you mind taking a look at it and giving me a second opinion?"

In my years as a contractor, I've made one rule I live by: I never work for friends or relatives. But I am happy to volunteer my services for free—because you can't fire free help, can you? So out to the house I went. The stucco American foursquare looked charming. Sure, it needed some fixing up, but I could easily understand why my friend was excited about it. Then I got to work. I headed straight to the base-ment because the foundation crack seemed like the most serious flaw of all. But when I got there, I found that it was just an ordinary crack, not a foundation-wrecking fissure by any means. I looked at the

A Twice-Annual Checkup

What's the best way to take care of your home? The same way you take care of your own health—by spotting small problems and fixing them before they turn into larger ones. To keep an eye out for what's wrong, conduct a twice-yearly inspection of your home from top to bottom, inside and out. Do this once in the spring and once again in the fall. Bring a notepad along to catalog what needs your attention. And remember: Structural things go first, the decorative ones go second.

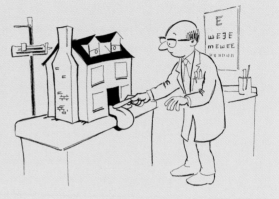

boiler next. No problem there, either; it just needed to be cleaned. Finally, I opened the electrical box. True, the dishwasher and refrigerator should have been hooked up to separate circuit breakers, but this was a task that an electrician—and even I—could have finished in about five minutes. "This place is great," I said to my friend, to her relief. She took my advice, ignored the comments from the professional inspector (whom she had just paid $300), and has been living in the place happily for, oh, about five years now.

The point here isn't that inspectors should be mistrusted. Just the opposite is true. Inspectors are a vital part of the home buying and maintenance process. But part of the obligation of being a homeowner is to learn how to tune in to the condition of a home yourself, whether you're buying a new one or simply trying to maintain an existing one. If you don't, you're at the mercy of home inspectors and contractors who will blithely tell you what they think is or isn't wrong with your home. A basement-to-attic inspection that you conduct yourself will help you assess what kind of condition your house is in, and alert you to what projects you'll need to add to your to-do list. And it will also give you the confidence you'll need to work with professionals—whether they are contractors, real estate agents, or professional inspectors. Put on your X-ray glasses and let me show you how I might look at your home to determine its condition.

An Outsider's Approach

Forget, for a moment, that the house you're studying is your own. Nothing clouds the analytical mind more than an emotional attachment. Instead, you need to adopt the coldly observant attitude of, say, Barnaby Jones and notice only what you see—not what you wish you were seeing.

Whenever I do a house inspection for a friend, they're quick to rush me inside and show me the well-lit living room or the gourmet kitchen. Instead, I start on the outside. I might pause briefly to admire the style of the house, or the great landscaping, or the beautiful view. But really what I'm looking for are clues to the home's structural integrity. The first thing I do is gaze up at the ridge of the roof. If it's perfectly straight, that's an excellent sign. If, however, it sways like the back of an old mare destined for the glue factory, I can all but assume it has roof leaks and rot.

I then walk around the perimeter of the home and see if the walls are standing straight. I don't use a level or a plumb bob or anything; I simply rely on my senses to see how things are aligned. If the walls seem to tilt or lean—which can happen even on a fairly new house—this can indicate a number of things about the shape of the place. It may hint that the house was built on squishy soil and the foundation is settling, or that the foundation and the footings aren't adequate. If a home is more

Choosing a Home Inspector

If you have a toothache, I'll bet the chances are pretty slim you would just call up any dentist you happened to find in the phone book. Who wants to take a risk like that with something as important as your mouth? The same is true of your home. When hiring an inspector—which you need to do if you're buying a home and applying for a mortgage—make sure you have someone experienced doing the job. But where do you find someone like this?

Try calling your local building department or a few real estate agents and ask for recommendations. Before you hire the inspector, ask what his credentials are. You want someone who is accredited by the American Society of Home Inspectors—which is sort of the American Medical Association of home inspectors. Beyond that, ask a few questions about just what the inspector plans to do. Mediocre inspectors will simply run through a checklist as they go through your home. For the $300 or so you're going to be paying, you deserve more. Rather than a routine checklist, insist on a detailed report listing specific major problems and specific recommendations for repairing them. Look for someone who has long experience as an inspector—five years or longer—or who worked as a contractor and knows the field well.

Most important of all, make sure you accompany the inspector on his tour. You'll not only be able to check the caliber of the inspector's work, you'll learn a great deal about the condition of your home.

than fifty years old, some sort of tilt is probably inevitable. But on a house younger than that, and certainly on one under twenty years old, this is a sign that you've got major structural problems under way.

While you're looking outside, make sure you take your eyes off the house and look at what surrounds it. I don't care about the landscaping, the views, or the neighbor's antique satellite dish that's visible from the backyard. But I do care about the grading in the yard. If the house lies at the bottom of a hill, for instance, everything from that slope could be draining into the basement. Look for signs that water has been puddling or pooling, which can also add to leaks. I also care about the pitch and slope of the driveway, patio, and sidewalk. They should be pitched slightly away from the house so that water drains away from the foundation. Fill up a bucket of water and dump it on them to check for yourself. If the water doesn't run away from the house, that means it's running toward the foundation and can contribute to basement dampness.

Now I focus on the details. I look at the roof shingles (for which a pair of binoculars is handy) and check for any missing or broken shingles, which can lead to leaks. I look at the gutters around the house, to make sure none of them are clogged and overflowing, and that the downspouts drain water away from the house rather than pouring it alongside the foundation. The best way to accomplish this is to check their performance in the pouring rain, since everything seems to be shipshape in dry weather.

I walk around to look at the siding, to make sure that any trees or landscaping planted close to the house isn't brushing against it. This can severly damage the siding and roofing, even in the gentlest of winds. Sometimes it's possible to save an overgrown tree or shrub with some careful pruning. But in other cases—such as if that little spruce tree you planted two feet from the foundation now resembles something closer to a giant sequoia—your only choice is to remove it. Next, I check the windows, especially the surrounding edge where they meet the exterior of the home. Whether the house has brick, stucco, or wood siding, this gap around the windows has to be filled with caulk. If the caulk is missing or deteriorated, cold air—as well as moisture—may be infiltrating inside.

From the Bottom Up

Next, it's straight to the basement. Structural problems upstairs can often be camouflaged with paint and décor. But this is not the case in the basement, where any dampness or decay literally assaults your nose upon entering. In fact, I start by taking a good sniff of air. I don't expect it to smell like a bowl of narcissus. It is, after all, a basement. But I do expect it to smell free

How to Shop for a New Home

Congratulations: You've found the home of your dreams.

It's in the perfect neighborhood, with the right number of bedrooms and bath-rooms—and nothing has ever looked so appealing. But before you sign the sales contract, take a step back to make sure you're falling in love for the right reasons. Buying a home can be an astonishingly emotional proposition as well as an astonishingly risky one. Hidden rot and dangerously antiquated systems can turn a routine real-estate excursion into a budget-busting disaster. To make sure you know what you're getting into from the beginning, take your own inves-tigative tour.

To begin, stand in the front yard and look at the exterior of your would-be home. Does it stand straight and tall, with a strong horizontal line along the roof? Or does it sag like a hammock? Look up close to where the house meets the foundation on all four sides. This should be rot-free; any signs of trouble here could signal the need for extensive structural work. Take a look at the drive-way, the sidewalks, and the landscaping. Does everything pitch away from the house, which provides proper drainage of rainwater? Or does it slant toward the foundation, which is an invitation to flooding?

Now enter the house. Begin with the front door and ask yourself how it feels. The handle should be secure, not tinny; the door should close with a sturdy thud, rather than feeling like plywood. Continue this tactile exploration inside. Do the doors feel soundproof or hollow? Does the banister on the staircase seem sturdy, or does it wiggle when you grab hold of it? Go into the kitchen and open and close every cabinet door and drawer. They should close squarely, and the drawers should glide smoothly.

Remember, décor is not the issue here, since you'll probably want to change it anyway. What you want to examine is the structure of the house underneath—which, after all, is really what makes a house feel durable and comfortable. Turn on the faucets to check if the water pressure is adequate, and take a close look at all the fixtures. Whether they're new or not, they should be in tip-top order. In the bathrooms, press the tiled walls in shower or tub areas with your hands. Do they move? If they do, there is inevitably rot beneath the walls, which could involve huge repairs. Next, head to the basement and take a long, deep breath. Things should smell fresh, not like mildew—which would be a sure sign of dampness.

Now comes the hard part. After you've looked at everything, rate the house on a scale of 1 to 10. If you don't give it at least a 7, keep hunting. Ultimately, you'll still need to hire a professional inspector when you find a place that passes the test, but you'll have earned something no inspector can give you—the confidence that comes from knowing your decision is being guided by practicality.

And that, more than anything, is what produces happy homeowners.

of mold and mildew. With a flashlight, I take an up-close look at the foundation walls. Are they crumbling and flaking? Is there a whitish powder all over them, formed by a process called efflorescence? These are signs that moisture is soaking through the walls—and a hint of bigger trouble to come. I also like to tap with a hammer on some of the structural beams and floor joists in the ceiling. The hammer should make a solid thunk. If the wood sounds hollow or, worse, is soft and easily dented by the hammer, this could be a sign of rot or insect damage. Especially troublesome would be to find little openings and channels in the wood—a sure sign of termites.

Unglamorous as it may be, I take a look at the mechanical systems down here. What's the age of the furnace, and what is the age of the water heater? These typically have the manufacturing dates stamped somewhere on the outer cover, so you don't have to guess. If you have a furnace that's more than twenty years old, it's time for a new one. I don't care how well tuned up it is; the efficiency level simply can't compete with that of a newer model. The same is true of a water heater, but after only ten years. With furnaces and water heaters older than this, you're lucky if you get 50 percent efficiency, which, as I've said, means that 50 cents out of every dollar is going to waste. It doesn't take an accountant to show the money that you can save by buying new ones.

At last, I head to the first floor. As I walk around, I continue to use all of my senses—not just my eyesight. I begin by walking across the floor. Does it creak excessively, which could signify structural problems with the subfloor? Head to the staircase and tug on the banister. Is it snug, or does it wiggle? I walk around opening and closing the doors—both the front door and closet doors, and doors to the rooms—to see how they operate. If they function smoothly and close with a solid sound, I'm happy. If they're warped or hollow-sounding, or if they feel thin, I'm not. I take a look at the frame around the door as well. It should have square corners, close to perfect 90-degree angles that would make Pythagoras proud. If there's any shifting, or if the doors have been cut in weird shapes by previous homeowners, it shows that the house is leaning and

When to Run Away

How many times have you heard a real estate agent say that a home "just needs a little TLC"? Sometimes it's the truth—and the work you put in can save you a pile of money. But sometimes it can end up costing you a pile of money because the problems go way beyond cosmetic. Unless you're an experienced home renovator or have the budget to hire one, don't even think about buying a place that shows any one of these obvious signs of distress.

● *Crumbled or bowed foundation walls.* This is a sure sign that the foundation is ready to cave in. No foundation, no house. Get the picture? The remedy involves jacking the house up, excavating a new foundation, then setting it down again. This is not something you can tackle on weekends.

● *Excessive mold, mildew, or standing water in the basement.* Slight water problems in the basement can be managed with sump pumps and dehumidifiers. But chronic seepage and dampness is a different matter. If you can smell or see the trouble, you're looking at a maddening fix that could cost many thousands of dollars to pinpoint and fix. Better look elsewhere.

● *The walls list by 3 inches or more from top to bottom.* A slight tilt in an exterior wall can be okay, but anything more than 3 inches indicates major structural issues that require massive amounts of work. Unless George Washington slept there and you can apply for a grant for a historical renovation, don't sign the contract.

● *The electrical system contains old knob-and-tube wiring.* Uh-oh. This is positively the worst thing you can find. I wouldn't even recommend plugging in a lamp with this type of antiquated, deteriorated arrangement. It's a fire waiting to happen. Either look for a different home or spend the $10,000 or more you'll need to replace it *before* you move in.

● *Decayed or broken rafters visible when you climb into the attic.* This signifies a massive amount of rot, probably from a leaky roof. Fixing it requires ripping the top half of the house down, rebuilding the rafters, and constructing a new roof. Does this sound cheap?

Looking for Trouble

Friends of mine built a new home, but when they moved in and turned on the faucet in one of the bathrooms, nothing came out. The plumber forgot to connect it, and the building inspector working for the local government didn't take much notice either. Not everything can be perfect with a new home or a major renovation, to be sure; a house is, after all, a truly handmade object. Yet whether you spend $150,000 or $500,000 on construction, I believe you're entitled to a new house or addition that's well built—and the best way to get that is by hiring a private building inspector to follow the process for you.

We've become accustomed to building inspectors as civil servants, people who work for a city or town and make whirlwind visits to construction sites to see that everything's in order. Many homeowners think this will also guarantee them a good house—but public building inspectors only check to make sure that the house conforms to the building code. They don't pay any attention at all to how neatly or well it's being built. To protect yourself, you need to hire an additional inspector who reports to you—and keeps you informed of how he thinks the construction is going.

The most effective way to use a private inspector is to involve one at the beginning of the building process. Ideally, I'd have your inspector make five or six different visits. The first would come at the time of the excavation for the foundation. He'd make sure the footings that actually hold the house up are set

sagging. This might just add to a home's charm. Then again, it might be a sign of major structural decay lurking just beneath the walls. As you're walking through the house, pay attention to the walls and ceiling as well—again, not their color or whether the wallpaper looks nice. Notice instead the condition of the actual drywall and plaster. Does it appear to be solid, or do you notice a large number of cracks? Cracks may not mean there are structural issues, but smooth walls go a long way toward the overall look and feel of a home in good repair.

on solid soil and that the foundation, whether cement or masonry, is reinforced with steel bars. Have the inspector come back again during the framing to make sure that the walls are straight and all the corners built at 90-degree angles. Carpenters blast through a house so fast these days, I don't think most of them even remember what a level is—or if they do, they never use it. Your own inspector can catch these mistakes, and you can request that your builder have them fixed. You'll need to schedule a third visit for the inspector to look at the mechanical systems—plumbing, wiring, and heating.

Most important of all, schedule an inspection just before the drywall goes up. I can't tell you how many sins of carpentry have been cleverly concealed by walls and ceilings. Taking a look at this stage, an inspector can check to make sure everything is well insulated, which will add to your comfort and cut down on your heating and cooling bills. After that comes the final inspection—to make sure the finish coat of paint looks great, the carpeting is installed correctly, and the finished floors and tiling are done correctly.

Paying for an inspector is pricey, especially to homeowners on a budget. A single visit might run you between $175 to $300; expect to pay $1,000 to $1,500 over the course of the project. Yet while that may seem like a lot of money, trust me: You'll appreciate moving into a home that works—every time you turn on the faucet.

Now it's time for the kitchen. Test out the cabinet doors and drawers to see if they operate smoothly and without sticking. Then take a deep sniff inside the cabinets. Any mildew here could be a sign that the kitchen plumbing is leaking and water is being trapped behind the cabinets. Pay special attention to the cabinet beneath the sink. Any dampness here is a sure sign of leakage, which can cause major structural damage in a short period. Feel the P-trap with your hand to detect any moisture beading on it, and look for signs of corrosion in the chrome, which also points to a small leak. If you find it, you may need to replace the pipes. Make sure faucets, soap dispensers, and any kind of accoutrements in the kitchen operate well. Check to make sure the exhaust hood works, and then stick your head as far as you can into it to see if there's a buildup of grease or grime, which can be a fire hazard during cooking.

Bathrooms and Beyond

Next, I look for the bathrooms, and here I make an inspection similar to what I did in the kitchen—especially checking for dampness under the sink. In the bathroom, I also pay particular attention to the corners of the walls and ceilings. If you have poor ventilation in the bathroom, moisture accumulates—and this is where it will show up. If you see brown patchy areas, you've got something to worry about that can't be painted away.

In the bathroom, I also test the toilet. You need to actually sit on the toilet (with the lid down) and rock back and forth, to make sure it's attached tightly to the floor. If it wiggles and rocks, it means the bolts holding the toilet in place have pulled loose from the floor. Usually, this means there's been a leak and that the subfloor and other structural members have begun to decay. I then check the water supply line for leaks. In the bathroom, it's hard to tell the difference between condensation and leaks, so I do a simple test. I take tissues and wipe the supply line clean. Then I wrap a dry tissue around the supply line for a while. Even the slightest moisture will get picked up by that paper and will tell me if there's a leak.

Because this is a room that is regularly doused with water, you have to pay special attention to the tile walls. Check the grout lines of both the floors and walls to make sure they're solid, with no cracks in them to allow water to leak through. Look to see that sinks, showers, and tubs are properly caulked in place to seal water leakage. If the caulk looks gloppy and covered with mold or mildew, you'll definitely want to replace this. It might not affect the structure of the home, but who wants to jump in the bath or shower every morning and look at that?

Now, head to the bedrooms. There's little that can go wrong in a bedroom in terms of overall systems of a house. Instead, you're paying more attention to simple things—like whether the doors open and close properly, and the overall look and feel of the walls and the closet doors. Here, and elsewhere around the house, check that the light switches function properly and that there are an adequate number of outlets in a room. According to electrical codes, there is supposed to be one outlet every 6 feet along the wall. If you have fewer than this, you run the risk of overloading circuits as you plug in lamps, fish tank filters, radios, and air conditioners. Before you know it, you've turned the room into a lair for the extension cord octopus. Instead of running another extension cord, hire an electrician to run an additional receptacle or two. It's a smart—and safe—investment.

To the Top

When I'm finished looking around in the living areas of a home, I head up to the attic. Whether it's finished or unfinished, accessible by a staircase or a pull-down ladder, the attic can tell you a great deal about the health of your home. The first thing you're trying to find out is if you have adequate insulation for the region where you live. But even more important, you're trying to find out if the space is properly ventilated. Look for a continuous ridge vent, gable vents with fans, or mushroom-type vents protruding through the roof every 10 feet. Check the underside of the sheathing just beneath a roof with a flashlight. Do you notice any moisture here, or are there any blackish areas where mildew or fungus have been able to sprout?

If there's a brick chimney that runs up through the attic, take a close look at it for signs of flaking or other deterioration. This can be a sign of leaks due to poor flashing, and can damage not just the chimney but the wood structure around it. Here and elsewhere around the house, take a look to see if the previous owners did anything funky, especially with wiring. Sometimes I'll find fixtures connecting to the rooms below that have so many strange wires popping out of them, they look like spaghetti. This can be a real mess, and a real fire hazard as well. If you find old knob-and-tube wiring—an antiquated system that I describe in Chapter 3—which is most visible in the attic—call an electrician at once. Take a look also at how the exhaust fans in the bathrooms and kitchen are vented. They should be routed through pipes that connect directly outside and should never vent directly into the attic space. That can create huge moisture problems in the wintertime.

Choosing Your Priorities

Many of us have things in our home that we've always wanted to get around to—and then five years later we still haven't done them. Probably the best way to manage this is to create a list of different projects that you organize during your sixty-minute inspection.

To start, break projects into different groupings. There can be a list of things that you can accomplish for under $100, another list of things that will cost under $500, and then a list of major projects for which there is no limit. To begin, take care of the obvious structural problems first. Leaks in the basement or roof, any rotten structure, and decayed windows—these things have to be addressed first. Ignore these for another year and you'll only end up with a more extreme version of the same problem. But then comes the difficult task of choosing what else to do. Here, you have to make a list of your priorities. If the tile wall in the shower is squishy, you need to replace it. But rather than spending $25,000 on a entire bathroom overhaul, maybe you can get by with the new shower surround—and maybe spend a few hundred dollars on a paint job and new towel bars.

This sort of list works whether you live in a home or an apartment, or whether your place is brand-new or a hundred years old. Home owner-ship, after all, isn't only about the amount of money you paid for a place. It's also about the amount of money you put into it. Not all of us can afford to buy a house that's done exactly the way we want before we move in. For most of us, a home becomes a work in progress—one that needs to strike a balance between maintenance and improvements.

Conducting your own clear-eyed inspection and setting a list of prior-ities for your home renovations projects is the only sure way to guaran-tee that your home doesn't become a money pit.

chapter SIXTEEN

A Homeowner's Survival Guide

Stress, anyone? Here's how to handle contractors, finances, and the chaos of home improvement

My wife and I bought and renovated our first home in 1990, and to say that we did so on a shoestring budget would be an insult to shoestrings. After the closing, the bankers handed us a check for all of $43, which represented the interest on the money they held as a down payment. To celebrate, we went out to a local burger-and-pie joint for lunch—leaving with our entire life savings, then about $19 and change, in my pocket.

Fortunately, I was rich with the sort of can-do optimism displayed only by first-time home buyers. I knew that we could turn my home into a palace, with some help from my friends. As it stood, however, the place represented the ultimate handyman's special. In terms of style, it had none other than, perhaps, its color. The outside was dark brown, with an even darker brown trim. The inside was covered with dark paneling from the 1960s (was it brown? I couldn't really tell). We called it the House of Brown. With nine days to go before we had to leave our apartment, I assured my wife that I could freshen everything up—including pulling all that paneling off to expose what I was sure were solid plaster walls beneath it.

After taking possession of our house that evening at 7 P.M., we were joined by some friends who brought champagne. I explained my plans and, as we passed the bottle around, my friend Dave said, "Why wait? Why not get started now?" Fortified by Korbel, that Budweiser of champagnes, I heartily agreed and went out to grab my crowbar from the back of my pickup. I tore into a piece of paneling in the dining room, and down it came—along with the entire wall of plaster behind it. "My God!" cried my wife as the dust swirled and settled revealing only the bare structure of the wall. "What did you do?" "Well, there's no point stopping here," Dave said, and we quickly brought the party to a halt and worked until 2 a.m. ripping off all the paneling and plaster downstairs. We had owned the house for just five hours and already it had depreciated in value!

Home ownership, as I quickly discovered, is an act of faith—and not just for those with do-it-yourself ambitions. Even if you're not planning a big renovation, all of us struggle with finances, the boredom of maintenance projects, and the often wild chasm that exists between the image we have of what we would like our home to be and the often bleaker reality. At times it's enough to make you want to erect a teepee and move to the backyard. Anyone who imagines that owning real estate will grant them some sort of life of leisure is in for some bitter disappointment. Yet at the same time, few things in life can be more rewarding—especially if you approach your home with an eye toward the long term. You'll be buoyed by the knowledge that the improvements you make, however small they may seem, will add value when it comes time to sell. And unlike pouring your money into mutual funds with vague plans of cashing them in someday, you'll benefit from an investment in your home because you'll be able to live with the changes you've made every day. Even so, the stress of renovations, finances, and working with contractors can sometimes be overwhelming. Let me conclude our introduction to your house by suggesting some ways to manage it all—in short, to maintain the dream within your dream home.

A Question of Character

The ancient Greeks had a rule to govern people's behavior: "Know thyself." It was a straightforward command to help separate the mortals from the gods. And the same thing can apply today with home renovation. There are those who have no stomach for it whatsoever (let's call them mortals), and there are those who actually thrive on it (let's call them relatives of mine).

To put this rule to work, take an honest look at your character—or, more important if you're married, your *spouse's* character—and ask what sort of project you can reasonably tolerate. Simply stated, big home renovations can make a mess of our lives. As much as we dream about our plans, and as much as we feel we're organized, this is one of the most difficult projects for a family to live through—especially a family with children. Everyone has a different threshold of what they can withstand, and it's essential to get a sense of this before committing yourself to buying a home or apartment that needs major work.

My friend Mike, for instance, is an extremely talented builder. A decade ago, I helped him build the house where he now lives. His family has grown since then to include three children, and what he could really use is an extra bedroom—similar to one that I happened to be adding on to my own house. Mike could have done the same, but when he brought his wife over one night to take a look she focused more on the havoc that the process had created. The living room had been turned into a workshop, with sawhorses everywhere. Plastic buckets filled with plaster and debris lined the hallway. Halogen work lights glowed in the yard, making the whole thing look something like a crime scene. "This will be beautiful," Mike's wife said, brushing dust from her pants. "But I just know I could never live through it."

She will never have to, either, because the mess would present too great an obstacle to their daily lives. Instead, when they need a larger house, Mike will build an entirely new one. There's nothing wrong with this, either; in fact, I applaud them for choosing the approach that suits them best. The point is that by realistically assessing who you are, you can steer yourself clear of domestic trouble. A renovated house can be a beautiful thing—but only if you're still living together when it's done.

In addition to trying to take on renovation projects they're not suited for, many homeowners sometimes make a mistake by trying to do complicated work themselves. In principle, I think this is a great thing to do. It's satisfying to take care of your own home—which I know firsthand— and it can save you money. But, it can also lead to a Pandora's box of troubles if you have no training for the task you're doing. Trying to sand a hardwood floor without ever having done it before is an invitation to disaster. And I've seen more than one botched tiling job, obviously the product of people who, on a whim, woke up one morning and imagined themselves as tile setters.

Working on a home requires skill and craftsmanship. If you've got it, terrific. If you don't, then pay someone for it. If you're still determined to take on the work yourself, at least take time to get the training you'll need. Find how-to books and videos in the library, or take courses at a community college. Or volunteer for an organization like Habitat for Humanity; not only do you get training from their team leaders, but you get the satisfaction of helping a family in need. Most important, get some practice before, say, hacking into your roof with a reciprocating saw to add that living room skylight. This may sound obvious, but I can't tell you the amount of damage I've seen perpetrated by homeowners who should know better. One otherwise clever person I know, for

instance, decided to install a set of windows in his living room. His carpentry was flawless, but there was one little problem: He forgot to add headers, which are the structural beams needed to carry the weight of the wall above. He couldn't understand why the windows kept cracking until I reminded him of this essential element he had somehow overlooked.

When it came time to rip the windows out and reinstall them, with headers in place, he decided to leave the job to me.

Meet the Contractor

When you're hiring a general contractor for a major project, you're doing more than just paying a professional to do their job. You're also inviting into your home someone who will inevitably become an intimate member of the household for the duration of the work.

For one thing, contractors tend to show up early—like at about 7 A.M., when everyone is running around with wet hair and bathrobes. Not everyone is prepared for this sort of intrusion, of course. I worked with one couple who had young children and found themselves constantly behind schedule every morning. Each time I showed up, I knew just what my first job would be. It wasn't plugging in my circular saw or hauling out the sawhorses. Instead, I would drive their three children to school so Mom and Dad could get to work. I'm not saying you should look for a contractor who can be both a friend and a nanny. But I am saying that you need to be very selective in order to make sure you find people you can trust—and be willing to pay for them.

Many people try to take a cost-cutting approach when they have work done on their homes, and this is all wrong. Some try to do it by being their own contractor—knowing that between 15 and 20 percent of the construction price goes to the general contractor for profit and overhead. If they do this without having had any experience in it, however, they're in for a great deal of trouble. If it were easy to be a contractor, after all, then that's all anyone would want to be; there would be no more lawyers or accountants or bakers or grocers. But this job is a difficult

How to Hire a Contractor

Think of a renovation project as the equivalent of surgery on your home. You wouldn't trust your body to a surgeon you happened to find in the yellow pages; why should you be any less rigorous in choosing a contractor? Here are a few steps to guide you through the process:

● *Get recommendations.* Start with your friends and family and then check in with the National Association of the Remodeling Industry for a list of members in your area. You could also talk with your local building inspector, who will surely have an opinion about the quality of local contractors—especially those who routinely meet building code requirements.

● *Make phone calls.* First, ask your prospective contractors if they would be willing to take on a project of the size you're proposing. It may be too small—or too big—for some. Ask if they'll provide references for work they've done.

● *Meet in person.* Based on the phone interviews, pick three or four contractors to meet for further discussion. Good contractors should be able to answer your questions in a way that puts you at ease. Personality is crucial here. If they make you bristle during this meeting, things are only going to worsen.

● *Check references.* It's nice they've supplied references. Now contact the references and arrange to meet them *in person*. Take a firsthand look at the work that

one. It requires you to be part visionary, part diplomat, part drill sergeant, and 100 percent energetic, even after an exhausting day spent raising roof trusses. The key difficulty is to find good workers called subcontractors—such as electricians, plumbers, and carpenters—then coax them to show up when they're supposed to. As things proceed, this turns into an incredibly intricate dance of timing and budgeting, and it is why being a contractor is such a challenge.

Beyond making things run smoothly, good contractors can also save you money as well. That roster of subcontractors they work with often was done and see if you like it. Then ask the homeowners how the projects went. Did the contractors show up on time? Did they disappear for days and weeks? Was work completed on schedule? Also, visit a current job site to make sure that it's being run neatly and safely.

● *Take bids.* A good contractor will want a complete set of blueprints, as well as a sense of what homeowners expect out of the project. To compare bids, ask everyone to break down the cost of materials, labor, profit margins, and other expenses. Generally, materials account for 40 percent of the total cost; the rest covers overhead and the typical profit margin, which is 15 to 20 percent. Be prepared to spend a lot to get good work, especially if you're choosing a contractor with whom you can communicate well.

● *Be prepared to wait.* Good contractors usually aren't sitting by the phone eager for your call. If you've found someone you think you can trust but who won't be available to start work on your project for six months, it's far better to wait than to turn to someone less qualified.

Finally, put in writing whatever agreement you make regarding fees and a schedule of payments. This isn't a sign of mistrust between you and the contractor. Just the opposite—it's the foundation on which a good working relationship can stand.

offer their services at a discounted rate in return for steady work. If you were to go out and hire an electrician for a day to upgrade your wiring, for instance, you might end up paying $100 per hour. If I were to hire that same contractor, one who has worked with me every few weeks for the last decade, I might only have to pay him $75. The same is true with hardware stores, lumberyards, and other suppliers. Individual homeowners end up either paying retail rates or getting a slight discount if they open an account with the store. Major contractors can negotiate much bigger cuts—as much as 40 percent or even

The Ideal Homeowner

Everyone has a clear picture of the ideal contractor—someone who shows up on time, finishes on time and on budget, does great work, and keeps everything neat and tidy. But let's take a look at this from the contractor's view. Who are the ideal homeowners? Surprisingly, they're not necessarily the ones who serve coffee and doughnuts (although this surely helps).

To me, the best clients are those who have realistic expectations about what they're embarking on. Because as much as they think they're just beginning a small renovation, work inevitably expands as the project begins. A kitchen overhaul, for instance, can soon become a major interference in a household. The homeowners who manage this best are the ones who have a plan: Who's going to get the children off to school when the workers arrive? Who's going to be available to answer questions over the course of the day? And how are they going to be able to function without the use of a kitchen, a bathroom, or other vital areas of a house? The other thing I look for on the part of homeowners is patience and confidence in me as a contractor. If the electricians don't show up on a Tuesday as they were supposed to, for instance, the homeowners don't get agitated. They understand that the electricians probably had some other emergency and will get to their job as soon as they can.

By being flexible and tolerant, homeowners can create a place where workers look forward to showing up. And that, more than anything, is the best way to guarantee a job well done.

more—because they're steady customers who buy in bulk. What supplier wouldn't want to offer them big price breaks?

Unfortunately, contractors as a profession get only slightly more respect than do lawyers. You'll seldom hear how wonderful they are; you'll often hear people describe how horrible they are. People complain about shoddy workmanship, long delays, and even criminal contractors who abscond with down payments. These sorts of things do indeed happen, but all of this can be avoided if you keep one thing in mind: When you hire a contractor, you are entering into a business transaction with someone and need to arrange it as such. That means coming up with a contract rather than a vague agreement of what work is to be done, setting a timetable and a deadline, and creating a schedule for payments.

Most problems begin for homeowners when they try to have work done at bargain prices. Let's look at it this way—if you were about to have your appendix removed and took the novel approach of bidding the job out to a bunch of surgeons, would you take the lowest bidder? Probably not. And the same is true for work on your home. If you take the lowest bid, the least experienced contractor, or the person with no references, you become a coconspirator when the project goes awry. Instead, be prepared to pay for high-quality services, which means you should focus on the middle or in some case even the highest bids.

Good contractors can do just about anything for you—but they cannot manage your money. This remains your chief responsibility, yet it is where most mistakes are made. If there is one guiding principle here, it is this: Don't pay for work until it is completed to your satisfaction. Not ever. Sometimes, contractors will ask homeowners to give them a lump sum payment at the start of the project in order to get started. This is common on smaller jobs with contractors just starting in the business. While it seems like it might be reasonable, I have seen this arrangement unravel too many times to trust it. You pay someone $3,000 to buy supplies, and then he disappears. Where does this leave you? Nowhere. Think of it another way. When you go to the grocery store, you pay at the checkout line once you have the groceries in your basket. You don't pay the week before. It's a cash-on-delivery basis. The same is true with reputable contractors.

On small projects, this means you pay when everything is finished. On larger projects, it means you set up a schedule of payments pegged to the completion of certain stages of work—usually upon completion of the excavation, the framing, the drywall, and then the entire project. This way, subcontractors and suppliers are never kept waiting more than thirty days for their money. If the contractor asks for a small deposit of, say, 5 percent to make sure you're sincere about following through with your plans—well, okay. But if the person asks you for a third up front, you say no. Then you find another contractor.

The worst thing that can happen when paying a contractor, of course, is that he uses your money to complete other jobs that have already been started—the "borrow from Peter to pay Paul" principle. Or, more accurately, the "steal from Peter to pay Paul" principle. (You're Peter, by the way, and never Paul.) The way to protect yourself from this is by agreeing in writing at the outset of the project to a specified payment schedule. Then you will have nothing to worry about. As things are finished and you're content with the work, you pay. If the work is not completed at any stage or if it's not satisfactory, you don't. And you won't be out any money because you haven't *paid* any money.

This is a basic fundamental of business, but I am continually amazed at how many people I run into who have forgotten it—including one guy who was the CEO of a big company. He called me a few years ago, after a kitchen renovation and addition turned into a financial fiasco. He had hired a contractor who bid $200,000 for the job, but before the guy started work he demanded a sixth of that up front—rounded off to a cool $30,000. The contractor said he needed the money to order cabinets and supplies and, amazingly, the homeowner paid him. Then he asked for a second $30,000 to get the project moving. And, again, the homeowner paid him. The contractor actually did order some supplies and even

Lien On Me

Major renovation and building projects involve a simple equation among homeowners, contractors, and subcontractors. Specifically, the homeowners pay the contractors, and the contractors then pay the subcontractors. Or at least they *should*. If contractors suddenly find themselves with financial problems, they may fail to make those payments—and in turn you may find the subcontractors attaching liens to your property and demanding payment.

One smart way to protect yourself is to have proof that the subcontractors are being paid. The easiest way to do this is by asking your contractor to supply you with copies of what are called lien waivers. When the subs are paid, they fill out these waivers, which signify that they've been paid in full for their work and will not hold you, the homeowner, legally responsible for anything further. Seeing copies of the lien waivers is just another way to double-check that workers are being paid as work progresses during a lengthy project. Similarly, you should request to see copies of receipts for purchases such as windows, doors, cabinets, and supplies. This way, you'll know that the money you're handing over to the contractor is going where it's supposed to go.

Make your request for the lien waivers and receipts known at the start of the project—before you sign anything. If the contractor balks, there's only one thing to do: Find another contractor.

showed up for a few days here and there to rip things apart. But then he disappeared. "He seemed like a nice guy," said the homeowner, who ultimately lost about half of that $60,000 and had to take legal action to try to recoup the rest.

What I don't understand is why people would be so trusting with their money, particularly with someone whose only real qualification is that he's a "nice guy." Haven't we all seen Alfred Hitchcock movies? On one level, your relationship with a contractor has to be personal. This is wonderful. But it is, above anything else, a business relationship. The sooner you start conducting it like one, the better. Insist on a schedule for work and payments in writing. Keep in mind that costs do tend to vary, especially in old houses. That simple plumbing job, for example, can expose a deteriorated system that needs replacement. You have to pay for that. Whatever cost overruns there are, make sure you find out about them as they occur. Make sure the contractor asks your approval for any unbudgeted expenses and gives you a weekly accounting of any cost overruns. You sure don't want this to come as a surprise at the end of the project.

Creating a Safe Haven

A major home renovation can become an all-encompassing affair. With a few whacks of a crowbar, a home can quickly turn into a flurry of dust and noise, one in which not a single square inch can escape the intrusion. If this were to last just a week or so, it would be bearable. But big projects can drag on for months or even a year. What could be more stressful than this? To counteract this, my wife and I have developed the concept of what we call a "safe haven" when renovating. It is a portion of the house that remains untouched so that you can continue your daily life while the work swirls around.

When my wife became pregnant with our first child, it became clear that we would need an extra bedroom on the second floor. Simple enough. But this project involved ripping off the front of the house, the back of the house, and the roof to boot. It looked as if a tornado had hit, and my neighbors seriously wondered whether we were tearing the place down rather than fixing it up. Even as I banged around in the night, however, my wife didn't have to suffer (relatively speaking). That's because I left our upstairs bedroom perfectly intact. I put a little mat outside the door where I would take off my boots, and I would open up the beautifully trimmed six-panel door and move from a scene of destruction to one of absolute serenity. There would be my wife, resting on the bed in a room where everything was in place. It was a little like Dorothy stepping from black and white out

A Graceful Exit

Despite the best planning, your relationship with a contractor can sometimes sour to the point that things become unworkable. In short, you want a divorce. But how do you stop work and break the contract without creating an even bigger mess? The worst thing you can do in a case like this is to suddenly call a halt to the work and toss the contractor out. While it might solve the immediate problem, it will leave you with a half-finished project that will be difficult for someone else to step in and finish. Talk about chaos! Instead, there are natural milestones in building, whether that is completing a foundation, finishing the framing, or installing the drywall. Make it clear to the contractor that the relationship isn't working out, then tell him to stop work once the next milestone has been reached. Pay the contractor for the work he's done, then send him on his way. With the work completed up to a logical stage, the next contractor will have a much easier time knowing where to begin.

into the Technicolor of Munchkinland. My wife worked in an office at the time and still managed to leave in the morning looking rested and beautifully dressed—as if nothing in particular were going on inside our house. We were living through a nightmare, I suppose. But it was *our* nightmare, and we were very pleased with it.

The key to making a renovation manageable is the safe haven. If you're doing a kitchen, for instance, you have to set up a temporary kitchen somewhere—even if it's in the garage. You can't pretend you're going to be happy having to eat out for every meal, including breakfast. If you're renovating a bathroom, make sure that you have another one perfectly in order so that your household can function normally. If you're redoing the whole downstairs, you might want to think about turning an upstairs bedroom into a temporary family room, complete with a TV and a couch. These spaces, makeshift as they may be, are crucial to surviving this process.

Dollars and Sense

The stress of living with a renovation is one thing; the stress of paying for it is quite another. We all tend to be wildly unrealistic about the costs of construction work. Part of this is because we're hoping for bargains; another part is the fact that we can't predict what underlying difficulties might spring up, especially in an older house. Then there's the desire to add things as we go along, such as an extra set of windows in the living room or some handmade tiles around the fireplace. I've never met anyone who went through a big renovation and said, "Oh, and it came in under what we wanted to spend." Even if you're determined to stick to a tight budget, you will most likely end up having to scrimp on materials or labor to make ends meet. This is hardly an intelligent option. Instead, I always recommend accepting reality: You will absolutely spend more than you planned. Therefore, budget an extra 15 to 20 percent to cover these costs at the outset. Creating this cushion—even if it means scaling down your plans to accommodate it—will make you immune to financial shock. Now, what could be more stress-reducing than that?

A Home to Treasure

Despite the odds, the ordeal of my first house, which I told you about at the start of this chapter, had a happy ending. After working at my business all day, I would head straight to the new home to load up Dumpsters with broken chunks of plaster, string electrical cable through the walls, and ultimately rush to patch everything back together. I even sanded the wood floors myself—a first for me. Fueled by Pepsi and Ho-Hos, I'd work until about three or four in the morning, head back to my apartment, shower, crawl into bed, and pop back up at six. My wife and I moved in nine days later as scheduled, to a home that looked renewed and livable.

What were the rewards for all these efforts? For one thing, we now owned a place that was worth a lot more than what we spent on it. Yet there was also something deeper that came with the experience. We

A Little Help from Some Friends

Working alone on your own home renovation project can be a tedious, lengthy affair. Inevitably, the tasks take far longer than you ever could have expected, and the strain of squeezing all that work into the few hours you have available on weekends and after work can leave you exhausted. If you want to make the time pass with greater happiness, do what I often do—invite a few friends over to help.

The addition to my first house, especially, turned into a sort of Amish barn raising. As my wife kept the chuck wagon going with sandwiches and sodas, my friends and I raised the roof and added the framing for a new bedroom in one weekend. Between breaks, we sat in the yard on piles of rubble, eating sandwiches and telling stories. As an experience, it was amazing, and one we get nostalgic about to this day. When my friends had similar projects of their own, of course, my wife and I eagerly rushed over to help them.

Besides the low cost, one of the nice things about having friends work with you on your home is that you have a greater appreciation for the occasional imperfection they may leave behind. My friend Mike, for instance, painted our bedroom ceiling, but forgot to touch up around the ceiling fan one late night. At first I was going to fix it, but then I decided to leave it just as it was. After all, this was sort of Mike's signature up there, a memento of the time when our friends pulled together and helped us settle into our new home.

found ourselves truly at home—living in a place that we had grown to love, one that was filled with our work, our memories, and our hopes for the future. This, I believe, can become true of any home. Whether new or old, in move-in condition or facing a brush with the bulldozer, a house is a wonder. It represents the ultimate handmade object, full of imperfections but charming in part *because* of those imperfections. This is not some car churned out in a factory, where the paint job is sprayed on by a robot. Instead, it has a soul of its own. Buying a house, I learned, represents not so much an acquisition as a commitment—to care for it, understand it, and lead it through whatever crises the seasons may bring.

The sooner you accept this, the sooner home ownership can become a joy. You'll be able to attune yourself to the steady pulse of your home, and know just what it takes to keep it alive.

Tooling Around

A small collection of easy-to-use tools is all you'll need to master the basics of home repair

An acquaintance of mine loves tools—not so much as useful items to help him with home repair, but more as a collection to show off in his basement workshop. On a tour recently, I noticed he had a $500 radial arm saw. Now, even *I* don't own a radial arm saw, and I work on home building and renovation every day. You might use one if you were a carpenter working on dozens of houses at the same time and needed to cut hundreds of pieces of wood to exactly the same length. But it's way more than what you need to, say, trim a little piece of molding to replace a piece that's missing or broken. Talk about killing a fly with a sledgehammer. "Why on earth do you own this?" I finally asked him point-blank. "Well," he said, "it was on sale." And had he ever used it? Of course not.

Tools are this way with some people. With the same justification that spurred Edmund Hillary up Mount Everest ("Because it was there"), they stock up on scary-sounding tools they'll never use—routers, planers, reciprocating saws, and those boxed sets that contain 177 different wrenches. If you're going into woodworking or planning on rebuilding your car engine, great. But if you're a

essential tools

typical homeowner, you don't need this much stuff at all. Instead, you can tackle most simple repairs with a collection of tools that will fit into a 5-gallon bucket. Here's what's on the short list:

A good screwdriver. You don't need dozens of these. One will do, as long as it's one that can be fitted with a number of different heads, from Phillips to slotted.

An adjustable wrench. One single wrench will all but eliminate the need for those entire sets of socket wrenches and open-ended wrenches.

Three types of pliers. Often sold as a set, this would include an ordinary pair of pliers, a pair of needle-nose pliers, which are great for grasping hold of things in tight places, and a pair of wire cutters, which can be useful around the house even if you're not doing electrical work.

A set of Allen wrenches. These are more like screwdrivers, which are used to tighten bolts that have six-sided holes in the tops of them instead of ordinary slots. They're essential if you're going to remove a doorknob, among other things. Look for the kind that has wrenches of different sizes that fold in place like the blades of a pocketknife.

A level. This will help you make sure that pictures, shelves, or curtain rods are straight when you hang them. Choose between a 2-foot long standard level and a compact "torpedo" variety about 6 inches long.

A tape measure. Great for measuring furniture, rugs, window heights, and so on. Some of them even have a tiny tape recorder in them, so you can call out the measurements instead of writing them down (is this luxury or what?).

A stud finder. This will cost about $10 and makes a beep when it locates a structural board behind the wall so that you can be sure you're nailing pictures into something solid.

A good hammer. Buy a 16-ounce claw hammer—rather than a dinky little one—which will help you do things like pound in nails to hang pictures or tap a can of paint closed with with ease.

A small handsaw. You do not need to, and should not buy, a power circular saw for small tasks. They're dangerous unless you take the time to learn how to use them correctly. Instead, a small handsaw will do. You can find one with a 12-inch blade that fits in a sheath for safety, like a giant carving knife.

A plunger. Skip the caustic liquid drain openers and buy one of these. It uses pressure and suction to clear clogged drains safely.

A Chisel. Paired with the hammer, this can help you chip out wood to reset a door hinge or adust a sticking latch.

A utility knife. With its retractable, replaceable blade, this makes a useful helpmate on any project—and is a favorite with carpenters for sharpening pencils. It gives them that rustic "I'm a pro" look.

Screws and nails. You don't need to buy these in bulk just yet, but they do come in handy. Look for small packets containing an assortment of each.

Things that stick. A roll of electrical tape, a bottle of carpenter's glue (the yellow stuff, not the white stuff), and a roll of the ever-versatile duct tape will get you through just about any household repair I can imagine.

A cordless drill. *This is the only power tool you will need unless you get into some serious home renovation.* Should I repeat that? You can find a good one for about $30. Look for one that not only drills holes but can be fitted with screwdriver attachments, which will help you do things such as assemble those bookcases you just bought from Ikea. The cordless aspect means you can work with it outside or climb up a ladder without tripping over it.

And that's it. All together, these might add up to $150, which is hardly a budget buster considering the money you'll save in house calls from a carpenter or plumber. After that, the only other thing you'll need is a tool box to hold everything. My favorite, by the way, is one that doubles as a step stool—where you'll be able to sit down and take a break after your new tools have helped you make quick work of your home repair chores.

Nouns (and a Few Verbs) You Should Know

To manage what's going on with your home, it helps to speak the language of maintenance and renovation

As a sixteen-year-old carpenter's apprentice, I remember knowing just about everything in the building trade—or at least acting like I did. So I didn't flinch when my boss sent me on a little errand after I had painstakingly cut some 2-by-4s for him for a job. "Aw, jeez. These came up a little short," he said, with 100 percent sincerity. "Do me a favor and get the lumber stretcher from the back of my truck—you know, the green one with the yellow handle." Hmmm, the lumber stretcher? This was a new one to me. But rather than admitting I had never heard of it, I went to look. After about ten minutes ransacking the place, I finally had to give up and tell my boss I couldn't find it—only to discover him and a big group of his coworkers huddled around, every one of them pointing at me and guffawing.

As a homeowner, no one is likely to stoop so low as to play a joke like this on you. But you'll nonetheless feel the same bewilderment and humiliation if you enter into a discussion about your house with a plumber, electrician, heating and cooling specialist, or any sort of carpenter. Before you know it, they'll be talking about jambs and sills and drain tiles—and you might as well be off scouting for the lumber stretcher yourself. When it comes to your house, ignorance isn't bliss; it's just ignorance. Save yourself the embarrassment, by brushing up on some key words now. This is not an exhaustive list, by any means, nor is it an exhausting one. It simply represents a few dozen of the more familiar terms you'll encounter as you care for your home.

Air duct: Pipes that carry warm air and cold air from the furnace or air-conditioning system to rooms throughout the house, then back again

Amperes (or amps): A unit of electrical volume that tells you how much current a wire can carry; modern homes tend to have 200-amp service, while older homes have 60- or 100-amp service

Antiscald valve: Also known as a pressure-balancing valve, this bathroom safety device detects sudden changes in hot- and cold-water pressure and keeps you from getting scalded in the shower or bath

Awning window: While casement windows open from the side, these crack open from the bottom—and are the only windows that can safely be left open in the rain

Backfill: The gravel or earth bulldozed into place after a foundation has been poured; can also be used as a verb

Beam: One of the main horizontal wooden or steel structural members in a house

Boiler: A system that heats water, which is then pumped throughout the house via pipes connected to radiators

Bridging: Small pieces of wood or metal nailed between floor joists to give them extra stability

Casement window: These windows crank open from the side and catch breezes that flow by a house

Caulking: This flexible and versatile material is squeezed from a tube into gaps between two surfaces; pure silicone caulk is used to form waterproof seals along sink, shower, and tub edges in bathrooms, while paintable latex caulk is used to seal gaps around windows and to cover up cracks between molding and drywall

Circuit breaker: A safety device in an electrical system that calibrates how much electric current is flowing through the wires and shuts the current down if the wires become overheated

Circuit breaker box: The cabinet that holds all the circuit breakers for your home; also called the service panel or electric panel

Compression chamber: A vertical, air-filled pipe in a plumbing system that prevents knocking sounds by absorbing pressure when water is shut off at a faucet or valve

Condensing unit: In a central air-conditioning system, this refers to the noise-making fan positioned outside the house that creates cool air and exhausts heat

Continuous ridge vent: An outlet for air that is installed along the very peak of a roof and runs across its entire length

Crawl space: A shallow, unfinished space up to 4 feet tall underneath a house, which is used to give access to pipes and ducts

Double glazing: An insulating window pane formed by two layers of glass with a sealed air space between them

Double-hung windows: Windows with an upper and lower sash that glide past one another when opened

Drain tile: A pipe buried either inside or outside the perimeter of a house foundation in order to channel water into either a sump pump or sewer system

Drywall: Wallboard made of gypsum that is sandwiched between heavy paper

DWV: An abbreviation for "drain-waste-vent," which lists the principal components of all plumbing systems

Eaves: The overhang at the bottom of a sloping roof

Fascia: A vertical board that runs along the edge of a roof, usually behind a gutter

Ejector pump: A pump that sends wastewater from basement fixtures such as toilets and washing machines up and into the main sewer line

Flashing: Metal strips that protect against water seepage by joining various planes of a roof, or by covering gaps between the roof and the chimney or the roof and a wall

Flue: The pipe that carries the spent gases from your boiler, furnace, or water heater out through the chimney

Footing: The concrete base on which a foundation sits

Framing: The rough lumber of a house, including joists, rafters, studs, and beams

Furnace: A system that heats air, which is then distributed throughout the house via ducts made of sheet metal

Gable: The triangular side of a wall that rises up to a point beneath the inverted V of the roofline

Glazing: The technical term for glass in a window; also refers to the act of replacing a broken pane

Ground: In an electrical system, this refers to a safety wire that gives electricity an "escape route" if the neutral wire fails

Ground fault circuit interrupter (GFCI): A circuit breaker located within an electrical outlet that is used as safety device in bathrooms, kitchens, and outdoors

Hardwood: The close-grained wood from leafy trees such as oak, maple, or cherry

Header: In wood framing, a short, horizontal beam positioned above windows and doors

Heat pump: An energy-efficient geothermal heating and cooling unit, in which water is forced through a loop into the ground, where it either absorbs or releases energy

Hollow-core door: A door made from two veneer surfaces with a hollow interior

House wrap: A water-repellent sheeting that is installed just beneath the exterior siding

HVAC: An abbreviation for "heating, ventilation, and air-conditioning," which lists the principal components used to control indoor climate

Ice dam: The accumulation of ice and melted snow on a roof, which can result in horrendous leaks

Jamb: The two vertical sections of a door frame that attach to the hinges on one side and to the door latch on the other

Joists: A series of horizontal boards stretching between the walls of a house, which form the structural base for both the floors and the ceilings

Knob-and-tube wiring: An outdated and extremely fire-prone electrical system that involved stretching pairs of wires through a wall, holding them in place with porcelain knobs to prevent them from touching, and covering them with cloth sheathing

Leaders: The downspouts that transfer water flow from gutters to the ground

Load-bearing wall: A strong wall, including any exterior wall, positioned so that it carries the weight of the house above it; one of the home's principal structural elements

Main water valve: The valve that controls all the flow of water to your home

Masonry: This term refers to walls built by a mason, whether they're composed of brick, stone, tile, or other materials

Oil-based paint: This recipe uses oil as the vehicle to apply pigment; the extremely durable finish has become the professional painter's choice for interior and exterior trim

P-trap: The invention that made indoor plumbing practical, this simple bend in the drain pipe beneath a sink creates a water-filled "plug" that prevents sewer gases from belching back into the home

Partition wall: Used to divide up space and create rooms and closets, these walls serve no structural role in keeping a house standing and can easily be moved

Pitch: The angle or slope of a roof, measured as a ratio of the "rise" over the "run"—as in an 8-over-12 roof, which rises 8 feet for every 12 horizontally

Programmable thermostat: A money-saving thermostat with a clock that can be programmed to various temperatures at different times of the day or week

R-value: A measure of the ability of insulation to restrict heat flow; the higher the R-value, the better the insulation

Radiant floor heat: Coils of electricity, hot water, or steam pipes embedded in floors to heat rooms

Rafter: A structural roof member that spans an angle from an exterior wall to a center ridge beam

Receptacle: An electrician's term for an outlet

Sash: The movable part of a window that contains the glass

Septic tank: An underground sewage tank in which solids settle; the remaining waste is discharged by gravity into a sewage leaching field

Sheathing: The covering of plywood (or boards, on older houses) on an exterior wall or roof, which lies beneath the finished siding or roofing

Sill plate: Also called the mud sill, this is the lowest member of the house framing, which rests directly on top of the foundation wall

Slab: A concrete floor poured directly on an earth or gravel base

Soffit vents: Inlets on the underside of a roof overhang that allow air to be drawn under the roof to prevent ice dams

Softwood: Wood from a cone-bearing tree (such as pine) that can be easily worked

Studs: The vertical framing of 2-by-4s or 2-by-6s that supports a wall

Subfloor: A layer of plywood laid directly on joists that supports a finished wood or tile floor

Sump pump: A pump in a basement or crawl space that removes water

Sump pump pit: A recessed cavity in the floor of a basement or crawl space that collects water and holds the sump pump

Swamp cooler: Also called "eevaps," these energy-efficient cooling systems popular in the South rely on evaporation of water to create cold air

Three-pole switch: Light switches used in pairs to control a single fixture from two locations

Tuckpointing: A process where new mortar is installed in the joints of a masonry home, both to improve its appearance and protect against weather

Vapor barrier: An impervious layer of plastic or treated paper used to prevent humidity from migrating into the exterior walls and top-floor ceiling of a house

Volt: A unit of electrical pressure; most home circuits carry 120 volts, while heavy-duty appliances use 240 volts

Waste riser: Plumbing pipes that run vertically and carry waste water to a sewer or septic tank

Water-based paint: This recipe uses water as the vehicle to apply pigment; also called latex or acrylic latex, this is the professional painter's choice for interior and exterior walls

Water shield: This waterproof rubber membrane is applied beneath the roof shingles to prevent leaks from ice dams

Water stops: These valves, positioned under sinks and toilets, control water flow to individual fixtures

Watt: A unit of electrical power, which is calculated by multiplying amperage by voltage; the wattage rating tells you how much power an electrical fixture can handle

Weatherstripping: Metal, wood, plastic, or other material installed around door and window openings to prevent air infiltration

Essential Resources
Not sure where to turn to find out more about your home? Let Mr. Fix-It lead the way

Whenever I'm learning about something new, I always face the same problem: Where do I go to find reliable information? I rarely find everything I need all in one place. Instead, it becomes a continuing process, in which one thing leads to another, until I'm eventually confident that I know enough to be able to make the right choices. When it comes to your home, I can help you along in this process by directing you to a few organizations and trade associations that I know firsthand will provide you with valuable resources. You can call these organizations by telephone if you want, but there's no reason to waste the dime, since all of them have comprehensive Web sites for quick access to the best information. This is not an all-inclusive list by any means. Instead, think of it as a glimpse inside my Rolodex. With this list as a start, I'm confident you'll be able to continue the rest of your home improvement journey on your own.

resources

Alliance to Save Energy

www.ase.org

1200 18th St. NW

Suite 900

Washington, DC 20036

202-857-0666

The ASE Web site has a good section for consumers, with information on everything from energy-efficient appliances to how to reduce monthly electrical bills.

American Institute of Architects

www.aia.org

1735 New York Ave. NW

Washington, DC 20006

800-AIA-3837

Great Web site for finding architects, and the design resource center and bookstore can also be very helpful.

American Society of Interior Designers

www.asid.org

608 Massachusetts Ave. NE

Washington, DC 20002

202-546-3480

Not only can you find local certified designers, you can also find information on how to interview them, how to work with them, and how to understand how they set their fees.

American Society of Home Inspectors

www.ashi.com

932 Lee St.

Suite 101

Des Plaines, IL 60016

800-743-ASHI

The ASHI Web site has an FAQ on inspections, a guide for home buyers and home sellers, a listing of local inspectors—and even an online store where you can purchase a book called Preventive Home Maintenance.

American Society of Landscape Architects

www.asla.org

636 Eye St. NW

Washington, DC 20001

202-898-2444

A section on the Web site entitled "For the Public" includes details you'll need to find a qualified landscape architect in your area.

Association of Professional Landscape Designers

www.apld.org

1924 N. Second St.

Harrisburg, PA 17102

717-238-9780

This Web site covers the basics of garden design in a concise and useful way; ask for a free pamphlet entitled "Guidelines for Hiring a Landscape Designer."

Carpet and Rug Institute

www.carpet-rug.com

P.O. Box 2048

Dalton, GA 30722

800-882-8846

Here you'll find helpful guidelines on such things as choosing vacuum cleaners, selecting carpets and rugs, and cleaning and caring for your floor coverings.

Cedar Shake & Shingle Bureau

www.cedarbureau.org

P.O. Box 1178

Sumas, WA 98295

604-820-7700

This Web site contains everything you could want to know about cedar—including answers to questions such as "How resistant are cedar shakes and shingles to hail?" (The answer, not surprisingly, is very.)

Efficient Windows Collaborative

www.efficientwindows.org

Alliance to Save Energy

1200 18th St. NW

Suite 900

Washington, DC 20036

202-530-2245

Here you'll find information on how to select a window, what's new in window design, and detailed information about various types of glazing.

Electrical Safety Foundation International

www.esfi.org

1330 N. 17th St.

Suite 1847

Rosslyn, VA 22209

703-841-3229

This is a good Web site that covers the basics of home safety, including a useful safety checklist you can bring with you on a home inspection, and a kid-friendly home electrical safety quiz in which you play "spot the hazard" with an illustrated house.

Forest Products Society

www.forestprod.org

2801 Marshall Court

Madison, WI 53705

608-231-1361

This venerable not-for-profit research organization has a great publications catalogue, which you can request by telephone or simply download from the Web site. The catalogue contains useful and technically detailed books on such topics as deck building, selecting wood, and the fine points of exterior painting and paint selection.

The Hydronic Foundation

www.hydronics.org

119 East King Street

P.O. Box 1671

Johnson City, TN 37605

800-929-8548

Hydronics—that would mean piped water—can be used to heat and cool a house. This comprehensive Web site includes details on everything from pump maintenance to the basics of radiant floor heating.

International Ground Source Heat Pump Association (IGSHPA)

www.igshpa.okstate.edu

490 Cordell South

Oklahoma State University

Stillwater, OK 74078-8018

800-626-4747/405-744-5175

The "Visitors Center" on the Web site explains ground source heat pumps with great clarity, and includes a list of qualified installers around the country who can help you in this rapidly growing and energy-efficient field.

National Association of Home Builders

www.nahb.com

1201 15th St. NW

Washington, DC 20005

202-266-8200/800-368-5242

The NAHB Web site can be a good resource on topics ranging from buying a home to renovating one—including a special section for consumers containing information on home energy issues.

National Association of the Remodeling Industry

www.remodeltoday.com

780 Lee St.

Suite 200

Des Plaines, IL 60016

847-298-9200

The NARI Web site can help you find professional remodeling contractors, and includes tips on how to select them and what questions to ask them during interviews.

National Fenestration Rating Council

www.nfrc.org

1300 Spring Street, Suite 500

Silver Spring, MD 20910

301-589-6372

Fenestration refers to windows and doors, and this Web site contains just about everything you'll need to know to shop for them, including details that will help you compare various levels of energy performance.

National Fire Protection Association

www.nfpa.com

1 Batterymarch Park

Quincy, MA 02269

800-344-3555 or 617-770-3000

Here you'll find comprehensive information about fire safety in the home—including fact sheets and tips, information to educate children, as well as an online store to buy high-quality fire extinguishers.

National Kitchen and Bath Association

www.nkba.org

687 Willow Grove Street

Hackettstown, NJ 07840

877-NKBA-PRO

This Web site contains useful tips you'll need in order to remodel a kitchen or bath—including information on finding designers and contractors. You can also request a free workbook to get you started.

National Roofing Contractors Association

www.nrca.net

10255 West Higgins Road

Suite 600

Rosemont, IL 60018

The NRCA Web site offers homeowners roof checkup guidelines, buyers' guides to roofing materials, and listings of roofing contractors.

National Wood Flooring Association

www.woodfloors.org

16388 Westwoods Business Park

Ellisville, MO 63021

800-422-4556 (US)/800-848-8824 (Canada)

Not particular to any one kind of wood, this Web site has a wood floor "gallery" to help you make decisions, as well as good information on cleaning and caring for existing floors.

Wallcoverings Association

www.wallcoverings.org

401 N. Michigan Ave.

Chicago, IL 60611

312-644-6610

With this Web site, you can learn the basics of wallpapering, including a do-it-yourself guide, as well as information on the various types and styles of wallpaper available.

Water Quality Association

www.wqa.org

4151 Naperville Road

Lisle, IL 60532

630-505-0160

This Web site can help you diagnose problems with your water, including various smells and deposits, and includes information on contaminants ranging from arsenic to zinc.